Peterson's

MASTER AP

ENGLISH LANGUAGE

& COMPOSITION

2nd Edition

Margaret C. Moran
W. Frances Holder

PETERSON'S
A (n)elnet. COMPANY

PETERSON'S
A (n)elnet. COMPANY

About Peterson's, a Nelnet company

Peterson's (www.petersons.com) is a leading provider of education information and advice, with books and online resources focusing on education search, test preparation, and financial aid. Its Web site offers searchable databases and interactive tools for contacting educational institutions, online practice tests and instruction, and planning tools for securing financial aid. Peterson's serves 110 million education consumers annually.

For more information, contact Peterson's, 2000 Lenox Drive, Lawrenceville, NJ 08648; 800-338-3282; or find us on the World Wide Web at www.petersons.com/about.

Previously published as *Peterson's AP English Language & Composition* © 2005

Editor: Wallie Walker Hammond; Production Editor: Susan W. Dilts; Manufacturing Manager: Ray Golaszewski; Composition Manager: Gary Rozmierski

ISBN-13: 978-0-7689-2474-9
ISBN-10: 0-7689-2474-X

Printed in the United States of America

10 9 8 7 6 5 4 3 2   09 08 07

Second Edition

Petersons.com/publishing

Check out our Web site at www.petersons.com/publishing to see if there is any new information regarding the test and any revisions or corrections to the content of this book. We've made sure the information in this book is accurate and up-to-date; however, the test format or content may have changed since the time of publication.

OTHER RECOMMENDED TITLES

Peterson's Master AP Calculus AB & BC

Peterson's Master AP Chemistry

Peterson's Master AP English Literature & Composition

Peterson's Master AP U.S. Government & Politics

Peterson's Master AP U.S. History

Contents

PART III AP ENGLISH LANGUAGE & COMPOSITION STRATEGIES

PART IV: ENGLISH USAGE AND GRAMMAR REVIEW

PART V: TWO PRACTICE TESTS

APPENDIXES

Acknowledgments

Text from the Preface of *Modern American Poetry*, 5th Revised Edition, by Louis Untermeyer. Copyright 1919, 1921, 1925, 1930, 1936 by Harcourt, Brace & Co, Inc. Reprinted by permission of Professional Publishing Service.

Text excerpt from "Politics and the English Language" from *Shooting an Elephant and Other Essays* by George Orwell. Copyright 1946 by Sonia Brownell Orwell and renewed 1974 by Sonia Orwell. Reprinted by permission of Harcourt, Inc., and A. M. Heath & Company, Ltd.

"Addressing the Graduating Class" from *Essays, Speeches & Public Letters by William Faulkner,* ed. by James B. Meriweather. Copyright 1951 by William Faulkner. Reprinted by permission of Random House, Inc., and Chatto & Windus, Ltd.

Acknowledgments

Before You Begin

HOW THIS BOOK IS ORGANIZED

Whether you have five months, nine weeks, or just two short weeks to prepare for the exam, *Peterson's Master AP English Language & Composition* will help you develop a study plan that caters to your individual needs and timetable. These step-by-step plans are easy to follow and are remarkably effective.

- **Top 10 Strategies to Raise Your Score** gives you tried and true test-taking strategies

- **Part I** includes the basic information about the AP English Language & Composition test that you need to know.

- **Part II** provides a diagnostic test to determine your strengths and weaknesses. Use the diagnostic test as a tool to improve your test-taking skills.

- **Parts III** and **IV** provide the review and strategies for answering the different kinds of multiple-choice and essay questions and give you numerous opportunities to practice what you are learning. It is a good idea to read the answer explanations to all of the questions because you may find ideas or tips that will help you better analyze the answers to questions in the next practice test you take. You will also find reviews of grammar, mechanics, and usage.

- **Part V** includes two additional practice tests. Remember to apply the test-taking system carefully, work the system to get more correct responses, and be careful of your time in order to answer more questions in the time period.

- The **Appendixes** provide you with the new Peterson's College-by-College Guide to AP Credit and Placement (for more than 400 selective colleges and universities) as well as a review of literary and rhetorical terms you may encounter on the test.

SPECIAL STUDY FEATURES

Peterson's Master AP English Language & Composition was designed to be as user-friendly as it is complete. It includes several features to make your preparation easier.

Overview

Each chapter begins with a bulleted overview listing the topics that will be covered in the chapter. You know immediately where to look for a topic that you need to work on.

Summing It Up

Each strategy chapter ends with a point-by-point summary that captures the most important points. The summaries are a convenient way to review the content of these strategy chapters.

Bonus Information

Be sure to look in the page margins for the following test-prep tools:

NOTE

Notes highlight critical information about the test.

TIP

Tips draw your attention to valuable concepts, advice, and shortcuts for tackling the exam. By reading the tips, you will learn how to approach different question types, pace yourself, and remember what was discussed previously in the book.

ALERT!

Whenever you need to be careful of a common pitfall, you'll find an *Alert!* This information reveals and eliminates the misperceptions and wrong turns many people take on the exam. By taking full advantage of all features presented in *Peterson's Master AP English Language & Composition,* you will become much more comfortable with the exam and considerably more confident about getting a high score.

APPENDIXES

Peterson's **College-by-College Guide to AP Credit and Placement**, Appendix A, gives you the equivalent classes, scores, and credit awarded at more than 400 colleges and universities. Use this guide to find your possible placement status, credit, and/or exemption based on your AP English Language & Composition score. Appendix B provides a review of literary and rhetorical terms you may encounter on the test.

YOU'RE WELL ON YOUR WAY TO SUCCESS

Remember that knowledge is power. You will be studying the most comprehensive guide available and you will become extremely knowledgeable about the exam. We look forward to helping you raise your score.

GIVE US YOUR FEEDBACK

Peterson's, a Nelnet company, publishes a full line of resources to help guide you through the college admission process. Peterson's publications can be found at your local bookstore, library, and high school guidance office, and you can access us online at www.petersons.com.

We welcome any comments or suggestions you may have about this publication and invite you to complete our online survey at www.petersons.com/booksurvey. Or you can fill out the survey at the back of this book, tear it out, and mail it to us at:

Publishing Department
Peterson's
2000 Lenox Drive
Lawrenceville, NJ 08648

Your feedback will help us to provide personalized solutions for your educational advancement.

TABLE OF LITERARY WORKS

The following list represents all the works discussed in this book, broken out by chapter.

TOP 10 STRATEGIES TO RAISE YOUR SCORE

When it comes to taking an AP, some test-taking skills will do you more good than others. There are concepts you can learn and techniques you can follow that will help you do your best. Here are our picks for the top 10 strategies to raise your AP English Language & Composition score:

1. **Create or choose a study plan from this book and follow it.** The right study plan will help you get the most out of this book in whatever time you have.

2. **Choose a place and time to study every day,** and stick to your routine and your plan.

3. **Complete the diagnostic and practice tests in this book.** They will give you just what they promise: practice—practice in reading and following the directions, practice in pacing yourself, practice in understanding and answering multiple-choice questions, and practice in writing timed essays.

4. **Complete all of your assignments for your regular AP English Language & Composition class.** Ask questions in class, talk about what you read and write, and enjoy what you are doing. The test is supposed to measure your development as an educated and thinking reader.

5. **Highlight the key words in the question** so you will know what you are looking for in the answer choices.

6. **For a tiered or multi-step question,** decide what the correct answer is and then determine which answer choice contains ONLY that answer.

7. **All elements in an answer must be correct for the answer to be correct.**

8. **With *not/except* questions, ask yourself if an answer choice is true about the selection.** If it is, cross it out, and keep checking answers.

9. **If you aren't sure about an answer but know something about the question, eliminate what you know is wrong and make an educated guess.** Ignore the answers that are absolutely wrong, eliminate choices in which part of the answer is incorrect, check the time period of the question and of the answer choices, check the key words in the question again, and revisit remaining answers to discover which seems more correct.

10. **Finally, don't cram the night before the exam.** Relax. Go to a movie, visit a friend—but not one who is taking the test with you. Get a good night's sleep.

PART I

AP ENGLISH LANGUAGE & COMPOSITION BASICS

All About the AP English Language & Composition Test

chapter 1

OVERVIEW

- 10 facts about the AP English Language & Composition Test
- Scoring the AP English Language & Composition Test
- Suggested reading
- Practice plans for studying for the AP English Language & Composition Test
- Summing it up

10 FACTS ABOUT THE AP ENGLISH LANGUAGE & COMPOSITION TEST

1 **The Advanced Placement Program Offers High School Students an Opportunity to Receive College Credit for Courses They Take in High School.**

The AP program is a collaborative effort of secondary schools, colleges and universities, and the College Board through which students who are enrolled in AP or honors courses in any one or more of thirty-eight subject areas may receive credit or advanced placement for college-level work completed in high school. While the College Board makes recommendations about course content, it does not prescribe content. As a result, the annual testing program ensures a degree of comparability among courses in the same subject.

2 **Thousands of Colleges and Universities in the United States Participate in the AP Program.**

Neither the College Board nor your high school awards AP credit. You need to find out from the colleges to which you are planning to apply whether they grant credit and/or use AP scores for placement. It is IMPORTANT that you obtain each school's policy IN WRITING so that when you actually choose one college and register, you will have proof of what you were told.

❸ The AP English Language & Composition Test Measures Your Ability to Analyze the Rhetoric of Prose Passages and to Write Essays in Various Rhetorical Modes.

According to the College Board's course description, an AP course in language and composition will enable students to develop and refine their writing styles by writing extensively. The course will also provide extensive opportunities for students to read a variety of rhetorical modes to analyze how writers' choices affect style.

NOTE

See Chapter 3 for multiple-choice questions. See Chapter 4 for strategies for writing essays.

❹ The AP English Language and Composition Test Has Two Parts: Multiple Choice and Essays.

Section I, Multiple Choice, typically has between 50 and 60 questions divided among five or six prose passages. This section counts for 45 percent of your total score, and you have 60 minutes to complete it. In Section II, you have three essays to write. The questions usually consist of two essays that require analysis of rhetorical and stylistic strategies in selected prose passages and one that requires a synthesis of sources to support an argument—a persuasive essay based on an analysis and evaluation of sources. The essays count for 55 percent of your total score. You have 40 minutes to write each essay, 120 minutes total writing time. You will also have 15 minutes to read the sources for the synthesis essay.

NOTE

See "Suggested Reading," p. 8.

❺ The Prose Passages Are Taken from a Variety of Subject Areas.

According to the information from the College Board, you might find selections on the AP exam written by autobiographers, biographers, diarists, historians, critics, essayists, journalists, political writers and commentators, and science and nature writers. You may also find letters. Within the multiple-choice section, you will find one selection that has footnotes. One of the essay questions will be based on several, possibly as many as six, passages that you will need to synthesize for your answer. The styles will vary as the subject matter varies. There is no way you can read every possible piece of nonfiction, but you can hone your skills of rhetorical and stylistic analysis and argumentation and work on refining your own writing style.

❻ There Is No Required Length for Your Essays.

It is the quality, not the quantity, that counts. Realistically, a one-paragraph essay is not going to garner you a high mark because you cannot develop a well-reasoned analysis or argument and present it effectively in one paragraph. An essay of five paragraphs is a good goal. By following this model, you can set out your ideas with an interesting introduction, develop a reasoned body, and provide a solid ending.

NOTE

See "Scoring the AP English Language and Composition Test," below.

7 You Will Get a Composite Score for Your Test.

The College Board reports a single score from 1 to 5 for the two-part test, with 5 being the highest. By understanding how you can balance the number of correct answers in the multiple-choice section and the essay score you need in order to receive at least a "3," you can relieve some of your anxiety about passing the test.

8 Educated Guessing Can Help.

No points are deducted for questions that go unanswered on the multiple-choice section, and don't expect to have time to answer them all. A quarter of a point is deducted for each wrong answer. The College Board suggests guessing IF you know something about a question and can eliminate a couple of the answer choices. Call it "educated guessing."

9 The Test Is Given in Mid-May.

Most likely, the test will be given at your school, so you do not have to worry about finding a strange school building in a strange city. You will be in familiar surroundings—that should reduce your anxiety a bit. If the test is given in another school, be sure to take identification with you.

Plan your route to the other school and actually take the trip once before test day—drive or take public transportation, whichever way you will go on test day—to be sure you won't get lost the morning of the test. Add extra time because you may be going during the morning rush hour.

10 Studying for the Test Can Make a Difference.

The first step is to familiarize yourself with the format and directions for both parts of the test. Then, you will not waste time on the day of the test trying to understand what you are supposed to do. The second step is to put those analytical skills you have been learning to work, dissecting and understanding the kinds of questions you will be asked. The third step is to practice "writing-on-demand" for the essays.

SCORING THE AP ENGLISH LANGUAGE & COMPOSITION TEST

Around early July, you and the colleges you designate will receive a score from 1 to 5, with 5 being the highest, for your AP English Language & Composition Test, and your high school will receive its report a little later. The multiple-choice section is graded by machine, and your essays are graded during a marathon reading session by high school and college teachers.

A different reader grades each of your essays. None of the readers knows who you are (that's why you fill in identification information on your pink Section II booklet and then seal it) or how the others scored your other essays. Each reader is familiar with the work or works discussed in the essay question she or he is reading. The grading is done on a holistic system; that is, the overall essay is scored, not just the development of your ideas, your spelling, or your punctuation. For each essay, the College Board works out grading criteria for the readers to use, much as your teacher uses a rubric to evaluate your writing.

What the Composite Score Means

The College Board refers to the composite score as "weighted" because a factor of about 1.3 (the exact number varies from year to year) for the multiple-choice questions and a factor of 3.0556 for the essay questions are used to determine a raw score for each section. That is, the actual score you get on the multiple-choice questions—say 35—is multiplied by about 1.3 (1.2273 for 55 questions in a recent year). The actual score that you get on the essay test—say 21—is multiplied by 3.0556. Those two numbers, your raw scores, are then added and the resulting score—somewhere between 0 and 150 (107, based on the above example)—is then equated to a number from 5 to 1.

A score of 107 would have been good enough to get you a "4" for the test in a recent year. But 5 more points—112—would have gotten you a "5." The range in a recent year was 112 to 150 for a "5."

What Does All This Mean to You?

You can leave blank or answer incorrectly some combination of 20 questions on a 55-question multiple-choice section, get a 7 for each of your three essays, and still get a "5." It is not as easy as it may seem, or the majority of students would not fall into the "3" range, although a 3 may be good enough to get you college credit or advanced placement. A score of 4 certainly will.

Take a look at the charts below. It takes work, but raising your score may not be that

POSSIBLE SCORE DISTRIBUTION FOR A 55-QUESTION MULTIPLE-CHOICE SECTION					
SCORE = 5		**SCORE = 4**		**SCORE = 3**	
MC	**Essays (3)**	**MC**	**Essays (3)**	**MC**	**Essays (3)**
25	25 (8.33)	25	21 (7)	25	14 (4.66)
30	23 (7.66)	30	19 (6.33)	30	12 (4)
35	21 (7)	35	17 (5.66)	35	10 (3.33)
40	19 (6.33)	40	15 (5)	40	8 (2.66)
45	17 (5.66)	45	13 (4.33)	45	6 (2)

AP Grade	AP Qualifier	Composite Scores	Probability of Receiving Credit
5	Extremely Well Qualified	112–150	Yes
4	Well Qualified	95–111	Yes
3	Qualified	76–94	Probably
2	Possibly Qualified	48–75	Rarely
1	No Recommendation	0–47	No

impossible. Sometimes, the difference between a 3 and a 4 or a 4 and a 5 is only a couple of points.

The highest score you can receive on an essay is a 9, so the highest total essay score is 27. It is possible to get a variety of scores on your essays—7, 5, and 5, for example. The chances are that you will not get a wide range of individual essay scores like 6, 2, and 5. Even if you did, you could still get at least a 3 and possibly a 4, depending on how many correct answers you have in the multiple-choice section weighed against how many wrong answers you have.

According to the College Board, about 62 percent of the students who took the test in a recent year received a 3 or better. The cut-off point for passing grades may change from year to year, but it remains around this range. This chart shows the actual conversion scale in a recent year. What it means is that you neither have to answer all the questions, nor do you have to answer them all correctly, nor write three "9" essays to receive your AP credit.

Five Things to Remember

1 The 50 to 60 question multiple-choice section is worth 45 percent of your total score.

2 Students who perform acceptably on the essays can receive a 3 if they answer correctly 50 to 60 percent of the multiple-choice questions.

3 There is no deduction for unanswered questions.

4 There is a quarter-point deduction for wrong answers.

5 The three essays together account for 55 percent of your total score.

Why Are We Telling You These Facts?

Because you can use them to your advantage.

1 It is important to spend time practicing the kinds of questions that you will find in the multiple-choice section, because 45 percent of your score comes from that section. You do not have to put all your emphasis on the essay questions.

NOTE

The *Diagnostic* and *Practice Tests* will help you pace yourself in the exam.

NOTE

See Chapter 3 for strategies on educated guessing.

2-3 You can leave some questions unanswered and still do well. Even though you will be practicing pacing yourself as you use this book, you may not be able to complete all 50-odd questions on the day of the test. If you come across a really incomprehensible passage, you can skip it and come back to it later and still feel that you are not doomed to a low score.

4 There is a guessing penalty. If you do not know anything about the question or the choices, do not take a chance. However, IF you know something about the question and can eliminate one or more of the answer choices, then it is probably worth your while to choose one of the other answers. You would need to answer four questions incorrectly to lose one point, but answering even one question correctly would gain you another point. Rather than calling it guessing, call it EDUCATED GUESSING. Even the College Board suggests this strategy.

5 In writing the essays, you need to pace yourself so that you spend approximately the same amount of time planning and writing each one. Remember that you will get an additional 15 minutes to read the sources for the synthesis essay. You are not expected to write perfect essays. As the College Board cautions its readers for the synthesis essay, ". . . the essay is not a finished product and should not be judged by standards that are appropriate for out-of-class writing assignments. Instead, evaluate the essay as a draft, making certain to reward students for what they do well. All essays, even those scored an 8 or a 9, may contain occasional flaws in analysis, prose style, or mechanics."

SUGGESTED READING

The following list of autobiographers, diarists, biographers, writers of history, critics, essayists, journalists, political writers and commentators, and science and nature writers draws heavily from the selection of writers that the College Board suggests students read during an AP English language and composition course. The works have been chosen from a variety of sources to provide a representative list. There are also suggestions for books on composition and critical analysis. Reading essays in magazines like *The New Yorker* and the *New Republic* and columnists on the Op-Ed page of the *New York Times* will introduce you to writers like Cynthia Ozick, Gary Wills, Thomas Friedman, and Maureen Dowd. In studying for the test, use this list as well as writers you are introduced to in class to practice developing essay responses. If you are looking for models of analysis, check page xiv for a list of all works discussed and analyzed in this book.

Autobiographers and Diarists

Angelou, Maya, *I Know Why the Caged Bird Sings, The Heart of a Woman*

Cofer, Judith Ortiz, "The Myth of the Latin American Woman," *Woman in Front of the Sun: On Becoming a Writer*

Dana, Charles, *Reminiscences of the Civil War, Notes of Travel*

De Quincey, Thomas, *Autobiographical Sketches*

Douglass, Frederick, *Narrative of the Life of Frederick Douglass, An American Slave*

Franklin, Benjamin, *The Autobiography of Benjamin Franklin*

Hellman, Lillian, *An Unfinished Woman, Scoundrel Time*

Hurston, Zora Neale, *Dust Tracks on a Road*

Keller, Helen, *The Story of My Life, Helen Keller's Journal*

Kingston, Maxine Hong, "No Name Woman"

Lawrence, T. E., *Seven Pillars of Wisdom*

Malcolm X, *The Autobiography of Malcolm X*

Newman, John Henry, *Apologia Pro Vita Sua*

Pepys, Samuel, *The Diary of Samuel Pepys*

Welty, Eudora, *One Writer's Beginnings*

Wright, Richard, *Black Boy*

Yezierska, Anzia, *Bread Givers, Red Ribbon on a White Horse: My Story*

Biographers and Historians

Bates, Walter Jackson, *The Achievement of Samuel Johnson, John Keats*

Boswell, James, *Life of Samuel Johnson*

Carlyle, Thomas, *On Heroes, Hero-Worship and the Heroic in History*

Catton, Bruce, *Mr. Lincoln's Army, A Stillness at Appomattox*

Churchill, Winston, *My Early Life*

DeLoria, Vine, Jr., *Custer Died for Your Sins*

Edel, Leon, 5-volume biography of Henry James, *James Joyce: The Last Journey*

Ellmann, Richard, *James Joyce*

Foote, Shelby, *The Civil War* in three volumes, *Chickamauga and Other Stories*

Franklin, John Hope, *From Slavery to Freedom, Race and History*

Fraser, Antonia, *The Weaker Vessel*

Gibbon, Edward, *The History of the Decline and Fall of the Roman Empire*

Holmes, Richard, *Firing Line, Redcoat*

Lerner, Gerda, *The Majority Finds Its Past, The Creation of Feminist Consciousness*

Macaulay, Thomas, "Milton," *History of England*

Morison, Samuel Eliot, *Admiral of the Ocean Sea, John Paul Jones*

Parkman, Francis, *The Oregon Trail*

Schama, Simon, *Landscape and Memory, Rembrandt's Eyes*

Schlesinger, Arthur M., *The Age of Jackson, A Thousand Days*

Takaki, Ronald, *A Different Mirror*

Trevelyan, George, *American Revolution*

Tuchman, Barbara, *The Guns of August, Practising History* (collection)

Critics

Allen, Paula Gunn, *Studies in American Indian Literature: Critical Essays,* "The Sacred Hoop"

Anzaldua, Gloria, *Borderlands/La Frontera: The New Mestiza, Making Face, Making Soul/Haciendo Caras: Creative and Critical Perspectives of Feminists of Color*

Arnold, Matthew, *Essays in Criticism, Culture and Anarchy*

Clark, Kenneth, *Civilisation*

Croce, Arlene, *Afterimages, Going to the Dance*

Emerson, Ralph Waldo, "Self-Reliance," "The Over-Soul"

Gates, Henry Louis, Jr., *Toward a Theory of Afro-American Literary Criticism, Loose Canons: Notes on the Culture Wars*

Hazlitt, William, *Sketches and Essays*

hooks, bell, *Teaching to Transgress*

Johnson, Samuel, *The Rambler, The Idler*

Kael, Pauline, *5001 Nights at the Movies*

Oates, Joyce Carol, *Where I've Been, And Where I'm Going: Essays, Reviews, and Prose; Contraries: Essays*

Pater, Walter, *The Renaissance, Appreciations*

Ruskin, John, *Modern Painters, The Stones of Venice*

Santayana, George, *The Sense of Beauty*

Sontag, Susan, *Against Interpretation*

West, Cornel, *Race Matters, Keeping Faith: Philosophy and Race in America, The African-American Century*

Wilson, Edmund, *Axel's Castle*

Essayists

Addison, Joseph, *The Tatler, The Spectator*

Agee, James, *Let Us Now Praise Famous Men*

Angelou, Maya, *Wouldn't Take Nothing for My Journey Now*

Bacon, Francis, *Essays, Colours of Good and Evil*

Baldwin, James, *Notes of a Native Son*

Chesterton, G.K., *Tremendous Trifles*

Didion, Joan, "Miami: The Cuban Presence," "The Liquid City"

Fussell, Paul, *Poetic Meter and Poetic Form*

Gallant, Mavis, *Paris Journals: Selected Essays and Reviews*

Gordimer, Nadine, *The Essential Gesture, Writing and Being*

Hoagland, Edward, *The Circle Home, The Courage of Turtles*

Lamb, Charles, *Essays of Elia*

Mailer, Norman, *The Armies of the Night, A Fire on the Moon, The Executioner's Song*

Mairs, Nancy, "On Being a Scientific Booby"

Márquez, Gabriel García, "Eye of a Blue Day"

McCarthy, Mary, *Ideas and the Novel, How I Grew*

Montaigne, *The Essays*

Naipaul, V.S., *The Return of Eva Peron: With the Killings in Trinidad*

Olsen, Tillie, *Silences*

Orwell, George, *Shooting an Elephant and Other Essays*

Ozick, Cynthia, *Metaphor and Memory, A Cynthia Ozick Reader*

Reed, Ishmael, *Shrovetide in Old New Orleans: Essays, God Made Alaska for the Indians: Selected Essays*

Rich, Adrienne, *What Is Found There: Notebooks on Poetry and Politics,*

Richler, Mordecai, *Hunting Tigers Under Glass: Essays and Reports, Notes on an Endangered Species and Others*

Selzer, Richard, *Mortal Lessons: Notes on the Art of Surgery,* "The Masked Marvel's Last Toehold"

Steele, Richard, *The Tatler, The Spectator*

Thoreau, Henry David, *Walden,* "Resistance to Civil Government"

Updike, John, *Picked-Up Pieces, Still Looking: Essays on American Art*

Walker, Alice, "In Search of Our Mothers' Gardens," "Beauty: When the Other Dancer Is the Self"

White, E.B., "The Ring of Time"

Williams, Terry Tempest, *Great and Peculiar Beauty: a Utah Centennial Reader*

Woolf, Virginia, *A Room of One's Own,* "Old Mrs. Grey"

Journalists

Angell, Roger, *The Summer Game, Once More Around the Park*

Baker, Russell, *Growing Up*

Dowd, Maureen, *Are Men Necessary?*

Drew, Elizabeth, *Washington Journal*

Ephron, Nora, *Crazy Salad*

Fitzgerald, Frances, *America Revised*

Goodman, Ellen, *Turning Points, Paper Trail*

Halberstam, David, *The Making of a Quagmire, The Breaks of the Game, The Children*

Logan, Andy, *The Man Who Robbed the Robber Barons*

Mencken, H.L., *Prejudices,* "The Feminine Mind"

Morris, Jan, *Pax Britannica* Trilogy

Smith, Red, *Views of Sports, The Red Smith Reader, Red Smith on Baseball*

Steffens, Lincoln, *The Shame of the Cities*

Trillin, Calvin, *American Fried: Adventures of a Happy Eater, An Education in Georgia*

Wolfe, Tom, *The Right Stuff*

Political Writers and Commentators

Arendt, Hannah, *The Origins of Totalitarianism*

de Beauvoir, Simone, *The Second Sex*

Buckley, William F., *Up from Liberalism*

de Crévecoeur, J. Hector St. John, *Letters from an American Farmer*

Du Bois, W. E. B., *The Souls of Black Folk*

Fuller, Margaret, *Woman in the Nineteenth Century*

Galbraith, John Kenneth, *The Affluent Society*

Gilman, Charlotte Perkins, *Women and Economics*

Hobbes, Thomas, *Leviathan*

Jefferson, Thomas, "The Declaration of Independence"

Kennan, George, *Memoirs*

King, Martin Luther, Jr., "Letter from a Birmingham Jail"

Lapham, Lewis H., *Money and Class in America, Waiting for the Barbarians*

Locke, John, *The Second Treatise on Civil Government*

Machiavelli, Niccolò, *The Prince*

Mill, John Stuart, *On Liberty*

Milton, John, *Areopagitica*

More, Thomas, *Utopia*

Paine, Thomas, *Common Sense, The Crisis*

Schreiner, Olive, *Women and Labour*

Swift, Jonathan, "A Modest Proposal"

de Tocqueville, Alexis, *Democracy in America*

Vidal, Gore, *Matters of Fact and Fiction, Decline and Fall of the American Empire, The American Presidency*

Will, George, *The Morning After: American Successes and Excesses, Suddenly: The American Idea Abroad and at Home*

Wills, Garry, *Nixon Agonistes, Explaining America: The Federalist, Lincoln at Gettysburg*

Wollstonecraft, Mary, *A Vindication of the Rights of Woman*

Science and Nature Writers

Abbey, Edward, *The Monkey Wrench Gang*

Berry, Wendell, *A Continuous Harmony: Essays Cultural and Agricultural, Standing on Earth, Late Harvest: Rural American Writing*

Bronowski, Jacob, *The Ascent of Man*

Carson, Rachel, *Silent Spring*

Darwin, Charles, *Origin of Species, The Descent of Man*

Dillard, Annie, *Teaching a Stone to Talk*

Ehrlich, Gretel, *The Solace of Open Spaces*

Eiseley, Loren, "The Brown Wasps"

Gould, Stephen Jay, *Ever Since Darwin, Hen's Teeth and Horse's Toes, The Hedgehog, the Fox, and the Magister's Pox: Mending the Gap Between Science and the Humanities*

Keller, Evelyn Fox, *Making Sense of Life, Refiguring Life*

Lopez, Barry, *Of Wolves and Men, Crossing Open Ground*

Matthiessen, Peter, *Wildlife in America, Under the Mountain Wall: A Chronicle of Two Seasons in the Stone Age, Tigers in the Snow*

McPhee, John, *Annals of the Former World*

Mead, Margaret, *Coming of Age in Samoa, Growing Up in New Guinea*

Muir, John, *John Muir: Nature Writings, Essays, My First Summer in the Sierra*

Sagan, Carl, *The Dragons of Eden, Cosmos*

Thomas, Lewis, *The Lives of Cells, The Youngest Science: Notes of a Medicine-Watcher*

Weiner, Jonathan, *Planet Earth, The Beak of the Finch*

Works on Composition and Analysis

Axelrod, Rise B., and Charles R. Cooper, *The St. Martin's Guide to Writing*

Barzun, Jacques, *Simple and Direct: A Rhetoric for Writers*

Berthoff, Ann E., *The Making of Meaning: Metaphors, Models and Maxims for Writing Teachers*

Cooley, Thomas, *The Norton Sampler: Short Essays for Composition*

Corbett, Edward P. J., *Classical Rhetoric for the Modern Student*

Costello, Karin Bergstrom, *Gendered Voices: Readings from the American Experience*

Cox, Don Richard and Elizabeth Giddnes, *Crafting Prose*

DiYanni, Robert, and Pat C. Hoy II, *The Scribner Handbook for Writers*

Elbow, Peter, *Writing with Power*

Gibson, Walker, *Persona: A Style Study for Readers and Writers*

Hall, Donald, ed., *The Contemporary Essay*

Lanham, Richard, *Analyzing Prose; The Electronic Word: Democracy, Technology, and the Arts; Revising Prose*

Murray, Donald, *The Craft of Revision*

Strunk, W., Jr., and E. B. White, *The Elements of Style*

Warriner, John E., *English Composition and Grammar: Complete Course*

Zinsser, William K., *On Writing Well: An Informal Guide to Writing Nonfiction*

PRACTICE PLANS FOR STUDYING FOR THE AP ENGLISH LANGUAGE & COMPOSITION TEST

The following plan is worked out for nine weeks. The best study plan is one that continues through a full semester so you have time to think about ideas, and to talk with your teacher and other students about what you are learning, and you will not feel rushed. Staying relaxed about the test is important. A full-semester study plan also means that you can apply what you are learning here to class work (your essay writing) and apply your class work to test preparation. The plan is worked out so that you should spend about 3 hours on each lesson.

Nine-Week Practice Plan

WEEK 1

First: Take the *Practice Test 1: Diagnostic*, pp. 33–68, and complete the self-scoring process. List the areas that you had difficulty with such as timing, question types, and writing on demand.

Then: Reread Chapter 1 about the basic facts of the test and its scoring.

WEEK 2

Lesson 1

Reread *Scoring the AP Language &Composition Test* on pp. 5–8 to remind yourself that at least a "3" is achievable.

Read Chapter 3, *About the Multiple-Choice Questions*, pp. 71–104.

Practice by completing *Exercise 1*.

Correct the activities with the *Answer Key and Explanations* for the exercise.

Note areas that need improvement.

Lesson 2

Read "Grammar for the Multiple-Choice Questions" in Chapter 5 and Appendix B, *A Quick Review of Literary and Rhetorical Terms*.

Practice answering multiple-choice questions by completing *Exercises 2* and *3* in Chapter 3.

Correct the activities with the *Answer Key and and Explanations* for the exercises.

Note those areas where you have improved and those areas that still need work.

WEEK 3

Lesson 1

Review Chapter 3, *About the Multiple-Choice Questions*, pp. 71–104; Chapter 5 for grammar, pp. 147–150; and Appendix B, *A Quick Review of Literary and Rhetorical Terms*, pp. 287–293.

Practice answering multiple-choice questions by completing *Exercise 4* in Chapter 3.

Correct the activities with the *Answer Key and Explanations* for the exercise.

Note those areas where you have improved and those areas that still need work.

Lesson 2

Read Chapter 4, *About the Free-Response and Synthesis Essays*.

Do *Exercise 1*. Time yourself to see how well-developed and complete an essay you can plan and write in 40 minutes.

Complete the self-evaluation and ask a responsible friend, an AP classmate, or a teacher to evaluate your essay against the scoring guide.

With your evaluator's and your comments in mind, revise your essay.

WEEK 4

Lesson 1

Reread Chapter 4, pp. 105–144, as needed. Do *Exercise 2* in 40 minutes.

Complete the self-evaluation and ask a responsible friend, an AP classmate, or a teacher to evaluate your essay against the scoring guide.

With your and your evaluator's comments in mind, revise your essay.

Lesson 2

Reread Chapter 4, pp. 105–144, as needed. Do *Exercise 3* in 40 minutes.

Complete the self-evaluation and ask a responsible friend, an AP classmate, or a teacher to evaluate your essay against the scoring guide.

With your evaluator's and your comments in mind, revise your essay.

WEEK 5

Lesson 1

Review the list you made after you took the *Practice Test 1: Diagnostic* to see what you need to review about the multiple-choice section.

With these areas in mind, reread Chapter 3, *About the Multiple-Choice Questions*.

Review the *Exercises* in the chapter and the *Answer Key and Explanations*. Pay particular attention to the strategies for answering the questions.

Determine if there are areas that you are still unsure of.

Lesson 2

Review the list you made after you took the *Practice Test 1: Diagnostic* to see what you need to review about the essay section of the AP exam.

Reread Chapter 4, pp. 105–144.

Revise the first two essays on the *Practice Test 1: Diagnostic*.

Use the *Self-Evaluation Rubric for the Free Response Essays* to assess how much you have improved since you originally wrote the two essays.

Note any areas that you think you still need to improve.

Revise the remaining essay if necessary.

WEEK 6

Lesson 1

Take *Practice Test 2*.

Score your answers against the *Answer Key* and evaluate your essay against the rubric.

Ask a responsible friend, an AP classmate, or a teacher to evaluate your essay against the scoring guide.

Read the *Answer Key and Explanations* for all the multiple-choice questions, including the ones you answered correctly.

Compare your scores on *Practice Test 2* to the scores on the *Practice Test 1: Diagnostic*. Where did you improve? What do you still need to work on?

Lesson 2

Choose a selection that is used for one of the essay questions in the *Diagnostic Test* and analyze it as though you were going to create your own multiple-choice test. Be sure to ask yourself about the mode of the piece, any literary devices that are employed, and the theme of the piece.

Choose one of the selections in the *Diagnostic Test* that is used as the basis for multiple-choice questions and turn it into a practice essay activity. Develop a question and then answer it in an essay.

WEEK 7

Lesson 1

Take *Practice Test 3*.

Score your answers against the *Answer Key* and evaluate your essay against the rubric.

Ask a responsible friend, an AP classmate, or a teacher to evaluate your essay against the scoring guide.

Read the explanations for all the multiple-choice questions, including the ones you answered correctly.

Compare your scores on *Practice Test 3* to the scores on the *Practice Test 1: Diagnostic* and *Practice Test 2*. Where did you improve? What do you still need to work on?

Lesson 2

Choose a selection that is used for one of the essay questions in the *Practice Test 1: Diagnostic* and analyze it as though you were going to create your own multiple-choice test. Be sure to ask yourself about the mode of the piece, any literary devices that are employed, and the theme of the piece.

Choose one of the selections in the *Practice Test 1: Diagnostic* that is used as the basis for multiple-choice questions and turn it into a practice essay activity. Develop a question and then answer it in an essay.

WEEK 8

Lesson 1

Choose a selection that is used for one of the essay questions in the *Diagnostic Test* and analyze it as though you were going to create your own multiple-choice test. Be sure to ask yourself about the mode of the piece, any literary devices that are employed, and the theme of the piece.

Choose one of the selections in the *Practice Test 1: Diagnostic* that is used as the basis for multiple-choice questions and turn it into a practice essay activity. Develop a question and then answer it in an essay.

Lesson 2

Read and analyze five articles in magazines such as *The New Yorker* and selections in anthologies to practice your skills. Be sure to ask yourself about the mode of each piece, any rhetorical devices that are used, and the theme of the piece.

Apply an essay question from one of the tests in this book to two of the articles and write a practice essay for each. Use the scoring guide to assess your answer.

WEEK 9

Lesson 1

Read and analyze articles in magazines such as *The New Yorker* and selections in anthologies to practice your skills.

Review Chapters 3 and 4.

Review Chapter 5.

Lesson 2

Randomly choose selections from Section I of the *Practice Test 1: Diagnostic* and the other *Practice Tests* and review the *Answer Key and Explanations* to remind yourself of the strategies you can use to unlock the answers.

Reread *Scoring the AP English Language & Composition Test*, pp. 5–8.

Assemble all materials you will need on test day: pens, pencils, a watch, and your registration information.

The Panic Plan

Eighteen weeks, nine weeks, how about two weeks? If you are the kind of person who puts everything off until the last possible minute, here is a two-week Panic Plan. Its objectives are to make you familiar with the test format and directions, to help you get as many correct answers as possible, and to write the best essays you can.

WEEK 1

Read and *Scoring the AP English Language & Composition Test*, pp. 5–8.

Take *Practice Test 1: Diagnostic:* Read the directions carefully and use a timer for each section.

Complete the self-scoring process. You can learn a lot about the types of questions in the multiple-choice section by working through the answers.

Read Chapters 3 and 4 and complete the *Exercises*.

Multiple Choice

Answer the multiple-choice section on *Practice Test 2*.

Complete the self-scoring process, and see where you may still be having problems with question types.

Read all the answer explanations, including those you identified correctly.

Essays

Complete the essay section on *Practice Test 2*.

Score your essays against the rubric, noting areas for improvement.

Ask a responsible friend, an AP classmate, or a teacher to evaluate your essays against the scoring guide as well. Compare your scores to those on the *Practice Test 1: Diagnostic*.

WEEK 2

Reread *Scoring the AP English Language & Composition Test*, pp. 5–8, and Chapters 3, 4, and 5.

Assemble all materials you will need on test day: pens, pencils, a watch, and your registration material.

Multiple Choice

Answer the multiple-choice questions in *Practice Test 3*.

Complete the self-scoring process.

Reread Chapters 1 and 3 if you are still unsure of any of the strategies or information about answering multiple-choice questions.

Essays

Write the essays from *Practice Test 3,* working on strengthening your areas of weakness.

Score the essays against the rubric.

Ask a responsible friend, an AP classmate, or a teacher to evaluate your essays against the scoring guide. Choose one essay to revise.

SUMMING IT UP

- The AP Program offers an opportunity to receive college credit for courses taken in high school.

- The AP English Language & Composition Test measures your ability to analyze the rhetoric of prose passages and to write essays in various rhetorical modes.

- Section I, Multiple Choice, contains about 50 questions on poetry and prose passages; Section II requires writing 3 essays.

- The multiple-choice questions include the following types:
    - main idea
    - detail
    - inference
    - definition
    - tone and purpose
    - form
    - factual knowledge

- The multiple-choice section is graded by machine and the essays are graded during a reading session by high school and college teachers.

- Section II includes three essays. Two of the essays usually require analysis of rhetorical and stylistic strategies in selected prose passages and one requires a synthesis of sources to support an argument—a persuasive essay based on an analysis and evaluation of sources.

- The highest score you can receive on an essay is a 9, so the highest total essay score is 27.

- The three essays together account for 55 percent of the total score

- The suggested reading list draws heavily from the selection of writers that the College Board suggests students read during their AP English Language & Composition course.

PART II

DIAGNOSING STRENGTHS AND WEAKNESSES

CHAPTER 2   Practice Test 1: Diagnostic

ANSWER SHEET PRACTICE TEST 1: DIAGNOSTIC

SECTION I

1. Ⓐ Ⓑ Ⓒ Ⓓ Ⓔ
2. Ⓐ Ⓑ Ⓒ Ⓓ Ⓔ
3. Ⓐ Ⓑ Ⓒ Ⓓ Ⓔ
4. Ⓐ Ⓑ Ⓒ Ⓓ Ⓔ
5. Ⓐ Ⓑ Ⓒ Ⓓ Ⓔ
6. Ⓐ Ⓑ Ⓒ Ⓓ Ⓔ
7. Ⓐ Ⓑ Ⓒ Ⓓ Ⓔ
8. Ⓐ Ⓑ Ⓒ Ⓓ Ⓔ
9. Ⓐ Ⓑ Ⓒ Ⓓ Ⓔ
10. Ⓐ Ⓑ Ⓒ Ⓓ Ⓔ
11. Ⓐ Ⓑ Ⓒ Ⓓ Ⓔ
12. Ⓐ Ⓑ Ⓒ Ⓓ Ⓔ
13. Ⓐ Ⓑ Ⓒ Ⓓ Ⓔ
14. Ⓐ Ⓑ Ⓒ Ⓓ Ⓔ
15. Ⓐ Ⓑ Ⓒ Ⓓ Ⓔ
16. Ⓐ Ⓑ Ⓒ Ⓓ Ⓔ
17. Ⓐ Ⓑ Ⓒ Ⓓ Ⓔ
18. Ⓐ Ⓑ Ⓒ Ⓓ Ⓔ

19. Ⓐ Ⓑ Ⓒ Ⓓ Ⓔ
20. Ⓐ Ⓑ Ⓒ Ⓓ Ⓔ
21. Ⓐ Ⓑ Ⓒ Ⓓ Ⓔ
22. Ⓐ Ⓑ Ⓒ Ⓓ Ⓔ
23. Ⓐ Ⓑ Ⓒ Ⓓ Ⓔ
24. Ⓐ Ⓑ Ⓒ Ⓓ Ⓔ
25. Ⓐ Ⓑ Ⓒ Ⓓ Ⓔ
26. Ⓐ Ⓑ Ⓒ Ⓓ Ⓔ
27. Ⓐ Ⓑ Ⓒ Ⓓ Ⓔ
28. Ⓐ Ⓑ Ⓒ Ⓓ Ⓔ
29. Ⓐ Ⓑ Ⓒ Ⓓ Ⓔ
30. Ⓐ Ⓑ Ⓒ Ⓓ Ⓔ
31. Ⓐ Ⓑ Ⓒ Ⓓ Ⓔ
32. Ⓐ Ⓑ Ⓒ Ⓓ Ⓔ
33. Ⓐ Ⓑ Ⓒ Ⓓ Ⓔ
34. Ⓐ Ⓑ Ⓒ Ⓓ Ⓔ
35. Ⓐ Ⓑ Ⓒ Ⓓ Ⓔ
36. Ⓐ Ⓑ Ⓒ Ⓓ Ⓔ

37. Ⓐ Ⓑ Ⓒ Ⓓ Ⓔ
38. Ⓐ Ⓑ Ⓒ Ⓓ Ⓔ
39. Ⓐ Ⓑ Ⓒ Ⓓ Ⓔ
40. Ⓐ Ⓑ Ⓒ Ⓓ Ⓔ
41. Ⓐ Ⓑ Ⓒ Ⓓ Ⓔ
42. Ⓐ Ⓑ Ⓒ Ⓓ Ⓔ
43. Ⓐ Ⓑ Ⓒ Ⓓ Ⓔ
44. Ⓐ Ⓑ Ⓒ Ⓓ Ⓔ
45. Ⓐ Ⓑ Ⓒ Ⓓ Ⓔ
46. Ⓐ Ⓑ Ⓒ Ⓓ Ⓔ
47. Ⓐ Ⓑ Ⓒ Ⓓ Ⓔ
48. Ⓐ Ⓑ Ⓒ Ⓓ Ⓔ
49. Ⓐ Ⓑ Ⓒ Ⓓ Ⓔ
50. Ⓐ Ⓑ Ⓒ Ⓓ Ⓔ
51. Ⓐ Ⓑ Ⓒ Ⓓ Ⓔ
52. Ⓐ Ⓑ Ⓒ Ⓓ Ⓔ
53. Ⓐ Ⓑ Ⓒ Ⓓ Ⓔ
54. Ⓐ Ⓑ Ⓒ Ⓓ Ⓔ

answer sheet

SECTION II

Question 1

_____

_____

_____

_____

_____

_____

_____

_____

_____

_____

_____

_____

_____

_____

_____

_____

_____

_____

_____

_____

_____

_____

_____

_____

_____

answer sheet

Question 2

_____

_____

_____

_____

_____

_____

_____

_____

_____

_____

_____

_____

_____

_____

_____

_____

_____

_____

_____

_____

_____

_____

_____

answer sheet

Question 3

_____

_____

_____

_____

_____

_____

_____

_____

_____

_____

_____

_____

_____

_____

_____

_____

_____

_____

_____

_____

_____

_____

_____

answer sheet

Practice Test 1: Diagnostic

SECTION I

54 QUESTIONS • 60 MINUTES

Directions: This section consists of selections of literature and questions on their content, style, and form. After you have read each passage, select the response that best answers the question and mark the corresponding space on the answer sheet.

QUESTIONS 1–11 REFER TO THE FOLLOWING SELECTION. READ THE PASSAGE CAREFULLY, AND THEN CHOOSE THE ANSWERS TO THE QUESTIONS.

This passage is taken from a report on nationwide literacy prepared by the National Endowment for the Arts.

Line   In a recent essay, "What use is literature?" Myron Magnet stated that "data are meaningless until we can articulate a story that makes sense out of them, and literature makes sense out of the data of human experience."[46]

5   Data from the 2002 Survey of Public Participation in the Arts (SPPA) demonstrate that many people enjoy literature. Novels, short stories, poetry, and plays attract almost one-half of those 18 or older (47 percent or about 96 million people). Each part of the literary puzzle examined in this monograph—novels, short stories, poetry, and plays—
10   attracts a significant number of people. Poetry (read by 25 million adults) is about as popular as attendance at jazz performances or at classical music events. About as many people read plays (7 million) as attend live opera or ballet. Novels and short stories have an audience (93 million) that is larger than almost any other cultural or leisure
15   pursuit. A number of people have a particularly strong attachment to books; about one in six literary readers (17 percent) read 12 or more books in 2002. Americans participate in literature in a variety of other ways. Almost one in ten (9 percent) listened to live or recorded readings of novels or books, and 6 percent listened to poetry readings
20   during the survey year. About 7 percent wrote creative works of their own, and 9 percent used the Internet to learn about, read, or discuss topics related to literature. Most literary readers are active in a wide range of other cultural and leisure pursuits. . . .

---

[46] In *City Journal,* Summer 2003, www.city-journal.org

25   It is not clear from the SPPA data how much influence TV watching has on literary reading. Not surprisingly, a statistical model created to analyze frequent readers found that watching four hours or more of TV per day had a negative impact on the chances of someone reading 12 books or more per year.[47] Watching no TV had a positive impact on the probability of someone reading 12 books or more. Literary readers watch slightly less TV each day than non-readers, and frequent readers watch

30 only slightly less TV per day than infrequent readers. The SPPA results cannot show whether non-readers would read more if they watched less TV, or whether they would use this extra time in other ways. . . . The percentage of U.S. adults reading literature dropped from 56.4 percent in 1982 to 46.7 percent in 2002—a decline of almost 10 percentage points. This may indicate a downward trend over the past two decades, but

35 it is important to note that the SPPA is not conducted on a yearly basis. This monograph looks at the surveys held in 1982, 1992, and 2002—ten-year snapshots. No information is available for non-SPPA years, and it is possible that the 2002 drop is a short, one-year change. If the 2002 data represent a declining trend, it is tempting to suggest that fewer people are reading literature and now prefer visual and audio

40 entertainment. Again, the data—both from SPPA and other sources—do not readily quantify this explanation. As discussed in Chapter 3, television does not seem to be the culprit. In 2002, those who do read and those who do not read literature watched about the same amount of TV per day—three hours' worth. The Internet, however, could have played a role. During the time period when the literature participation

45 rates declined, home Internet use soared. According to a 2000 Census Bureau report, 42 percent of households used the Internet at home—up dramatically from 26 percent in 1998, one of the earliest years of the Bureau's tracking.[48] By contrast, literary reading rates reported in 1982 and 1992 were virtually identical in a period before the Internet was widely available. It was not until 2002 that the reported percentage of adults reading literature dropped considerably.

---

[47] The details of the statistical models created for this report are included in Appendix C.

[48] U.S. Department of Commerce, U.S. Census Bureau, "Home Computers and Internet Use in the United States: August 2000." *Current Population Report,* P23-207, September 2001.

---

1. Which of the following most accurately states the subject of the passage?

  (A) The reading habits of Americans

  (B) The effects of television on reading

  (C) How the Internet makes people read less

  (D) The popularity of poetry and novels

  (E) The declining importance of literature

2. The source listed in which footnote would be the best source for information on statistics of home computer use?

  (A) 46

  (B) 47

  (C) 48

  (D) None of the above

  (E) Any of the above

3. Which of the following is closest to the meaning of "articulate" as used in the first sentence?

  (A) Enunciate

  (B) Convey

  (C) Clear up

  (D) Pronounce

  (E) Decry

4. Which of the following is the best description of the tone of this passage?

    (A) Informative and unbiased
    (B) Opinionated and persuasive
    (C) Appeals to emotions
    (D) Accurate and hopeful
    (E) Creative and informational

5. The purpose of footnote 48 is to inform the reader that the information in lines 45–47

    (A) is about the U.S. Department of Commerce
    (B) was first published in 2000
    (C) appears in *Current Population Report,* P23-207
    (D) was written by the U.S. Census Bureau and edited by the U.S. Department of Commerce
    (E) appears in a book called Home Computers and Internet Use

6. With which statement would the authors of this article most likely agree?

    (A) Literary readers watch as much, if not more, television than most non-readers.
    (B) Only literary readers are important in determining reading statistics for U.S. citizens; non-fiction readers do not count.
    (C) Internet use has had a very detrimental effect on the percentage of U.S. citizens who are literary readers.
    (D) All data must have a story to accompany them.
    (E) A decline in literary readers might be attributed to a growing preference for audio and visual entertainment, but there is no hard data to support this fact.

7. The phrase "about one in six literary readers (17 percent) read 12 or more books in 2002" in lines 16–17, is used to support the assertion that

    (A) as many people read poetry as attend jazz performances or classical music events
    (B) many people have a particularly strong attachment to books
    (C) a small percentage of the population wrote their own creative works
    (D) most literary readers read at least 12 books in a calendar year
    (E) since 2002, literary readers read less books per year than before 2002

8. The sentence "Most literary readers are active in a wide range of other cultural and leisure pursuits . . ." at the end of the second paragraph is most likely

    (A) an opinion based in anecdotal evidence not included in the report
    (B) included to convince people who read the article to be more cultured
    (C) a conclusion drawn from results of surveys on which the report is based
    (D) the authors' wishes for a more cultural society
    (E) untrue based on the information in the passage

9. "This monograph looks at the surveys held in 1982, 1992, and 2002—ten-year snapshots." What type of literary device is represented by the use of the world "snapshot" in this sentence?

    (A) Personification
    (B) Simile
    (C) Onomatopoeia
    (D) Iambic pentameter
    (E) Metaphor

10. The word that would have the *most accurate* meaning if used to replace the word "about" as used in lines 8, 11, 12, and 16 in the second paragraph is

(A) Precisely
(B) Near
(C) Approximately
(D) Exactly
(E) Around

11. Footnote 47 is included in order to

(A) guide the reader to details about statistical models used in the report
(B) show the reader that the passage should be taken seriously
(C) help the reader understand the importance of accurate statistical models
(D) properly cite the publisher of the statistical model that is mentioned in the passage
(E) remind the reader that there are some appendixes to the report

QUESTIONS 12–24 REFER TO THE FOLLOWING SELECTION. READ THE PASSAGE CAREFULLY, AND THEN CHOOSE THE ANSWERS TO THE QUESTIONS.

From the Preface to the 1855 Edition of *Leaves of Grass*

Line America does not repel the past or what it has produced under its forms or amid other politics or the idea of castes or the old religions . . . accepts the lesson with calmness . . . is not so impatient as has been supposed that the slough still sticks to opinions and manners and literature while the life which served its requirements has passed
5   into the new life of the new forms . . . perceives that the corpse is slowly borne from the eating and sleeping rooms of the house . . . perceives that it waits a little while in the door . . . that it was fittest for its days . . . that its action has descended to the stalwart and well-shaped heir who approaches . . . and that he shall be fittest for his days.
10   The Americans of all nations at any time upon the earth have probably the fullest poetical nature. The United States themselves are essentially the greatest poem. In the history of the earth hitherto the largest and most stirring appear tame and orderly to their ampler largeness and stir. Here at last is something in the doings of man that corresponds with the broadcast doings of the day and night. Here is not
15   merely a nation but a teeming nation of nations. Here is action untied from strings necessarily blind to particulars and details magnificently moving in vast masses. Here is the hospitality which forever indicates heroes . . . Here are the roughs and beards and space and ruggedness and nonchalance that the soul loves. Here the performance disdaining the trivial unapproached in the tremendous audacity of its crowds and
20   groupings and the push of its perspective spreads with crampless and flowing breadth and showers its prolific and splendid extravagance. One sees it must indeed own the riches of the summer and winter, and need never bankrupt while corn grows from the ground or orchards drop apples or the bays contain fish or men beget children upon women. . . .

—Walt Whitman

12. Which of the following is the best statement of the theme of this passage?

    (A) A portrait of the beauty of the United States.
    (B) A forecast of the future of poetry in the United States.
    (C) A merging of new and old literary styles.
    (D) A discussion of the resources and poetry of the United States.
    (E) A poetic definition of the United States.

13. In line 5, to what does the word "corpse" refer?

    (A) Old forms of poetry
    (B) The past
    (C) Slough
    (D) Older opinions and manners
    (E) Current politics

14. How does Whitman suggest that the past and the present are linked?

    I.   The past nourishes and educates the present.
    II. In the present, the past is viewed differently.
    III. The present is merely a mirror image of the past.
    IV. The present can be seen only in the context of the past.

    (A) I only
    (B) II only
    (C) III only
    (D) IV only
    (E) I, II, and IV only

15. Which of the following statements does NOT reflect Whitman's ideas about the United States?

    (A) It is larger than most other countries.
    (B) The population is more literate than that of other nations.
    (C) The people of the United States have built a unique nation.
    (D) It is a country of vast riches in people and nature.
    (E) It is a country in transition.

16. When Whitman wrote "perceives that the corpse is slowly borne from the eating and sleeping rooms of the house," (lines 5–6) he used what type of literary device?

    (A) Personification
    (B) Meter
    (C) Oxymoron
    (D) Conceit
    (E) Metaphor

17. Which is the best interpretation of Whitman's statement "the United States themselves are essentially the greatest poem" in line 11?

    (A) The greatest volume of good poetry is from the United States.
    (B) The nation's vibrancy, beauty, and diversity are poetic.
    (C) The people of the nation are very poetic.
    (D) The United States is the leader in finding new forms of poetry.
    (E) Literature in the United States has poetry at its root.

18. The sentence "Here are the roughs and beards and space and ruggedness and nonchalance that the soul loves" (lines 17–18) is intended as

    (A) a challenge presented to humanity
    (B) symbolic of emotional highs and lows
    (C) a metaphor for the American landscape: physical and cultural
    (D) a contrast between something easy and something difficult
    (E) a reference to style and dress at the time of writing

19. Which of the following descriptions would best characterize the United States, according to Whitman?

    (A) Rigid
    (B) Malleable
    (C) Anti-intellectual
    (D) Exuberant
    (E) Enshrining the past

20. What does Whitman mean when he comments that the United States "is not merely a nation but a teeming nation of nations" (lines 14–15)?

(A) New Americans have tremendously increased the population.

(B) The nation's resources can support a large population.

(C) People come to the United States to make their fortunes.

(D) Native Americans represent a nation within a nation.

(E) The United States is a culturally diverse nation.

21. In the second paragraph, Whitman uses the word "here" to begin numerous sentences. What effect does he create?

(A) A ponderous feeling

(B) A sense of predictability

(C) Formality

(D) Exuberance

(E) A musical, poetic feeling

22. The following sentence contains which of the elements listed?

Here the performance disdaining the trivial unapproached in the tremendous audacity of its crowds and groupings and the push of its perspective spreads with crampless and flowing breadth and showers its prolific and splendid extravagance.

(A) A gerund phrase

(B) A participial phrase

(C) An infinitive phrase

(D) All of the above

(E) None of the above

23. The compound verb in the sentence beginning, "Here the performance" (lines 18–21) is

(A) push and spreads

(B) unapproached and showers

(C) unapproached and disdaining

(D) spreads and showers

(E) crowds and showers

24. What is Whitman saying in the sentence "Here at last is something in the doings of man that corresponds with the broadcast doings of the day and night." (lines 13–14)?

(A) The people of the United States follow a pattern like day becomes night.

(B) The nation's actions are unpredictable.

(C) The influence of the United States spreads as widely as day and night.

(D) A person meets challenges on a day-to-day basis.

(E) People have found a place in the United States where their actions are compatible with nature.

QUESTIONS 25–38 REFER TO THE FOLLOWING SELECTION. READ THE PASSAGE CAREFULLY, AND THEN CHOOSE THE ANSWERS TO THE QUESTIONS. IN *POLITICS AND THE ENGLISH LANGUAGE*, GEORGE ORWELL EXPRESSES A CONCERN FOR THE ENGLISH LANGUAGE AND THE MANIPULATION OF LANGUAGE IN THE MODERN WORLD.

From *Politics and the English Language*

Line Most people who bother with the matter at all would admit that the English language is in a bad way, but it is generally assumed that we cannot by conscious action do anything about it. Our civilization is decadent and our language—so the argument runs—must inevitably share in the general collapse. It follows that any struggle
5 against the abuse of language is a sentimental archaism, like preferring candles to electric light or hansom cabs to aeroplanes. Underneath this lies the half-conscious belief that language is a natural growth and not an instrument which we shape for our own purposes. . . .
. . . The defense of the English language implies more than this, and perhaps it is
10 best to start by saying what it does not imply.
To begin with it has nothing to do with archaism, with salvaging of obsolete words and turns of speech, or with the setting up of a "standard English" which must never be departed from. On the contrary, it is especially concerned with the scrapping of every word or idiom which has out worn its usefulness. It has nothing to do with
15 correct grammar and syntax, which are of no importance so long as one makes one's meaning clear, or with the avoidance of Americanisms, or with having what is called a "good prose style." On the other hand it is not concerned with fake simplicity and the attempt to make written English colloquial. Nor does it even imply in every case preferring the Saxon word to the Latin one, though it does imply using the fewest and
20 the shortest words that will cover one's meaning. What is above all needed is to let the meaning choose the word, and not the other way about. In prose, the worst thing one can do with words is to surrender to them. When you think of a concrete object, you think wordless, and then, if you want to describe the thing you have been visualizing you probably hunt about till you find the exact words that seem to fit it. When you
25 think of something abstract you are more inclined to use words from the start, and unless you make a conscious effort to prevent it, the existing dialect will come rushing in and do the job for you, at the expense of blurring or even changing your meaning. Probably it is better to put off using words as long as possible and get one's meaning as clear as one can through pictures or sensations. Afterwards one can choose—not
30 simply *accept*—the phrases that will best cover the meaning, and then switch round and decide what impression one's words are likely to make on another person. This last effort of the mind cuts out all stale or mixed images, all prefabricated phrases, needless repetitions, and humbug and vagueness generally. But one can often be in doubt about the effect of a word or a phrase, and one needs rules that one can rely on
35 when instinct fails. I think the following rules will cover most cases:

    (i) Never use a metaphor, simile, or other figure of speech which you are used to seeing in print.
    (ii) Never use a long word where a short one will do.
    (iii) If it is possible to cut a word out, always cut it out.
40   (iv) Never use the passive where you can use the active.
    (v) Never use a foreign phrase, a scientific word, or a jargon word if you can think of an everyday English equivalent.
    (vi) Break any of these rules sooner than say anything outright barbarous.

These rules sound elementary, and so they are, but they demand a deep change in
45 attitude in anyone who has grown used to writing in the style now fashionable. One

GO ON TO THE NEXT PAGE ➤

could keep all of them and still write bad English, but one could not write the kind of stuff that I quoted in those five specimens at the beginning of this article.

I have not here been considering the literary use of language, but merely language as an instrument of expressing and not for concealing or preventing thought. . . . One
50 can at least change one's own habits, and from time to time one can even, if one jeers loudly enough, send some worn-out and useless phrase—some *jackboot, Achilles' heel, hotbed, melting pot, acid test, veritable inferno* or other lump of verbal refuse—into the dustbin where it belongs.

—George Orwell

25. The chief topic of this selection is

  (A) poor use of English
  (B) diction
  (C) chauvinistic disregard for foreign words and phrases
  (D) grammar and mechanics
  (E) scientific language and jargon

26. This passage is primarily concerned with

  (A) the meanings of words
  (B) the rules of syntax and structure in the English language
  (C) the use of colloquialisms in the English language
  (D) some rules to be used for better writing
  (E) integration of scientific and foreign words into the English language

27. Which of the following best expresses one of the author's goals?

  (A) To expand the use of the English language.
  (B) To introduce new grammar rules.
  (C) To teach creative writing.
  (D) To find new means of expression.
  (E) To simplify word use and sentence structure.

28. The author advocates which of the following actions?

  (A) Using simplicity to make English colloquial.
  (B) The use of detailed, descriptive phrasing.
  (C) Simple, direct word selection.
  (D) The use of common idioms.
  (E) The occasional use of foreign phrases to add interest.

29. The general tone of this passage is

  (A) subtly humorous
  (B) serious and persuasive
  (C) ironic
  (D) satirical
  (E) dramatic and portentous

30. George Orwell would agree with which of the following statements?

  (A) You can break the rules whenever you want.
  (B) You should never break the rules.
  (C) You can break the rules if the writing makes better sense.
  (D) You can break the rules early in a document if you are consistent.
  (E) Rules are useful conventions.

31. In the second paragraph, the author identifies what situation under which rules are necessary?

  (A) When vagueness is required.
  (B) When one's sense of what is good fails.
  (C) When there are no guidelines.
  (D) Whenever one is writing informally.
  (E) Rules are never required.

32. What does the author think will happen if his rules are followed?

    (A) Anything written will be good.
    (B) Writing will be easier to read.
    (C) More people will read.
    (D) Writing will be as good as possible.
    (E) More people will write.

33. What is the best paraphrase for the following sentence: "What is above all needed is to let the meaning choose the word, and not the other way about" (lines 20–21)?

    (A) Definitions of words should change depending on context.
    (B) A writer's meaning should determine word choice.
    (C) Words should always have the same meaning no matter how they are used.
    (D) A universal English system should be used.
    (E) The shortest and fewest words should be used.

34. According to Orwell's rules, why would he object to the following sentence: "The rich treasury of our language might go down the drain"?

    (A) Never use a metaphor, simile, or other figure of speech that you are used to seeing in print.
    (B) Never use a long word where a short one will do.
    (C) If it is possible to cut a word out, always cut it out.
    (D) Never use the passive where you can use the active.
    (E) Never use a foreign phrase, a scientific word, or a jargon word if you can think of an everyday English equivalent.

35. In the third paragraph, Orwell first uses the pronoun "one" and then switches to the pronoun "you." What is the effect of that change?

    (A) By so doing, he spotlights poor syntax.
    (B) By using "you," he relates more directly to the reader.
    (C) He is following his own advice: to simplify.
    (D) He is using an everyday English equivalent.
    (E) He is using standard English.

36. This sentence from the third paragraph, "In prose, the worst thing one can do with words is to surrender to them." (lines 21–22) contains which of the following?

    (A) Simile
    (B) Metaphor
    (C) Personification
    (D) Onomatopoeia
    (E) Alliteration

37. Which of the following is the best explanation of the author's rationale for saying that grammar and syntax are not important?

    (A) Grammar and syntax rules are too strict.
    (B) Grammar and syntax are never a major problem.
    (C) Grammar and syntax are not so important, as long as the meaning is clear.
    (D) Grammar and syntax rules are too lax.
    (E) Grammar and syntax are not universally understood.

38. What is the meaning of "colloquial" in line 18?

    (A) Fresh, colorful
    (B) Conversational, informal
    (C) Regional, provincial
    (D) Intriguing, fascinating
    (E) Understandable, comprehensible

GO ON TO THE NEXT PAGE

QUESTIONS 39–54 REFER TO THE FOLLOWING SELECTION. READ THE PASSAGE CAREFULLY, AND THEN CHOOSE THE ANSWERS TO THE QUESTIONS.

From *Roughing It*

Line It was always very cold on that lake shore* in the night, but we had plenty of blankets and were warm enough. We never moved a muscle all night, but waked at early dawn in the original positions, and got up at once, thoroughly refreshed, free from soreness, and brim full of friskiness. There is no end of wholesome medicine in such
5 an experience. That morning we could have whipped ten such people as we were the day before—sick ones at any rate. But the world is slow, and people will go to "water cures" and "movement cures" and to foreign lands for health. Three months of camp life on Lake Tahoe would restore an Egyptian mummy to his pristine vigor, and give him an appetite like an alligator. I do not mean the oldest and driest mummies, of
10 course, but the fresher ones. The air up there in the clouds is very pure and fine, bracing and delicious. And why shouldn't it be?—it is the same the angels breathe. I think that hardly any amount of fatigue can be gathered together that a man cannot sleep off in one night on the sand by its side. Not under a roof, but under the sky; it seldom or never rains there in the summertime. I know a man who went there to die.
15 But he made a failure of it. He was a skeleton when he came, and could barely stand. He had no appetite, and did nothing but read tracts and reflect on the future. Three months later he was sleeping out of doors regularly, eating all he could hold, three times a day, and chasing game over the mountains three thousand feet high for recreation. And he was a skeleton no longer, but weighed part of a ton. This is no
20 fancy sketch, but the truth. His disease was consumption. I confidently commend his experience to other skeletons.

—Mark Twain

---

* Lake Tahoe on the California–Nevada border

39. What is the tone of the passage?

(A) Witty
(B) Serious, scientific
(C) Insightful
(D) Argumentative
(E) Questioning, curious

40. Which of the following is the best statement of the theme of this passage?

(A) Lake Tahoe is beautiful.
(B) Going to Lake Tahoe can be helpful.
(C) The air and water quality of Lake Tahoe are outstanding.
(D) Lake Tahoe and its environs have recuperative powers.
(E) It is important to keep Lake Tahoe pristine.

41. This selection can be classified as a(n)

(A) expository essay
(B) dramatic dialogue
(C) exaggerated anecdote
(D) modern myth
(E) persuasive essay

42. The writer's purpose in this selection is to

(A) amuse and entertain his audience
(B) inform the audience about Lake Tahoe
(C) teach about the environment
(D) advocate a national park system through interesting readers in natural wonders
(E) subtly suggest a healthy lifestyle

43. What is the setting of this selection?

    (A) The Appalachian mountains in the mid-1800s.
    (B) The West in the late twentieth century.
    (C) The high deserts of the Southwest in the late 1700s.
    (D) The mountains of the West in the mid-1800s.
    (E) The Finger Lakes region of New York at the turn of the century.

44. Which of the following is the best characterization of Mark Twain's diction?

    (A) He uses a great deal of folksy language.
    (B) Twain's diction is erudite.
    (C) His style is very sophisticated.
    (D) He is somewhat careless and irresponsible in his word choices.
    (E) The passage is structured and static.

45. This passage from *Roughing It* could be considered an example of

    (A) romanticism
    (B) realism
    (C) naturalism
    (D) classicism
    (E) regionalism

46. When Twain writes, "But the world is slow," in line 6, he is saying that

    (A) people lack energy
    (B) it takes time to communicate
    (C) people take time to learn
    (D) it takes a long time to get to a new place
    (E) there is little that is new

47. The reference to the Egyptian mummy in line 8 emphasizes the

    (A) dryness of the region
    (B) age of the lake
    (C) rehabilitative powers of the region
    (D) spiritual aspects of the area
    (E) beauty of the region

48. When Twain writes "I think that hardly any amount of fatigue can be gathered together that a man cannot sleep off in one night on the sand by its side," (lines 11–13) he is saying that the speaker thinks

    (A) people never get enough sleep
    (B) many people sleep too much
    (C) sand forms a relaxing bed
    (D) anyone can get fully rested at Lake Tahoe
    (E) the sands at Lake Tahoe have medicinal qualities

49. The words "bracing" and "delicious" (line 11) suggest that the air is

    (A) cold and tasteful
    (B) supportive and tasty
    (C) invigorating and enjoyable
    (D) refreshing and supportive
    (E) invigorating and refreshing

50. Based on this passage, what conclusion can be drawn about Twain's feelings for the locale?

    I. He enjoys the environment of Lake Tahoe.
    II. He finds the mountain region invigorating.
    III. He feels it lacks the depth of the East.

    (A) I only
    (B) II only
    (C) III only
    (D) I and II only
    (E) I, II, and III

51. When Twain states, the air is what "angels breathe," (line 11) he is alluding to what aspect of the environment?

    (A) The altitude
    (B) The cold
    (C) The moisture
    (D) The heavenly scent from the pines
    (E) The perfection of the biosphere

52. Which of the following does NOT apply to Twain's style in this selection?

    (A) He uses specific details to create a sense of realism.
    (B) He captures the local color.
    (C) The speaker seems to be an ordinary person, the common man.
    (D) The language has the flavor and rhythms of common speech.
    (E) It imitates Shakespearean sentence structure.

53. How would you characterize the phrase "fancy sketch" (line 20)?

    (A) An elaborate drawing
    (B) A short, nonfiction anecdote
    (C) A medical tract discussing cures
    (D) A short skit or humorous act
    (E) A tall tale, a humorous account

54. All of the following rhetorical features are evident in this passage EXCEPT

    (A) personal anecdote
    (B) figures of speech
    (C) tall tale
    (D) colloquialism
    (E) simple sentence

STOP   If you finish before time is called, you may check your work on this section only. Do not turn to any other section in the test.

SECTION II

3 QUESTIONS • 2 HOURS 15 MINUTES

> **Directions:** Read the passage below carefully. Write a well-organized essay that evaluates the elements of rhetoric and style found in the passage. Explain how the writer uses these elements to communicate with his audience and to achieve his purpose.

Question 1

SUGGESTED TIME—40 MINUTES

"Addressing the Graduating Class"
University High School
Oxford, Mississippi, May 28, 1951

Years ago, before any of you were born, a wise Frenchman said, "If youth knew; if age could." We all know what he meant: that when you are young, you have the power to do anything, but you don't know what to do. Then, when you have got old and experience and observation have taught you answers, you are tired, frightened; you don't care, you want to be left alone as long as you yourself are safe; you no longer have the capacity or the will to grieve over any wrongs but your own.

So you young men and women in this room tonight, and in thousands of other rooms like this one about the earth today, have the power to change the world, rid it forever of war and injustice and suffering, provided you know how, know what to do. And so according to the old Frenchman, since you can't know what to do because you are young, then anyone standing here with a head full of white hair, should be able to tell you.

But maybe this one is not as old and wise as his white hairs pretend or claim. Because he can't give you a glib answer or pattern either. But he can tell you this, because he believes this. What threatens us today is fear. Not the atom bomb, nor even fear of it, because if the bomb fell on Oxford tonight, all it could do would be to kill us, which is nothing, since in doing that, it will have robbed itself of its only power over us: which is fear of it, the being afraid of it. Our danger is not that. Our danger is the forces in the world today which are trying to use man's fear to rob him of his individuality, his soul, trying to reduce him to an unthinking mass by fear and bribery—giving him free food which he has not earned, easy and valueless money which he has not worked for; the economies or ideologies or political systems, communist or socialist or democratic, whatever they wish to call themselves, the tyrants and the politicians, American or European or Asiatic, whatever they call themselves, who would reduce man to one obedient mass for their own aggrandizement and power, or because they themselves are baffled and afraid, afraid of, or incapable of, believing in man's capacity for courage and endurance and sacrifice.

That is what we must resist, if we are to change the world for man's peace and security. It is not men in the mass who can and will save Man. It is Man himself, created in the image of God so that he shall have the power and the will to choose right from wrong, and so be able to save himself because he is worth saving;—Man, the individual, men and women, who will refuse always to be tricked or frightened or bribed into surrendering, not just the right but the duty too, to choose between justice and injustice, courage and cowardice, sacrifice and greed, pity and self;—who will believe always not only in the right of man to be free of injustice and rapacity and deception, but the duty and responsibility of man to see that justice and truth and pity and compassion are done.

So, never be afraid. Never be afraid to raise your voice for honesty and truth and compassion, against injustice and lying and greed. If you, not just you in this room tonight, but in all the thousands of other rooms like this one about the world today and tomorrow and next week, will do this, not as a class or classes, but as individuals, men and women, you will change the earth; in one generation all the Napoleons and Hitlers and Caesars and Mussolinis and Stalins and all the other tyrants who want power and aggrandizement, and the simple politicians and time-servers who themselves are merely baffled or ignorant or afraid, who have used, or are using, or hope to use, man's fear and greed for man's enslavement, will have vanished from the face of it.

—William Faulkner

Directions: Read this passage about the accumulation and distribution of wealth carefully. Write a well-organized, persuasive essay that defends, challenges, or qualifies the assertions made by the author. Use evidence from your observations, experience, or reading to develop your position. Bear in mind the structure of an argument, the types of arguments, and the premises.

Question 2

SUGGESTED TIME—40 MINUTES

There remains, then, only one mode of using great fortunes; but in this we have the true antidote for the temporary unequal distribution of wealth, the reconciliation of the rich and the poor—a reign of harmony—another ideal, differing, indeed, from that of the Communist in requiring only the further evolution of existing conditions, not the total overthrow of our civilization. It is founded upon the present most intense individualism, and the race is prepared to put it in practice by degrees whenever it pleases. Under its sway we shall have an ideal state, in which the surplus wealth of the few will become, in the best sense, the property of the many, because administered for the common good; and this wealth, passing through the hands of the few, can be made a much more potent force for the elevation of our race than if it had been distributed in small sums to the people themselves. Even the poorest can be made to see this, and to agree that great sums gathered by some of their fellow citizens and spent for public purposes, from which the masses reap the principal benefit, are more valuable to them than if scattered among them through the course of many years in trifling amounts.

—Andrew Carnegie, "Wealth," 1889

GO ON TO THE NEXT PAGE

Directions: The following prompt is based on the following six sources. The assignment requires that you synthesize a number of the sources into a coherent, well-written essay that takes a position. Use at least three of the sources to support your position. Do not simply paraphrase or summarize the sources. Your argument should be the focus of your essay and the sources should support this argument. Remember to attribute both direct and indirect citations.

Question 3

SUGGESTED TIME—15 MINUTES FOR READING AND 40 MINUTES FOR WRITING

Introduction: Voter registration in the United States is higher than ever before. However, the number of Americans who are voting is lower than ever before. What might account for this gap? Why might people who register to vote not exercise their right to vote?

Assignment: Read the following sources (including any introductory information) carefully. **Then, write an essay that defends, challenges, or qualifies the claim that people who are registered to vote do not vote because they do not feel that their vote will make a difference. Synthesize at least three of the sources to support your position.**

You may refer to the sources by their titles (Source A, Source B, etc.) or by the descriptions in parentheses.

Source A (Smith)

Source B (Jenkins)

Source C (chart)

Source D (Allen)

Source E (Beggens)

Source F (Langevin)

> **SOURCE A**
>
> Smith, Andrew. "The Registration/Voter Gap," *Voter Rights Magazine,* April 9, 2005

The following passage is excerpted from an article about the gap between voter registration numbers and voter turnout in elections.

Why don't all people who can do so vote? It is an intrinsic right of every American citizen. Our government is run by elected officials. The premise is that these officials represent the will of the people, as evidenced by the fact that they have been voted into office. However, in reality, people often feel that their elected officials often don't represent them. But perhaps this is because those who don't feel that they are adequately represented did not vote in the first place. This can create a cycle in which voters do not vote because they have no confidence in elected officials, because they feel as if the elected officials do not represent *them,* so therefore, they don't vote, and the cycle begins again. But how can people who do not exercise their right to help choose their elected officials expect to be properly represented? What is perhaps most frustrating is the fact that a large number of these nonvoters are *registered* to vote.

Throughout the 1990s, voter registration as a percentage of the total voting age (eligible) population has risen dramatically. Why? Well, increased government interest in helping people register to vote is one factor. The National Voter Registration Act, passed by Congress in 1993 (also known as the Motor Voter program) shares a large part of the responsibility for the increase in voter registration. The Motor Voter act simply makes it easier for people to register to vote. It cuts out lots of bureaucratic red tape. Most states now allow people to register by mail. In addition, in most states, when a person registers a vehicle, they can also register to vote. During the first full year of the program, approximately 11 million people registered to vote or updated their registration information.

Yet, it is obvious that merely being *registered* to vote does not *cause* people to vote. The government has launched programs to increase registration in an effort to increase voter *participation;* but this is a fallacy. The registration programs do not get to the heart of the issue—the disillusionment of the American public with our political system.

SOURCE B

Jenkins, Angela. Editorial in the online magazine *Students Unite*, December 2003 issue.

The following is excerpted from an online editorial about the lack of political involvement of college students and how that might affect politics in the future.

My fellow students, we are shirking our responsibilities as U.S. citizens. Yes, we, dear reader, are allowing our prized political system to become a joke. We sit around in the dining hall and complain about the war. We complain about the president. We complain about, well, everything that has to do with government. We kick around conspiracy theories and spend hours lamenting how unfair our government system really is. We whine about criminals with too many rights, or maybe we whine about the fact that they don't have enough rights. It doesn't really matter what the subject is, we'll debate until the day grows long.

But, and this is an important but, what do we do about it? How many of us who were eligible to vote actually voted in the last presidential election? How many of us voted in a local election? In fact, how many of us even voted for our own student council members? Well, I promise you, I have seen the numbers, and they are low, my friends. So, why do we complain so much?

This letter is a call to action. This political apathy has got to stop. Actually, that is not entirely accurate—it is not apathy toward politics that is the problem, it is apathy toward *voting*. Vote and make a difference, people. Run for office and make a difference. Just do something!

SOURCE C
Report on voter registration in the November 2004 election, prepared by the United States Census Bureau.

The following table is adapted from the U.S. Census Bureau's report on voter registration in the 2004 election.

Table E.
Reasons for Not Registering by Selected Characteristics: 2004
(Numbers in Thousands)

Characteristic	Total[1]	Percent distribution of reasons for not registering								
		Not interested in the election or not involved in politics	Did not meet registration deadlines	Not eligible to vote	Don't know or refused	Permanent illness or disability	Other	Did not know where or how to register	Did not meet residency requirements	My vote would not make a difference
Total, 18 years and older	32,432	46.6	17.4	6.7	6.2	5.6	4.7	4.5	3.7	3.7
Age										
18 to 24 years	6,888	44.0	24.0	5.8	8.2	1.8	3.1	6.2	3.9	2.6
25 to 44 years	13,284	45.7	19.0	8.5	5.5	2.8	5.0	4.8	4.4	3.5
45 to 64 years	8,508	50.4	13.4	6.6	6.7	5.9	4.6	3.2	3.0	4.6
65 years and older	3,751	45.6	9.1	2.3	3.8	21.6	6.3	3.1	2.2	3.8

[1] Includes only those respondents who answered "no" to the question "Were you registered in the election of November 2004?"
Source: U.S. Census Bureau, Current Population Survey, November 2004.

SOURCE D

Allen, Mario. "Voting Rights in America." *The Magazine,* August 25, 2005.

The following is excerpted from an article that discusses the history of voting rights in America.

Voting rights in America have come a long way since the nation's founding. In the early years of our nation, only white, land-owning men could vote. By 1830, in most states requirements of property ownership or religious tests were abolished, but still, only white men could vote. Women began to fight for the right to vote in the years before the Civil War, but it was not until 1920 that the 19th Amendment was ratified, giving women the right to vote.

After the Civil War, the passage of the 15th Amendment gave all African American males the right to vote. However, this right was in practice denied to African Americans in the South in many ways, including the use of poll taxes and the "grandfather" clause. The 24th Amendment would eliminate poll taxes in federal elections in 1964.

In 1965, the Voting Rights Act was passed. This act eliminated literacy tests to vote. It also sent federal representatives to the south to oversee voting registration. This act increased voter registration and participation for southern African Americans. Voting participation was extended to 18 year-olds with the passage of the 26th Amendment. This increased registration and participation, as well, although those 18–24 have the lowest registration and turnout rates of any age group. Finally, the passage of the "Motor Voter" act in 1993 increased voter registration by millions.

SOURCE E

Beggens, Alicia. "Did the Generation Z Vote Campaign Work?" *Rolling Moss Magazine*, February 2006.

The following is excerpted from an article about a campaign to get people between the ages of 18 and 24 to vote in the most recent presidential election.

The Generation Z Vote Campaign seemed like genius. The nation's most popular music station, coupled with a huge amount of celebrity support, sought to change the way that young people participate in politics today. The idea was to make politics interesting. It was reasoned that because young people looked up to celebrities, that celebrity endorsement would make voting, well, cool. In addition, the campaign had a decidedly Democratic leaning, pushing a fairly liberal agenda. Even so, many Republicans came out in support of the campaign, reasoning that any type of political involvement was better than none at all.

Which begs the question: did it work? For almost 18 months, the campaign seemed to be everywhere: on college campuses, in malls, all over TV and radio. And it seemed as if the targeted group was responding. There was a real feeling for a while that this time, the 18- to 24-year-olds would make a difference. They might even swing an election.

Alas, it seems it was all for naught. Although voter turnout overall in the last presidential election seemed to slightly increase from the previous election, the 18- to 24-year-old turnout numbers were atrocious. There was barely a difference in the percentage voting from the last election.

SOURCE F

"Langevin Testifies on Voter Legislation," United States House of Representatives press release, June 2006, can be found at http://www.house.gov/list/press/ri02_langevin/prvoter62206.html

The following is excerpted from a government press release regarding Congressman Jim Langevin's (D-RI) testimony before Congress regarding voter registration and identification requirements. This excerpt contains background information on Congress's record of enfranchisement.

When I was elected Secretary of State, Rhode Island had the oldest voting equipment in the nation. Beginning in 1993, as a state Representative when I chaired a special legislative commission on election reform and then as Secretary of State, I worked with my colleagues in the legislature, the State Board of Elections, local canvassing authorities and the public to investigate voting problems throughout the state and develop an effective resolution. We successfully upgraded our election equipment, significantly reducing our error rates and making our polling places and machines accessible to people with disabilities. We also implemented the requirements of the National Voter Registration Act—popularly known as "Motor Voter"—which reduced certain longstanding obstacles to registration. These changes were significant, and we ultimately met our goal of increasing the number of registered voters in Rhode Island by nearly 60,000 between 1993 and 2000. Our efforts made Rhode Island a model for electoral participation and accessibility, and I was pleased to help translate those successes to the national level by participating in the development of the Help America Vote Act—a great bipartisan effort of this committee and the most recent success story in Congress's long history of expanding voting opportunities to Americans.

Congress should be proud of its record of removing barriers and increasing the opportunity of all Americans to vote. Though it took us far too long, Congress guaranteed the right to vote to citizens whose only disqualification was the color of their skin. It opened polling places to the disabled. It extended the franchise to Americans living overseas. It enabled all citizens in our mobile society to register and reregister with ease. It did all this on a bipartisan basis. It did this while maintaining the integrity of our elections.

STOP   If you finish before time is called, you may check your work on this section only. Do not turn to any other section in the test.

ANSWER KEY AND EXPLANATIONS

Section I

1. A	12. E	23. D	34. A	45. E
2. C	13. B	24. C	35. B	46. C
3. B	14. A	25. B	36. C	47. C
4. A	15. B	26. D	37. C	48. D
5. C	16. E	27. E	38. C	49. C
6. E	17. B	28. C	39. A	50. D
7. B	18. C	29. B	40. D	51. A
8. C	19. B	30. C	41. C	52. E
9. E	20. E	31. B	42. A	53. E
10. C	21. D	32. B	43. D	54. D
11. A	22. B	33. B	44. A	

1. **The correct answer is (A).** Choice (A) is the best answer to this question: the passage is part of a report about the reading habits of Americans. Choice (B) is incorrect, because although the passage does mention the effect of television on reading, this is not the focus of the passage. Choice (C) contains a conclusion that simply cannot be drawn from the information in the passage. The passage does mention poetry and novels but only as supporting details, so choice (D) is incorrect. There is no support anywhere in the passage for the claim made in choice (E), so it, too, is incorrect.

2. **The correct answer is (C).** This question tests your ability to read and understand the purpose of certain footnotes. Choice (C), footnote 48, refers to a study on home computers and Internet use, and would therefore be the best source of information on statistics on home computer use. Footnote 46 is a citation for the quotation that opens the passage, so choice (A) is incorrect. Footnote 47 refers to statistical models that appear in appendixes to the passage, so it is not the best source for information on home computer use.

3. **The correct answer is (B).** To answer this question correctly, you must use context clues to determine the meaning of the word "articulate" as it is used in the passage. For questions like this one, if you do not know the meaning of the word being tested, try rereading the sentence to yourself, replacing the word being tested with the answer choices. Choose the answer choice that makes the most sense. In this case, choice (B), convey, is closest in meaning to "articulate"—you can convey, or tell, a story. Choice (A), enunciate, does not work, because it deals with pronunciation. Choice (C) is incorrect because it implies that there is a problem to be solved and does not fit in the context of the sentence. Choice (D), pronounce, may be a tempting choice, as it does imply speaking or articulating. However, choice (B) is still the *best* answer to the question. Choice (E), decry, does not make sense in the context of the sentence.

4. **The correct answer is (A).** Tone refers to the mood of a passage. In reading this passage, you should note that it is a pretty straightforward presentation of facts, and the conclusions drawn are based on statistics. In addition, there is no bias present in the article. In fact, in the third paragraph, the writers are careful to warn against drawing unsupported conclusions, "If the 2002 data represent a declining trend, it is tempting to suggest that fewer people are reading literature and now prefer visual and audio entertainment. Again, the data—both from SPPA and other sources—do not

readily quantify this explanation." Therefore, choice (A) is the best answer. The article does not attempt to persuade the reader one way or another nor does it appeal to emotions, so choices (B) and (C) are incorrect. Choice (D) is tempting, because it contains the word accurate, but hopeful does not accurately describe the tone of the passage. Choice (E) contains the word "informational," which accurately describes the passage, but the passage is not particularly creative, so choice (E) is incorrect.

5. **The correct answer is (C).** Here, you must make sure you understand the citations in footnote 48. Choice (C) is correct because it is the only accurate citation of the footnote among the answer choices. The information is not about the Department of Commerce, it was *compiled* in part by the Department of Commerce, so choice (A) is incorrect. Choice (B) is incorrect because the report was published in *2001*. Choice (D) is incorrect because the report was compiled by *both* the Census Bureau and the Department of Commerce. Choice (E) is incorrect because Home Computers and Internet Use is not a book.

6. **The correct answer is (E).** Choice (E) is the only reasonable conclusion that can be drawn based on information in the passage. Choice (A) is simply untrue based on information in the passage. The passage specifically states that literary readers watch television as much as or slightly less than nonreaders. Choice (B) is not supported by the passage. The passage deals with literary fiction, but nowhere does it state or imply that nonfiction readers would not count in reading statistics. Choice (C) is also not supported by the passage. Choice (D) does not make sense.

7. **The correct answer is (B).** To answer this question correctly, reread the part of the passage where the quote appears. The statistic appears after the semicolon in the following sentence, "A number of people have a particularly strong attachment to books;" Therefore, you can conclude that choice (B) is correct. The other choices do not make sense when you read the sentence in context.

8. **The correct answer is (C).** In this case, based on the tone of the passage as a whole, choice (C) is the best answer among the choices. Choice (A) is incorrect because the straightforward and scholarly nature of the passage does not suggest the inclusion of any anecdotal evidence. The article makes no attempt to convince people to do anything, let alone be more cultured, so you can eliminate choice (B). The authors do not express wishes for a more cultural society anywhere in the passage, so choice (D) is not correct. Finally, there is nothing in the passage that would suggest the information is untrue, so eliminate choice (E).

9. **The correct answer is (E).** To answer this question correctly, you must recall what you know about the literary devices listed in the answer choices. Personification is the attribution of human characteristics to animals or inanimate objects. This does not fit the use of the word snapshot, therefore, choice (A) is incorrect. Simile describes something using a comparison using "like" or "as," such as "sly as a fox." This does not fit the use of snapshot, so choice (B) is incorrect. Choice (C) is incorrect: onomatopoeia is a word that represents a sound, such as "crack!" Choice (D), iambic pentameter, refers to the cadence of written words, often in poetry. Choice (D) is incorrect. This leaves you with choice (E). A metaphor is the use of a symbol to represent something, such as "He is a rock."

10. **The correct answer is (C).** Remember that in this case, you are looking for the word that *most* accurately matches the meaning of "about" as used in the paragraph. You can immediately eliminate choice (A), because "about" would never mean "precisely." Choice (D) is a synonym for precisely, so you can eliminate it as well. This leaves you with choices (B), (C), and (E), which can all have the same meaning as "about" as used in the

second paragraph. However, choice (C), *approximately,* is the most accurate and unequivocal of the remaining answer choices, and is therefore correct.

11. **The correct answer is (A).** Here, you must determine the purpose of a footnote. In this case, the footnote refers to a statistical report mentioned in the passage and tells the reader where to find it, in Appendix C. Therefore, choice (A) is correct. Choice (B) does not make sense. Choice (C) is untrue; the footnote makes reference to statistical models, but it is not meant to help the reader understand them. Choice (D) is incorrect because the footnote directs the reader to the appendix; it does not cite the publisher of the statistical models. Choice (E) does not make sense. Footnotes are not included as "reminders."

12. **The correct answer is (E).** While the passage touches on the beauty of the United States, that is not the main focus, so choice (A) is eliminated. Nothing really is said about poetry as literature, so choice (B) is incorrect. The past and the present are discussed, but not in terms of literature, so choice (C) cannot be the answer. Choice (D) has virtually nothing to do with the passage. That leaves choice (E).

13. **The correct answer is (B).** There is no mention of poetry in the paragraph, which eliminates choice (A). Slough, choice (C), literally means the skin of a snake that is cast off; figuratively, it means a layer is cast off. You might not know that, but from the context, you could at least figure out that slough was something extraneous—maybe like fuzz—that stuck to something else. It would not seem important enough to be a corpse. Choice (D) is related to choice (C). Line 2 mentions politics but in the context of creating the past. Choices (C), (D), and (E) all relate in some way to the past, which is choice (B).

14. **The correct answer is (A).** Whitman suggests that America accepts the lesson of the past with calmness and that the past informs and educates the present, so point I seems to be a correct statement about the passage. Points II and III are incorrect restatements of the passage's theme. Point IV has a subtle implication that the past is always present, whereas Whitman suggests that the past nurtures the present for a time and then leaves, so point IV is also incorrect. Only choice (A) has item I, so it is the correct answer.

15. **The correct answer is (B).** Using the process of elimination, choice (A) is out because the writer plainly states that the United States is large. Choices (C) and (D) contradict Whitman's assertions that diversity makes the nation unique. Certainly, the United States is a nation that is changing, so choice (E) is not the answer. That leaves choice (B), and nowhere does the writer speak of Americans' ability to read.

16. **The correct answer is (E).** When Whitman writes about the past, he calls it a corpse. Personification, choice (A), gives human characteristics to nonhuman things, including concepts, but in this instance, metaphor is a more accurate identification of how Whitman uses the figure of speech in context. The passage is prose, so choice (B) is incorrect. Oxymoron, choice (C), combines two contradictory ideas and is wrong in this context. A conceit, choice (D), is an extended metaphor comparing two or more ideas and is, therefore, incorrect.

17. **The correct answer is (B).** The poet states that the nation is a poem. The only answer that indicates the same thing is choice (B), that the nation is poetic. While choices (A), (C), (D), and (E) mention poetry, they do not indicate that it is the United States itself that is the poem.

18. **The correct answer is (C).** This is a difficult question. By logically examining the choices, you can see that choice (E) is much too simplistic. Humanity is not Whitman's subject, choice (A), nor are emotions, choice (B). A contrast is possible but not between

easy and difficult, choice (D), which do not relate to the passage. That leaves the physical and cultural landscape.

19. **The correct answer is (B).** To choose the right answer here is really an issue of vocabulary. Even if you do not know what choice (B) means, choices (A) and (E) can be eliminated because they contradict what Whitman says about the United States. He does not mention education, so eliminate choice (C). Whitman's tone in the passage is one of exuberance, choice (D), but he does not characterize the nation that way. That leaves choice (B), which means that something is not rigid and can be changed and molded.

20. **The correct answer is (E).** Whitman stresses the diversity of the United States, which he finds positive. While aspects of choices (A), (B), (C), and (D) may be true, they are not points that Whitman makes in this selection.

21. **The correct answer is (D).** The tone of this paragraph is neither ponderous, choice (A), nor formal, choice (C), but joyous. The repetition of the word *here* helps develop that tone. One might argue that the repetition is stylistically poetic, choice (E), the writer using it purposely to create unity and a sense of rhythm, but that better fits the definition of parallelism.

22. **The correct answer is (B).** Because the construction *to* and a verb form is not part of the sentence, there is no infinitive, thus eliminating choices (C) and (D). A gerund is a form of the verb that acts as a noun. No verbal form functions as a noun in this sentence, so choice (A) can be eliminated. There are several participles, forms of a verb acting as an adjective, and several participial phrases, participles modified by an adverb or adverbial phrase or that have a complement, choice (B). Since there are participial phrases, choice (E) is incorrect.

23. **The correct answer is (D).** This is a very complex sentence, but you can eliminate choices (A), (B), and (C) because a compound verb has the same tenses for both or all verbs. *Crowds* and *showers*, choice (E), could be *nouns* or *verbs*, but in this sentence, *crowds* is a noun, the object of the preposition *of*.

24. **The correct answer is (C).** Choice (E) may sound important but has no relationship to the passage. Choice (A) is too simplistic. Choices (B) and (D) may be true but do not relate to the passage.

25. **The correct answer is (B).** Because all of these answer choices are touched on in the passage, the answer that covers the broadest portion of the selection is the correct response. Diction deals with the choice of words in written or spoken language, and, therefore, choice (B) is the most encompassing of the available responses.

26. **The correct answer is (D).** The question asks for the primary concern of the passage. The author discusses all of these answers at some point in the passage, but he spends most of his time listing and discussing some rules for better writing.

27. **The correct answer is (E).** The best approach to this question is to work through the answers, eliminating the incorrect answers. Orwell does not propose the expanded use of the English language, the introduction of new grammar rules, or the teaching of creative writing, choices (A), (B), and (C). He may imply a search for new means of expression, choice (D), but he clearly states a predilection for word and sentence simplification, choice (E).

28. **The correct answer is (C).** Orwell states that he is an advocate of simple, direct word selection. Each of the remaining four responses are counter to his fundamental thesis of simplicity.

29. **The correct answer is (B).** The question asks the reader to determine the feel or tone of the excerpt. The passage cannot be viewed as humorous, choice (A); ironic, choice (C); satirical, choice (D); or dramatic, choice (E). Orwell is quite serious in his concern for language, and his essay is meant to be persuasive, choice (B).

30. **The correct answer is (C).** The author lists six rules that he believes will improve writing. The last of these states "Break any of these rules sooner that say anything outright barbarous." That rule is consistent with choice (C). He does not advocate irresponsible or unreasoned breaking of rules, choices (A) and (D), nor does he advocate rigid adherence to rules, choice (B). Choice (E) is a statement of opinion that Orwell would probably agree with, but it is not the most accurate restatement of the essay. Be careful of such distracters that seem to be reasonable answers; check to see if they most accurately reflect the content.

31. **The correct answer is (B).** In the second paragraph, Orwell says, "But one can often be in doubt about the effect of a word or a phrase, and one needs rules that one can rely on when instinct fails." Only choice (B) reflects Orwell's statement.

32. **The correct answer is (B).** In the last sentence of the second paragraph, the author expresses the sentiment that these rules will not make bad writing good, the opposite of choice (A). On the other hand, good writing does not employ these rules. Choices (B) and (D) are similar. The difference is that components other than following the rules are needed to make writing "as good as possible," choice (D). Regardless of the other components, writing will be "easier to follow" if the writer follows the rules. Choice (C) is irrelevant to the passage.

33. **The correct answer is (B).** The author is stating that what a writer intends to say should determine word selection. The chosen words should not alter the writer's meaning. Choices (A) and (C) incorrectly deal with the definitions of words. Orwell does not address the responses contained in choices (D) and (E) in the lines cited.

34. **The correct answer is (A).** In the sentence given, there is figurative language that is a cliché, "go down the drain." Orwell would also object to the redundant phrase "rich treasury." However, there is no response that deals with redundancy. Choice (C) deals with wordiness, not redundancy. The given sentence has no long words, choice (B); is not in the passive voice, choice (D); and contains no foreign phrases, scientific words, or jargon, choice (E). A cliché is not jargon.

35. **The correct answer is (B).** At first, you might think that several of these are possible answers. Remember that the writer states that it is acceptable to break rules if the meaning becomes clearer by doing so. Orwell wants the reader to pay close attention here, so he directly addresses the audience. The other responses do not make sense in context.

36. **The correct answer is (C).** The definition of personification is a figure of speech in which inanimate objects or abstractions are endowed with human characteristics. In this sentence, *words* is given a human characteristic that suggests that a person can surrender to them. A simile uses *like* or *as* for comparison, choice (A), while a metaphor states that something is something else, choice (B). Words that sound like their meanings are onomatopoeia, choice (D), and words in a series that repeat an initial consonant sound are examples of alliteration, choice (E).

37. **The correct answer is (C).** The readers of your essays may not agree with Orwell, but he states in the second paragraph, "It has nothing to do with correct grammar and syntax, which are of no importance so long as one makes one's meaning clear . . ." The context does not support choices (A), (D), or (E). Choice (B) is only half right. The statement from Orwell has the qualifier "so long as one's meaning is clear," thus eliminating choice (B).

38. **The correct answer is (C).** Orwell lists some phrases that were popular at the time he wrote this article. He suggests that they be thrown in the trash can. Choice (A) is the opposite of what Orwell is saying. Choice (B) would be correct only if you were asked a question about metaphor. Orwell may be advocating choice (D) at some point in the essay, but the question asks what Orwell is saying in the last sentence, and choice (C) restates his idea. Choice (E) is irrelevant to the sentence.

39. **The correct answer is (A).** The tone of the passage could not be considered serious or deep. Any answer with that sense would be incorrect, so choices (B), (C), and (D) can be eliminated. Humor and wit are more evident in the writing than questioning or curiosity, choice (E), so choice (A) is the better response.

40. **The correct answer is (D).** Each of the five answers has an element of Twain's commentary in them; therefore, you must look for the response that best matches or sums up the main idea. Much of the selection links Lake Tahoe with improving health. Choice (D) is the only choice that recognizes the recuperative powers of the area. Choices (A) and (E) focus more on the scenic beauty, and choices (B) and (C) touch on aspects of the area that might be helpful to good health, and thus support choice (D).

41. **The correct answer is (C).** This selection should not be viewed as a serious piece of writing, and any response that suggests that view is incorrect. That includes choices (A), (B), and (E). Of the two remaining answers, the passage is an anecdote, a short narrative, choice (C), rather than a myth, a story once believed to be true, choice (D).

42. **The correct answer is (A).** The speaker is not a teacher or an advocate, so choices (B), (C), and (D) must be eliminated. Choice (E) suggests a more indirect approach, but there is nothing subtle about the speaker; he tells his audience what they should do. The simple answer, to amuse and entertain, is the best response.

43. **The correct answer is (D).** The possible correct answers can quickly be reduced by two, choices (A) and (E), because the excerpt states that Lake Tahoe is on the California-Nevada border. The locale is not set in a desert, so that eliminates choice (C). Mark Twain wrote in the 1800s, choice (B), and the lake is in the mountains. This identifies choice (D) as the correct answer.

44. **The correct answer is (A).** The correct answer can be determined by the process of elimination. Twain's diction could not be called erudite, choice (B), and his style is not sophisticated, choice (C). Although he chooses words of common speech, he does so with care to paint vivid images, thus eliminating choice (D). The passage is dynamic rather than static, so choice (E) can be eliminated. Examples like "brim full of friskiness" (line 5) support choice (A) as the correct answer.

45. **The correct answer is (E).** This is not a romantic passage, choice (A); it does not express great emotion or devotion, even though nature is prominently featured. Considering the amount of exaggeration, it certainly is not realistic, choice (B). Neither is it an example of naturalism or classicism, choices (C) and (D). The focus of this passage is clearly on a specific area of the country. This type of advocacy for a territory is known as regionalism.

46. **The correct answer is (C).** It is important to put the question in context. The phrase represents a transition from Twain's listing of health benefits at Lake Tahoe to other approaches that were then in vogue. The reference to slowness shows that the author was indicating that it will take time for people to learn about something new and to change. Choices (A) and (E) have no relationship to the passage. On a quick reading, you might think that choice (D) could be correct, but choice (D) relates to real movement. In the context of the question, the author is not speaking about literal movement. Choice (B) might seem correct, but the author is implying that people have to change their ways— rather than that the information about new things will be delayed.

47. **The correct answer is (C).** As Mark Twain often does, he is using an exaggerated comparison to make a point about Lake Tahoe. In this case, he uses a figure of speech that includes a long-dead mummy to make the point that Lake Tahoe has significant recuperative powers. Choices (A) and (B) are incorrect because the author mentions neither the region's dryness nor the lake's age. Nor does he refer to spiritual aspects of the area, choice (D), or its beauty, choice (E).

48. **The correct answer is (D).** The question is asking about sleep, the topic of the sentence. The items to note in reading the sentence are the antecedent of *its* (Lake Tahoe) and the recuperative powers of the lake. These elements identify choice (D) as the answer. Choices (A), (B), and (C) do not mention the lake, while choice (E) does not mention sleep.

49. **The correct answer is (C).** While delicious may mean tasty, it does not mean tasteful, so you can eliminate choice (A). Both sets of words in choices (D) and (E) mean *bracing*, so they can be eliminated. Although *bracing* can mean supportive, choice (B), *invigorating,* is a better meaning in the context of air, and *delicious* when referring to the senses means enjoyable, choice (C).

50. **The correct answer is (D).** The identification of the correct answer requires you to make an inference about the author's feelings. It is clear from Twain's comments that he has a positive feeling for the area. Points I and II reflect this attitude, whereas point III negatively compares Lake Tahoe with the East. Only choice (D) has both I and II.

51. **The correct answer is (A).** Taken with the phrase "the air up there in the clouds," the reference to angels points directly to height as an element in the correct answer. Since angels are said to be "up" in the heavens, altitude, choice (A), is the answer. Choices (D) and (E) may distract you, but the question asks about the environment—in the mountains. Choices (B) and (C) do not relate to angels.

52. **The correct answer is (E).** If you do not readily see that Twain does not use classical Shakespearean sentence structure, try the process of elimination. The author uses both specific details, choice (A), and local color, choice (B), to make his points. The speaker is also an ordinary person using common speech, choices (C) and (D).

53. **The correct answer is (E).** On a quick reading, you might select choice (A) without bothering to read a sentence or two above and below the cited lines. Avoid this temptation and go back to the selection. If you do, you will see that choice (A) is a distracter. Choice (C) can also be considered a distracter. It, too, is a very literal answer, and Twain is not to be taken literally, so eliminate choice (C). While brief, the example Twain gives should not be taken literally, so eliminate choice (B), which asks you to consider this example as a nonfiction account. Choice (D) is incorrect because there is no skit involved.

54. **The correct answer is (D).** You must choose which of the answer choices is not found in the passage. The passage is personal, as evidenced by the use of the first person pronoun, and fits the definition of an anecdote, making choice (A) a true statement about the passage and, therefore, an incorrect answer. There are several figures of speech, so choice (B) is not the answer. The entire passage is a tall tale, so choice (C) is also incorrect. There are several simple sentences—for example, sentence 3 and the final sentence—so choice (E) is also incorrect. Although Twain is known for using colloquialisms in his writing, none appear in this passage.

Section II

SUGGESTIONS FOR QUESTION 1

The following are points you might have chosen to include in your essay on Faulkner's speech to the graduating class. Consider them as you complete your self-evaluation. Revise your essay once, using points from this list to strengthen it.

Form or Mode

- Prose; a speech

- Persuasive

Theme

- Individuals can and must choose to change the world for the better.

- "It is man himself, created in the image of God so that he shall have the power and the will to choose right from wrong, and so be able to save himself because he is worth saving."

Characters

- Faulkner, the speaker

- Audience, the graduating high school students

Conflict/Issue/Challenge

- Good versus evil

Content/Important Points

- Beginning quotation

- Youth has power to rid the world of war and injustice

- Fear danger in the world

- Danger in those who use human fear to control humankind

- Right and duty to choose justice, courage, sacrifice, compassion

- If people choose right actions, tyrants will disappear.

Setting

- Speech given at graduation

- Contemporary times—the bomb

Point of View

- First person

Diction/Syntax/Style

- Offers no proof to support opening quotation; abandons point in third paragraph

- Speaking directly to students; use of second person, *you*

- Long, complex sentences

- Much parallel construction: "giving him free food which he has not earned, easy and valueless money which he has not worked for"

- Cadence ministerial, almost musical

- Word choice sophisticated but comprehensible: "glib," "baffled," "aggrandizement"

SUGGESTIONS FOR QUESTION 2

This question asks for a synthesis essay to support, oppose, or qualify Carnegie's comments about the responsibilities of the wealthy. Consider them as you complete your self-evaluation. Revise your essay once, using points from this list to strengthen it.

Form or Mode

- Persuasive essay

Theme

- The extra wealth of the few should become the property of all

Conflict/Issue/Challenge

- How to resolve the unequal distribution of wealth and reconcile the rich and the poor

Content/Important Points

- The wealthy should spend their excess wealth for public purposes and for the public good.

- Not Communist because the change that Carnegie advocates requires an evolution, not an overthrow of existing civilization

- The concept is based on the American ideal of individualism.

- Wealth should be administered by the few for the public good.

- Such a system is more beneficial to the poor than direct distribution of small sums of money to them.

- The result is a powerful force that will improve public conditions.

Point of View

- First-person plural to include all readers

Diction/Syntax/Style

- Long, complicated sentences with many clauses or prepositional phrases

- Persuasive language: "only one mode," "true antidote," "ideal state," "in the best sense"

- Use of active and passive voices

- Sentence variety

- Some parallel structure: "to see this, and to agree that"

- Strong adjectives: "ideal," "surplus," "potent," "great," "principal," "trifling"

SUGGESTIONS FOR QUESTION 3

This question asks for a synthesis essay that supports, qualifies, or disputes the argument that people do not vote because they do not feel a sense of political efficacy. It does not matter which position you take as long as you provide adequate support for your argument using your own opinions along with information from the sources. Consider the following as you complete your self-evaluation. Revise your essay using points from the list to strengthen it if necessary. Remember to proofread your response and make sure your grammar, syntax, and spelling are correct.

Thesis statement/introduction

- Clear definition of the issue—in this case, a lack of voter participation in the United States

- Clear statement of your position on the issue: why you agree or disagree with the statement that people do not vote because they do not feel their vote will make a difference

Supporting details

- Support is based on your own opinions about the position you take but information in the sources should also be used.

- Show a clear connection between the sources you choose to cite

- Sources are seamlessly integrated with appropriate transitions

- At least three of the six sources are used

- Explain the logic of how you arrived at the conclusion you did, based on the information provided in the sources

- Acknowledge opposing arguments and refute them

- Attribute both direct and indirect citations

Conclusion

- Include a restatement of your thesis tied into the supporting evidence you used. (ex: In sum, there can be no other conclusion drawn from the evidence except to say that people do not vote because of feelings of a lack of political efficacy.)

- Conclusion neatly sums up your argument.

SELF-EVALUATION RUBRIC FOR THE FREE RESPONSE ESSAYS

	8–9	6–7	5	3–4	1–2	0
Overall Impression	Demonstrates excellent control of the literature and outstanding writing competence; thorough and effective; incisive	Demonstrates good control of the literature and good writing competence; less thorough and incisive than the highest papers	Reveals simplistic thinking and/or immature writing; adequate skills	Incomplete thinking; fails to respond adequately to part or parts of the question; may paraphrase rather than analyze	Unacceptably brief; fails to respond to the question; little clarity	Lacking skill and competence
Understanding of the Text	Excellent understanding of the text; exhibits perception and clarity; original or unique approach; includes apt and specific references	Good understanding of the text; exhibits perception and clarity; includes specific references	Superficial understanding of the text; elements of literature vague, mechanical, overgeneralized	Misreadings and lack of persuasive evidence from the text; meager and unconvincing treatment of literary elements	Serious misreadings and little supporting evidence from the text; erroneous treatment of literary elements	A response with no more than a reference to the literature; blank response, or one completely off the topic
Organization and Development	Meticulously organized and thoroughly developed; coherent and unified	Well organized and developed; coherent and unified	Reasonably organized and developed; mostly coherent and unified	Somewhat organized and developed; some incoherence and lack of unity	Little or no organization and development; incoherent and void of unity	No apparent organization or development; incoherent
Use of Sentences	Effectively varied and engaging; virtually error free	Varied and interesting; a few errors	Adequately varied; some errors	Somewhat varied and marginally interesting; one or more major errors	Little or no variation; dull and uninteresting; some major errors	Numerous major errors
Word Choice	Interesting and effective; virtually error free	Generally interesting and effective; a few errors	Occasionally interesting and effective; several errors	Somewhat dull and ordinary; some errors in diction	Mostly dull and conventional; numerous errors	Numerous major errors; extremely immature
Grammar and Usage	Virtually error free	Occasional minor errors	Several minor errors	Some major errors	Severely flawed; frequent major errors	Extremely flawed

SELF-EVALUATION RUBRIC FOR THE SYNTHESIS ESSAYS

	8–9	6–7	5	3–4	1–2	0
Overall Impression	Demonstrates excellent control of effective writing techniques, sophisticated argumentation, and well integrated synthesis of source information; uses citations convincingly	Demonstrates good control of effective writing techniques; somewhat thorough and incisive; uses citations appropriately	Demonstrates general competence in stating and defending a position; some inconsistencies and weaknesses in argumentation	Demonstrates some skill but lacks understanding of question and sources	Demonstrates little skill in taking a coherent position and defending it or in using sources	Lacks skill and competence
Understanding of the Text	Takes a clear position that defends, challenges, or qualifies the question accurately	Demonstrates a somewhat superficial understanding of the sources	Displays some misreading of the sources or some stretching of information to support the chosen position	Takes a position that may misread or simplify the sources; may present overly simple argument	Misreads sources, or lacks an argument, or summarizes the sources rather than using them to support a position	Position does not accurately reflect the sources; no more than a listing of the sources
Organization and Development	Clearly states a position; uses at least three sources to support that position convincingly and effectively; coherent and unified	Clearly states a position; uses at least three sources to support that position; adequate development of ideas but less convincing; coherent and unified	Generally clearly stated position and links between position and cited sources; some weaknesses in logic; cites three sources	Creates weak connections between argument and cited sources; cites only two sources	Lacks coherent development or organization; cites one or no sources	No apparent organization or development; incoherent; cites no sources
Use of Sentences	Effectively varied and engaging; close to error free	Varied and interesting; a few errors	Adequately varied; some errors	Somewhat varied and marginally interesting; one or more major errors	Little or no variation; dull and uninteresting; some major errors	Numerous major errors
Word Choice	Uses the vocabulary of the topic as evident in the sources; interesting and effective; virtually error free	Demonstrates ease in using vocabulary from the sources	Occasional use of vocabulary from the sources; occasionally interesting and effective	Somewhat dull and ordinary; some errors in diction; no attempt to integrate vocabulary from the sources	Mostly dull and conventional; no attempt to integrate vocabulary from the sources	Numerous major errors; extremely immature
Grammar and Usage	Virtually error free	Occasional minor errors	Several minor errors	Some major errors	Severely flawed; frequent major errors	Extremely flawed

Using the rubrics on the previous pages, rate yourself in each of the categories below for each essay on the test. Enter on the lines below the number from the rubric that most accurately reflects your performance in each category. Then calculate the average of the six numbers to determine your final score. It is difficult to score yourself objectively, so you may wish to ask a respected friend or teacher to assess your writing for a more accurate reflection of its strengths and weaknesses. On the AP test itself, a reader will rate your essay on a scale of 0 to 9, with 9 being the highest.

Rate each category from 9 (high) to 0 (low).

Question 1

SELF-EVALUATION

Overall Impression	_____
Understanding of the Text	_____
Organization and Development	_____
Use of Sentences	_____
Word Choice (Diction)	_____
Grammar and Usage	_____
TOTAL	_____
Divide by 6 for final score	_____

OBJECTIVE EVALUATION

Overall Impression	_____
Understanding of the Text	_____
Organization and Development	_____
Use of Sentences	_____
Word Choice (Diction)	_____
Grammar and Usage	_____
TOTAL	_____
Divide by 6 for final score	_____

Question 2

SELF-EVALUATION

Overall Impression	_____
Understanding of the Text	_____
Organization and Development	_____
Use of Sentences	_____
Word Choice (Diction)	_____
Grammar and Usage	_____
TOTAL	_____
Divide by 6 for final score	_____

OBJECTIVE EVALUATION

Overall Impression	_____
Understanding of the Text	_____
Organization and Development	_____
Use of Sentences	_____
Word Choice (Diction)	_____
Grammar and Usage	_____
TOTAL	_____
Divide by 6 for final score	_____

Question 3

SELF-EVALUATION

Overall Impression	_____
Understanding of the Text	_____
Organization and Development	_____
Use of Sentences	_____
Word Choice (Diction)	_____
Grammar and Usage	_____
TOTAL	_____
Divide by 6 for final score	_____

OBJECTIVE EVALUATION

Overall Impression	_____
Understanding of the Text	_____
Organization and Development	_____
Use of Sentences	_____
Word Choice (Diction)	_____
Grammar and Usage	_____
TOTAL	_____
Divide by 6 for final score	_____

PART III

AP ENGLISH LANGUAGE & COMPOSITION STRATEGIES

About the Multiple-Choice Questions

OVERVIEW

- **Basic information about section I**
- **Acing the multiple-choice questions**
- **Analyzing the question types**
- **Attacking the questions**
- **A final word of advice: educated guessing**
- **Practicing**
- **Summing it up**

The questions in the multiple-choice section of the AP English Language & Composition Test ask you about passages from a variety of sources, rhetorical modes, historical eras, and literary periods and disciplines. You may read passages from commentaries, autobiographies, diaries and journals, biographies, or historical accounts or passages from essays about politics, science, nature, and the arts. In this chapter, you will find some basic information about Section I of the test, and you will develop an effective strategy for acing the multiple-choice section of the test.

On the Advanced Placement examination, you will discover that most of the multiple-choice questions assess how carefully you read, how well you interpret what you read, and how well you analyze literature. Some questions will ask you about grammar, mechanics, rhetorical modes of writing, structure, organization, development, or footnotes.

You may have taken hundreds of multiple-choice tests during your time in school. The multiple-choice questions on the AP English Language & Composition test really are not that different. Of course, there is a lot riding on the AP test, but, just like any other standardized test, if you have studied and you know some test-taking techniques, you can do well.

chapter 3

This chapter presents some general strategies for taking the objective portion of the Advanced Placement test. In addition, you will learn some special techniques that will allow you to score your highest. You will also have opportunities to practice what you are learning.

Use the *Practice Test 1: Diagnostic* and *Practice Test 2* as tools to improve your objective test-taking skills. Use the techniques explained in this chapter to practice answering multiple-choice questions on the selections. Correct your responses with the *Answer Key* provided for each test. If you do not understand why an answer is incorrect, refer to the explanations given. It is a good idea to read the answer explanations to all the questions—even the ones you answered correctly—because you may find ideas or tips that will help you better analyze the answer choices to questions on the next *Practice Test* that you take and on the real test.

After you have finished reviewing all the answers, ask yourself what your weak points are and what you can do to improve. Review the strategies in this chapter. Then try taking the next *Practice Test*. Remember the following test-taking tips:

- Carefully apply the test-taking system that you will be learning in this chapter.

- Work the system to get more correct responses.

- Pay attention to your time, and strive to answer more questions in the time period.

See how much you can improve your score each time you take a *Practice Test*.

BASIC INFORMATION ABOUT SECTION I

1. Section I consists of approximately 50 multiple-choice questions, with five choices for each.

2. Section I has four to five prose passages, and each selection has approximately 10 to 15 questions.

3. You will have 60 minutes to answer all of the questions.

4. The multiple-choice questions require the ability to:

  - Analyze rhetorical and linguistic choices

  - Identify stylistic effects that result from word choice

  - Critically examine prose selections

  - Understand an author's meaning and purpose

  - Recognize structural organization

  - Evaluate the legitimacy and purpose of sources

  - Comprehend rhetorical modes

  - Analyze syntax, figurative language, style, and tone

⑤   The test requires that you understand the terms and conventions of English and use the skills of critical reading and literary analysis.

⑥   You receive 1 point for each correct answer you give. You receive no points for each question you leave blank. If you answer incorrectly, one-quarter point is subtracted. This is the guessing penalty. We will discuss this penalty in detail later in this chapter.

⑦   Section I accounts for 45 percent of your final composite score.

In addition to the obvious importance of understanding the material, you have probably discovered during your educational career that there are three significant considerations when taking multiple-choice tests:

- Effective reading and analysis of test material
- Time management
- Educated guesses

The consequences of failing at any of these can affect your score:

- If you fail to read the selections or the questions skillfully, you may make errors that are unnecessary.
- If you neglect time, you may miss opportunities for showing what you know.
- If you do not make educated guesses to answer questions about which you are not positive, then you are missing out on a higher score.

How do you prevent these things from happening and ensure your highest score? You need to develop a plan to read effectively, to manage your time well, and to use all your knowledge to the best possible effect.

ACING THE MULTIPLE-CHOICE QUESTIONS

Pacing Yourself

The first part of the strategy for acing the multiple-choice section is time awareness. Since you have 60 minutes for Section I, give yourself approximately 11 to 14 minutes for each of the passages, depending on whether there are four or five selections. (You will see under *Setting Priorities* why it's not 12 to 15 minutes.) Use that 11-to-14-minute time period as a guideline. If you find you are spending significantly more time per section, speed up. In the event that you finish with time to spare, revisit any problem passages to see if you can answer questions that you left blank.

If, as the hour comes to an end, you find that you have only 5 or so minutes and another passage to complete, try this technique. Do not read the passage; read the questions instead. Some questions, such as those that ask about vocabulary, can be answered by reading the lines identified and a few lines above and below to understand the context. Other questions

NOTE

Be sure to take a watch so you can pace yourself, but don't take one with an alarm.

ask specific information about specific portions of the selection. Answer these sorts of questions when time is short.

Setting Priorities

The first active step to take is prioritizing the passages. Quickly scan the passages (this is where the extra 4 to 5 minutes come in) to find which ones seem difficult to you and which seem easier. You do not have to complete questions or passages in the order they appear on the test. Do the most difficult one last and the easiest one first. Read and answer the other passages according to how difficult they seem. Don't spend time agonizing over the order, or you'll lose your advantage in answering the easiest selection first.

Effective Strategies for Reading Selections

The first step is obvious: Read the selections. The passages can vary from a few short paragraphs to lengthy sections. Some selections may be from fictional works, but more than likely, the passages will be taken from essays, articles, letters, histories, and other types of nonfiction.

- Begin by skimming the selection. Take only 30 seconds or so to do this. You want an overview at this point; don't worry about the details.

- Then, concentrate and read the selection carefully. Read for a clear, specific understanding of the writer's main idea—the underlying communication that the writer is trying to make. It is not details but the fundamental message that you, the reader, are supposed to receive.

- In reading a selection with footnotes, pay attention to the author, the title, and the publication. Note the date as well. All this information may be useful to you in answering questions about the footnote. It may also help you better understand the selection itself.

ANALYZING THE QUESTION TYPES

The ideal is to know the correct answer as soon as you read the question, but that does not always happen. If you can identify the type of question you are facing, you can employ the best strategies to answer it correctly.

Comprehension Questions

Most of the multiple-choice questions will test how carefully you read and how well you interpret what you read. These comprehension questions fall into several categories: main idea, rhetoric, modes of discourse, definitions, meaning and purpose, form, organization, structure, and development.

MAIN IDEA QUESTIONS

This type of question frequently appears on the AP English Language & Composition Test. The question measures your ability to identify the author's ideas, attitude, and tone. A main idea question may also require you to identify the subject of the passage or to select the choice that best tells what the passage is about. You may also be asked to determine the elements of a footnote. Often, main idea questions about a passage require that you piece together facts and make an inference based on those facts.

Most inference questions will include one of these key words: *think*, *predict*, *indicate*, *feel*, *probably*, *seem*, *imply*, *suggest*, *assume*, *infer*, and *most likely*. When you come upon a question that contains one of these terms, return to the selection to find specific sentences that the question refers to, and make a sound generalization based on the clues. Skimming the first and last paragraphs of a passage is another helpful technique for answering these questions because writers often state their topic in the beginning or the end of a selection. Remember that in answering an inference question, you are making a guess, but the best guess is based on facts from the selection.

RHETORIC QUESTIONS

A great many of the questions on the exam are in this category. Questions about rhetoric might ask about syntax, point of view, or figurative language. To answer these questions, you must know how language works within a given passage. Not only must you be able to recognize these devices, but you must understand the effects these elements have on the piece of writing.

MODE QUESTIONS

A few questions ask you to identify the various rhetorical modes that writers employ. You must understand the differences among narration, exposition, description, and persuasion. Knowing why an author is particularly effective at using a specific mode will help you with other types of questions.

DEFINITION QUESTIONS

These are basically vocabulary questions about difficult words in a passage or about ordinary words that are used with a special meaning. Use the context surrounding the word or phrase in the question to arrive at its meaning. Reread the sentence in which the word appears, and then substitute each of the possible choices to see which is closest in meaning. To get the full sense of the idea, you may need to read the sentences that surround the one containing the word or phrase in question. Avoid choosing a word or phrase that looks or sounds like the word to be defined, unless you have checked it in context.

NOTE

As you answer multiple-choice questions in the *Practice Tests,* try to identify the category of each one. Knowing the question type will help you to identify the best strategy to use for answering the question.

TONE OR PURPOSE QUESTIONS

These frequently asked questions ask you to determine how or why the author wrote the material. The tone reflects the writer's attitude toward the subject and the audience. The purpose defines the effect the author wants to have upon the audience. Understanding the tone helps you to understand the purpose. Writers convey purpose through their choice of words and the impression those words create. Some possible tones are *admiration, adoration, optimism, contempt, pride, objectivity, disappointment, respect, surprise, anger, regret, irony, indignation, suspicion, pessimism,* and *amusement.* You may also find a multiple-choice question that asks you to determine the purpose of a footnote. These are fairly straightforward comprehension questions. The answer choices offer possible restatements of the footnote. A close reading of the footnote against the answer choices will help you determine the correct answer.

FORM QUESTIONS

Form is the method of organization that a writer uses. As you read, observe the patterns of organization used. While some authors will use only one form, others may use a combination. Be aware of structure, organization, and development. Look for comparison and contrast, cause and effect, order of importance, logical sequence of events, and spatial order.

Factual Knowledge Questions

There may be a few other question types that appear on the test.

- **English Language Questions.** These questions may test your knowledge of English grammar, punctuation, or mechanics, or they may test your understanding of literary terminology.

- **Cultural Questions.** This kind of question tests your knowledge of facts that are a part of our civilization. Well-educated people should know this type of information.

ATTACKING THE QUESTIONS

Remember that the more multiple-choice questions you answer correctly, the less pressure you will have to do exceptionally well on the three essays. The following test-taking strategies, combined with your use of critical reading skills, will help you do well on Section I.

Learning the Directions

It is a good idea to familiarize yourself with the instructions for each part of the test before the real test day. Knowing ahead of time what you have to do can save you time—perhaps enough to answer another one or two questions.

GENERAL DIRECTIONS FOR THE AP ENGLISH LANGUAGE AND COMPOSITION TEST

On the front page of your test booklet, you will find some information about the test. Because you have studied this book, none of it should be new to you, and much of it is similar to other standardized tests you have taken.

The page will tell you that the following exam will take approximately 3 hours—1 hour for the multiple-choice section and 2 hours and 15 minutes for the three essays—and that there are two booklets for this exam, one for the multiple-choice section and one for the essays.

The page will also tell you that Section I:

- Is 1 hour
- Has 50 questions (or some number from 50 to 60)
- Counts for 45 percent of your total grade

Then, you will find a sentence in capital letters that tells you not to open your exam booklet until the monitor tells you to open it.

Other instructions will tell you to be careful to fill in only ovals 1 through 50 (or whatever the number is) in Section I on your separate answer sheet. Fill in each oval completely. If you erase an answer, erase it completely. You will not receive any credit for work done in the test booklet, but you may use it for making notes.

You will find not only a paragraph about the guessing penalty—deduction of one-quarter point for every wrong answer—but also words of advice about guessing if you know something about the question and can eliminate several of the answers.

The final paragraph will remind you to work effectively and to pace yourself. You are told that not everyone will be able to answer all the questions. The page suggests that you skip questions that are difficult and come back to them if you have time.

DIRECTIONS FOR THE MULTIPLE-CHOICE SECTION

The specific directions for Section I read like this:

SECTION I

54 QUESTIONS • 60 MINUTES

Directions: This section consists of selections of literature and questions on their content, style, and form. After you have read each passage, select the response that best answers the question, and mark the space on the answer sheet.

In general, the directions for each selection and its accompanying multiple-choice questions read like this:

QUESTIONS 1–15. READ THE PASSAGE CAREFULLY AND THEN CHOOSE THE ANSWERS TO THE QUESTIONS.

Reading the Selections

- Most passages have no titles. If a selection is titled, think about what it tells you about the work. You may get a sense of the subject and theme just from the title.

- If there is no title, and there probably won't be, look for the topic sentence or thesis statement. In most writing, you will find it near the beginning. However, since AP exams ask you about challenging literature, you may find the topic sentence at the end or in the middle of the selection. Or you may find that the thesis is implied as opposed to stated.

- Scan the passages to decide the order in which you want to answer them. You do not have to answer the selections in the order presented. You can and should answer the selections and then the questions for each selection in the order that works for you. By showing yourself that you know answers, you build self-confidence.

- After you have decided the order in which you wish to answer the selections, skim for an overall impression of the selection. Then, read the selection carefully. Do not skip over confusing sentences. Read the footnotes carefully. Skim them when you first read the selection and then read them again when you have finished reading the selection.

- As you read, highlight words and sentences that seem significant. However, don't spend a great deal of time on this.

- As you read, observe patterns of organization that the writer employs. Patterns may follow a certain sequence or order, set up a compare-and-contrast situation, offer a problem and solution, show cause and effect, or offer a series of examples. Some authors may use more than one system of organization across paragraphs.

- Mentally paraphrase the passages. Paraphrasing helps you to discover the subject and the organization of the selection or the thesis and supporting arguments. The writer's style, transitions, sentence types, language, and literary devices become clear. You can see the framework of the passage in a paraphrase.

- Recall what you can about the author, the literary form, and the historical period.

Identifying the Question Type

- Remember that there are six major types of multiple-choice questions: *main idea, rhetoric, mode, definition, tone* or *purpose,* and *form.* You may also find a few factual knowledge or cultural questions.

- When answering a main-idea question, the correct choice must be entirely true and include as much relevant information as possible. In many questions, two or three choices might be correct. However, the answer that is most complete is the one to choose.

- When you are asked to make judgments about what is inferred or implied in a selection, you must put together clues from the passage. You must be able to support your answer with specific facts or examples from the selection.

- Questions that ask about the meaning of words or phrases are best answered by substituting your choice in the sentence or paragraph. If the choice makes sense, you have the correct answer.

- In answering a question about tone or purpose, pay attention to word choice. This type of question asks you to determine how or why the writer created the selection. Authors convey that information through diction.

Answering the Questions

- Reread lines, sentences, or paragraphs that are identified in the questions. In fact, scan or reread any selection if you do not immediately know the answer to a question.

- Just as you choose the order to attack the passages, choose how you wish to answer the multiple-choice questions. If you understand the passage, answer the questions in order.

STRATEGIES FOR ANSWERING OBJECTIVE QUESTIONS/ MAKING EDUCATED GUESSES	
ANSWER CHOICE	**REASON TO ELIMINATE**
1. Too narrow	Too small a section of the selection covered, based on the question
2. Too broad	An area wider than the selection covered, based on the question
3. Irrelevant	• Nothing to do with the passage • Relevant to the selection but not the question
4. Incorrect	• Distortion of the facts in the selection • Contradiction of the facts in the selection
5. Illogical	• Not supported by facts in the passage • Not supported by cited passage from the selection
6. Similar choices	GO BACK AND REVIEW 1–5 TO TEASE OUT THE DIFFERENCES.
7. *Not/except*	Answers that correctly represent the selection

- If you are not confident about a passage, skip difficult questions, and answer the easy ones first. Be sure to mark in the test booklet the ones you have not answered. If you skip questions, check to be sure that you also skip that number on your answer sheet.

- Read the question stem carefully, and be sure to read all the answer choices. Since the directions often ask for the best answer, several choices may be logical. Look for the most inclusive answer or the generalization.

- Look for consistency in the answers to the questions about a passage. If a choice seems contradictory to other answers you have given, rethink that choice.

- Many times, the key to finding the correct answer is to narrow the choices and to make an intelligent guess. Eliminate some answers by finding those that are obviously unrelated, illogical, or incorrect. Having reduced the number of choices, you can make an educated guess from among the remaining possibilities. Use the techniques presented in the chart above to reduce the number of choices.

- The *not/except* questions are tricky. You can forget what it is you are looking for and choose a correct answer for the selection but the wrong answer for the question. Convoluted? Yes; as you go through each answer, ask yourself, "Is this statement true about the selection?" If you answer "yes," cross off the answer and keep going until you find a choice to which you can answer "no."

A FINAL WORD OF ADVICE: EDUCATED GUESSING

One technique that is especially helpful for achieving your best score is educated guessing. Use this technique when you do not immediately know the correct answer as follows:

- Ignore answers that are obviously wrong. See the table on page 79, "Strategies for Answering Objective Questions/Making Educated Guesses," for reasons why you should eliminate certain types of answer choices.

- Discard choices in which part of the response is incorrect.

- Revisit remaining answers to discover which seems more correct. Remember to eliminate any response that has anything wrong about it.

- Choose the answer you feel is right. Trust yourself. Your subconscious usually will guide you to the correct choice. Do not argue with yourself.

ALERT!

A partially correct answer is a partially incorrect answer—and a quarter-point deduction.

You're probably thinking about the quarter-point penalty for an incorrect answer and are wondering if taking a chance is worth the possible point loss. Recognize that if you use this technique, your chances of scoring higher are excellent. You are not guessing but making an educated guess. You will have to answer 4 questions incorrectly to lose a single point, but answering even 1 question out of 4 correctly that you are not sure about will give you a quarter-point edge. If you have an idea about which choice is correct, act on it. Even the College Board suggests that you try—as long as you can eliminate some answer choices.

PRACTICING

Now, take the time to practice what you have just learned. Read the selection in Exercise 1, to follow, that was written in the eighteenth century by Hector St. John de Crèvecoeur. Apply the suggestions and strategies to determine the right answer. Circle the correct answer, and then write out your reasoning on the lines provided below each question.

If you do not understand the question, you may check the explanation immediately. You may refer to the answers question by question, or you may wish to score the entire section at one time. No matter which method you choose, read all the explanations against your own. See where your reasoning and ours differ. If your answer is incorrect, what is the flaw in your reasoning? If your answer is correct, is your reasoning the same as ours, or did we add to your understanding of the question and the process of arriving at the answer?

NOTE

Always read all the explanations given for correct answers in the *Answer Key and Explanations* sections in this book. The logic might offer you an insight that will help you with other questions.

EXERCISE 1

Directions: This section consists of selections of literature and questions on their content, style, and form. After you have read each passage, choose the best response to each question.

QUESTIONS 1–10. READ THE PASSAGE CAREFULLY, AND THEN CHOOSE THE ANSWERS TO THE QUESTIONS.

From the third essay of *Letters from an American Farmer*

Line   What attachment can a poor European emigrant have for a country where he had nothing? The knowledge of the language, the love of a few kindred as
5   poor as himself, were the only cords that tied him: his country is now that which gives him land, bread, protection, and consequence. *Ubi panis ibi patria** is the motto of all emigrants.
10   What then is the American, this new man? He is either an European, or the descendant of an European, hence that strange mixture of blood, which you will find in no other country. I could
15   point out to you a family whose grandfather was an Englishman, whose wife was Dutch, whose son married a French woman, and whose present four sons have now four wives
20   of different nations. *He* is an American, who, leaving behind him all his ancient prejudices and manners, receives new ones from the new mode of life he has embraced, the government he obeys,
25   and the new rank he holds. He becomes an American by being received in the broad lap of our great *Alma Mater.*** Here individuals of all nations are melted into a new race of men,
30   whose labors and posterity will one day cause great changes in the world. Americans are the western pilgrims, who are carrying along with them that great mass of arts, sciences, vigor, and
35   industry which began long since in the east; they will finish the great circle.

The Americans were once scattered all over Europe; here they are incorporated into one of the finest systems of
40   population which has ever appeared, and which will hereafter become distinct by the power of the different climates they inhabit. The American ought therefore to love this country
45   much better than that wherein either he or his forefathers were born. Here the rewards of his industry follow with equal steps the progress of his labor; his labor is founded on the basis of
50   nature, *self-interest;* can it want a stronger allurement? Wives and children, who before in vain demanded of him a morsel of bread, now, fat and frolicsome, gladly help their father to
55   clear those fields whence exuberant crops are to arise to feed and to clothe them all; without any part being claimed, either by a despotic prince, a rich abbot, or a mighty lord. Here
60   religion demands but little of him; a small voluntary salary to the minister, and gratitude to God; can he refuse these? The American is a new man, who acts upon principles; he must
65   therefore entertain new ideas, and form new opinions. From involuntary idleness, servile dependence, penury, and useless labor, he has passed to toils of a very different nature, re-
70   warded by ample subsistence.—This is an American.

_____
* Where bread is, there is one's country
** Beloved mother

1. Which of the following best describes the author's view of American society?

   (A) A melting pot
   (B) Lacking in prejudices
   (C) Devoid of principles
   (D) Class conscious
   (E) Lawless

   _____

   _____

   _____

   _____

2. Considering diction, tone, and rhetorical mode, how can this selection best be characterized?

   (A) An eloquent expression of the American dream
   (B) A charming narrative
   (C) An ironic discourse
   (D) A subtle criticism of the new American nation
   (E) A commentary directed at reforming European countries

   _____

   _____

   _____

   _____

3. Which of the following is NOT a reason for Americans to love this country more than that of their ancestors?

   (A) Religion demands little of them.
   (B) Rewards follow their labor.
   (C) Abbots, princes, or lords do not set a levy on crops.
   (D) The labor of Americans is founded on their own self-interest.
   (E) Charity is freely given.

   _____

   _____

   _____

   _____

4. In the next to the last sentence of the excerpt (line 67), what is the meaning of the word "penury"?

   (A) Largess
   (B) Imprisonment
   (C) Destitution
   (D) Hard work
   (E) Corporal punishment

   _____

   _____

   _____

   _____

5. The semicolon after the word "Europe" in line 38 serves which of the following purposes?

   (A) It sets off two or more independent clauses.
   (B) It separates items in a series.
   (C) It separates parenthetical elements.
   (D) It establishes a new thought.
   (E) It sets off an introductory phrase.

   _____

   _____

   _____

   _____

exercises

6. What literary device is used to describe the new American in this sentence, "He becomes an American by being received in the broad lap of our great *Alma Mater*"?

   (A) Simile
   (B) Personification
   (C) Metaphor
   (D) Apostrophe
   (E) Hyperbole

   _____

   _____

   _____

   _____

   _____

7. The organization of the selection could best be characterized as

   (A) stream of consciousness
   (B) comparison
   (C) order of importance
   (D) contrast
   (E) argumentation

   _____

   _____

   _____

   _____

8. Which of the following is the literary form that the writer has chosen to employ?

   (A) Narrative
   (B) Personal letter
   (C) Expository article
   (D) Epistle
   (E) Dialogue

   _____

   _____

   _____

   _____

   _____

9. What is the best synonym for the word "exuberant" in line 55?

   (A) Sparse
   (B) Abundant
   (C) Harvested
   (D) Withered
   (E) Enthusiastic

   _____

   _____

   _____

   _____

   _____

10. Which of the following statements best presents the writer's theme?

    (A) Americans will become self-absorbed.
    (B) The new nation will become an imperialist power.
    (C) America will cause worldwide changes.
    (D) American citizens will develop a rigid class structure.
    (E) The people will destroy their own country because of their excesses.

    _____

    _____

    _____

    _____

    _____

ANSWER KEY AND EXPLANATIONS

1. A	3. E	5. A	7. C	9. B
2. A	4. C	6. B	8. D	10. C

1. **The correct answer is (A).** The challenge of this question is to sift through the responses to select the one that most accurately describes the author's vision of America. Choice (E) is not mentioned in the selection and can be eliminated immediately. The information in each of choices (A) through (D) is mentioned in the passage in one form or another, so you might select one of these four because they sound familiar. A scanning of the passage, however, shows that the only response that truly reflects the author's words is choice (A), "a melting pot." Choice (B) is a detail that supports choice (A). Choices (C) and (D) contradict the attitude of the passage.

2. **The correct answer is (A).** Sometimes, the obvious choice is the correct answer. Choices (C), (D), and (E) do not reflect the tone, mode, or subject matter that is addressed by the author. Your decision should have been between choices (A) and (B). Choice (B) is in the running only because of the word *charming*. The style is arguably charming, but it is not a narrative.

3. **The correct answer is (E).** The key to choosing the correct answer for this question is in noting the word *not* in the question. You are looking for the one answer in the series that is either opposite to or not included in the writer's thesis. In this case, the subject of "charity," choice (E), is never mentioned in the passage.

4. **The correct answer is (C).** This is a straightforward vocabulary question, which makes it easy if you know the meaning of the word. If you are uncertain of the meaning, find the given word in context, and substitute each of the answer choices. By doing so, some answers may be eliminated, and one may clearly stand out as the correct answer. In this case, inserting the answer choices in context of line 67 easily eliminates choices (A) and (D) because gifts and hard work would not logically appear in the same series as involuntary idleness and useless labor. Because involuntary idleness might mean either imprisonment or unemployment, eliminate choices (B) and (E) because the author probably would not repeat the same idea. Also corporal punishment, choice (E), does not seem to fit in a series about working or not working. That leaves choice (C), which means destitute or penniless.

5. **The correct answer is (A).** Choice (B) can be eliminated because there is neither a series nor a parenthetical element, which eliminates choice (C). Choice (D) does not follow any grammar rule, and there is no introductory phrase, choice (E), in the sentence. There are, however, two independent clauses, choice (A).

6. **The correct answer is (B).** The process of elimination is a good strategy to use for determining the answer when you are not sure about the responses. You can eliminate choice (A) immediately because a simile is a figure of speech that includes *as* or *like*. Choice (B) might be correct because the author is attributing a lap to America, which seems like it is personification, but keep reading the answer choices. Reject choice (C) because a metaphor is an implied comparison. Apostrophe, choice (D), is a literary device of calling out to an imaginary, dead, or absent person; to a place, thing, or personified abstraction; or to begin a poem or make a dramatic break. Neither that nor choice (E), hyperbole, an obvious, lavish exaggeration or overstatement, fits the sentence. That leaves choice (B) as the only correct response.

7. **The correct answer is (C).** This question tests your ability to recognize types of organization and structure. Eliminate choices (A) and (E) because they do not apply to the selection. There is nothing that could be considered stream of consciousness about the selection. It might be persuasive, a form of argumentation, but argumentation is a mode of discourse, not a form of organization. While the writer does seem to compare, choice (B), and contrast, choice (D), he has arranged his thoughts to rise in power and conclude on a very strong note.

8. **The correct answer is (D).** The author is writing an epistle, or literary letter, which is a formal composition written in the form of a letter that is addressed to a distant person or group of people. Unlike personal letters, choice (B), which are more conversational and private, epistles are carefully crafted literary works that are intended for a general audience. Your best hint for this is in the title of the selection. Eliminate choices (A) and (E) since there is no story being told and no discussion among people. While you may have considered choice (C), the passage is less expository than persuasive.

9. **The correct answer is (B).** This is not so much a vocabulary drill as it is a test of your comprehension. None of the responses is an exact synonym for the word *exuberant* as we use the word today. You must determine the definition from the context of the sentence. Substitute each of the proposed responses, and select the one that makes the most sense, keeping in mind the tone and theme of the author. Neither *sparse*, choice (A), nor *withered*, choice (D), would likely be the correct response given the rest of the sentence. *Harvested*, choice (C), does not make sense before the crops grow. *Enthusiastic*, choice (E), is a synonym for *exuberant*, but it does not make sense in context. *Abundant*, choice (B), best captures the author's meaning.

10. **The correct answer is (C).** You can eliminate all but the correct answer in this question by keeping in mind the general tone of the author. The writer is very positive about America and America's future. Four of the five possibilities, choices (A), (B), (D), and (E), are negative. A clue to the answer can be found in the sentence, "Here individuals of all nations are melted into a new race of men, whose labors and posterity will one day cause great changes in the world." (lines 28–31)

Now that you have a sense of the logic involved in acing Section I of the test, try *Exercises 2* and *3*. Study the explanations for choosing the correct answers. If you are still unsure of your ability with multiple-choice questions, continue on with *Exercises 4* and *5*.

EXERCISE 2

Directions: This section consists of selections of literature and questions on their content, style, and form. After you have read each passage, choose the best response to each question.

QUESTIONS 1–10. READ THE PASSAGE CAREFULLY, AND THEN CHOOSE THE ANSWERS TO THE QUESTIONS.

From *The Law of the Great Peace* from the Iroquois Confederacy

Line When a candidate is to be installed, he
shall furnish four strings of shells or
wampum one span in length bound
together at one end. Such will consti-
5 tute the evidence of his pledge to the
chiefs of the League that he will live
according to the Constitution of the
Great Peace and exercise justice in all
affairs. When the pledge is furnished,
10 the Speaker of the Council must hold
the shell strings in his hand and
address the opposite side of the Council
Fire, and he shall begin his
address saying:

15 Now behold him. He has now
become a chief of the League. See
how splendid he looks.

An address may then follow. At the
end of it he shall send the bunch of
20 shell strings to the opposite side, and
they shall be received as evidence of
the pledge. Then shall the opposite
side say:

We now do crown you with the
25 sacred emblem of the deer's
antlers, the emblem of your
chieftainship. You shall now
become a mentor of the people of
the Five Nations. The thickness of
30 your skin shall be seven spans,
which is to say that you will be
proof against anger, offensive
actions, and criticism. Your heart
shall be filled with peace and good
35 will. Your mind shall be filled
with a yearning for the welfare of
the people of the League. With

endless patience you shall carry
out your duty and your firmness
40 shall be tempered with tenderness
for your people. Neither anger nor
fury shall find lodging in your
mind. All your words and actions
shall be marked with calm
45 deliberation. In all your delibera-
tions in law-making, in all your
official acts, self-interest shall be
cast away. Do not cast over your
shoulder behind you the warnings
50 of your nephews and nieces
should they chide you for any
error or wrong you may do, but
return to the way of the Great
Lake which is right and just. Look
55 and listen for the welfare of the
whole people, and have always in
view not only the present, but
also the coming generations, even
those whose faces are yet beneath
60 the surace of the ground—the
unborn of the future Nation.

1. According to this passage, which of the following is conduct that the leaders would be LEAST likely to encourage in a new chief?

    (A) Punish criticism and offensive behavior.
    (B) Be mindful of future genera-tions.
    (C) Be calm in words and actions.
    (D) Consider the welfare of all people.
    (E) Be a stern but fair lawmaker.

2. The clause "The thickness of your skin shall be seven spans" (lines 29–30) is an example of which of the following?

   (A) Simile
   (B) Analogy
   (C) Visual imagery
   (D) Metaphor
   (E) Alliteration

3. How does the speaker use rhetoric and style in the second speech of the selection to communicate the conduct expected of a new chief?

   (A) Declarative sentences, formal diction
   (B) Declarative sentences, future tenses
   (C) Imperative sentences, formal diction
   (D) Imperative sentences, future tenses
   (E) Imperative sentences, active verbs

4. In the context of this passage, the best interpretation of the word "span" (line 30) is

   (A) span of a life
   (B) span of a hand
   (C) span of an arrow
   (D) the wing span of an eagle
   (E) span of an arm

5. Which of the following is the best interpretation of the sentence "Neither anger nor fury shall find lodging in your mind" (lines 41–43)?

   (A) A chief does not become angry.
   (B) A chief does not rule with anger.
   (C) A chief does not remain angry.
   (D) A chief does not display anger.
   (E) A chief does not let anger rule him.

6. Which of the following can you infer about Native American culture from the imperatives and admonitions included in the installation ceremony?

   I. Family is important.
   II. A chief's conduct is important.
   III. Anger is offensive.

   (A) I only
   (B) II only
   (C) III only
   (D) I and II only
   (E) I and III only

7. The mode of this selection as a whole is best described as

   (A) argumentative
   (B) narrative
   (C) exposition
   (D) historical treatise
   (E) description

8. After careful rhetorical analysis of the selection, which of the following best describes the genesis of the speech?

   (A) Tribal customs
   (B) Logic
   (C) Ethics
   (D) Emotion
   (E) Spirituality

9. The sentence "With endless patience you shall carry out your duty and your firmness shall be tempered with tenderness for your people" contains all of the following EXCEPT

   (A) a verb in the passive voice
   (B) parallel structure
   (C) specific details
   (D) a participial phrase
   (E) courtly diction

10. In the sentence "Do not cast . . . right and just" (lines 48–54), what is the best meaning of the word "chide"?

   (A) Judge
   (B) Blame
   (C) Reprove
   (D) Criticism
   (E) Reprimand

ANSWER KEY AND EXPLANATIONS

1. A	3. C	5. E	7. C	9. D
2. C	4. B	6. B	8. C	10. C

1. **The correct answer is (A).** This question asks you to find the one answer that is incorrect. You could return to the passage and skim to find the behaviors required. Or you could also use common sense to recognize that choices (B), (C), (D), and (E) are behaviors that are desirable in a leader, which eliminates those as the answer, because you are being asked to find the behavior that is least likely to be encouraged in a leader. Choice (A) is not behavior that is desirable in a leader, so it is the correct answer. If you found the probable answer by using this logic, you could confirm your answer choice by scanning the selection.

2. **The correct answer is (C).** This question requires your knowledge of literary elements. Choice (A), simile, is a comparison that requires the word *like* or *as*, so it can be eliminated. Choice (B), an analogy, or comparison of similar things, is incorrect because there is no comparison in the sentence. A metaphor, choice (D), is another type of comparison in which one thing is referred to as another; it, too, is incorrect. Choice (E), alliteration, requires a series of words beginning with the same sound, so it can be eliminated.

3. **The correct answer is (C).** This question tests your knowledge of English grammar. The sentence is imperative; the use of *shall* instead of the usual *will* indicates a demand. *Shall* is not a form of the verb *to be*, but it is a helping verb. A declarative sentence, choices (A) and (B), simply states an idea, which is not the case here. One clue that the sentences are not exclamatory, choice (D), is the lack of an exclamation point as the end mark. Because the sentences do not ask a question, they cannot be interrogative, choice (E).

4. **The correct answer is (B).** This question asks you to be logical. Thickness of skin could not relate to life span, making choice (A) incorrect. Choices (C), (D), and (E) are illogical, too; seven times the span of either an arrow, a wing, or an arm would not be related to the depth of skin. As you probably have learned through your study of history, the hand was commonly used as a measure, making choice (B) the most logical interpretation.

5. **The correct answer is (E).** This is a comprehension question. Choices (B), (C), and (D) all seem appropriate, but the question is asking you for the "best interpretation." Choice (E) is the best because it includes the ideas in choices (B), (C), and (D). Choice (A) is a distracter because the selection does not say a chief cannot become angry, only that that anger should not affect his rule.

6. **The correct answer is (B).** Although anger and family (nephews and nieces) are mentioned in the passage, the fundamental message is the importance of a chief's conduct. Therefore, only choice (B), which mentions the chief's conduct, can be correct. Choice (A), family, and choice (C), the offensiveness of anger, are incorrect because they do not mention conduct. Choice (D) is only partially correct because only conduct is correct. Choice (E) is entirely wrong.

7. **The correct answer is (C).** The question asks you to identify the type of discourse used in the selection. If you recognized that the purpose is to explain how a candidate is installed as a chief of the Iroquois, selecting choice (C), exposition, is easy. If you did not see that, you could use the process of elimination to find the best choice. There is no

answers exercises

argument or persuasion occurring, so choice (A) can be ruled out. A narrative, choice (B), tells a story, which is not the mode used here. While there is a great deal of description, choice (E), the purpose of the selection is to present the stages of the ceremony. Choice (D) is a distracter; this is a not a mode of discourse.

8. **The correct answer is (C).** Don't be fooled. This is obviously a tribal custom, choice (A), and there may be some unspoken spiritual overtones, choice (E), but remember the conventions of rhetoric—logic, ethics, and emotion. This passage discusses the conduct that is expected of new chiefs and, hence, clearly evolves from ethics.

9. **The correct answer is (D).** This question tests your understanding of rhetoric and the conventions of English. You must identify what is NOT in the sentence. The sentence contains a verb, "shall be tempered," in the passive voice, so choice (A) is wrong. The coordinating conjunction, *and,* which joins two independent clauses, establishes parallel structure, thus eliminating choice (B). There are specific details, and the language is courtly, formal, and elegant, so choices (C) and (E) are incorrect. A participial phrase, choice (D), is a verb form that functions as an adjective or adverb. There is no such structure, which makes the only incorrect choice the right answer!

10. **The correct answer is (C).** This is a difficult vocabulary question. Most of the choices make sense in the context of the sentence. Think about the sense of the sentence, and use the process of elimination to find the best definition. You can eliminate choice (D) immediately because, while it suggests a very good possibility, it is a noun, and *chide* is a verb. Look for a verb among the other four choices that is similar in meaning to *criticism.* Since the youth are chiding a chief, you can safely assume that choices (A), (B), and (D) are too harsh. *Reprove,* close in meaning to criticize, is gentler and the best choice.

EXERCISE 3

Directions: This section consists of selections of literature and questions on their content, style, and form. After you have read each passage, choose the best response to each question.

QUESTIONS 1–10. READ THE PASSAGE CAREFULLY, AND THEN CHOOSE THE ANSWERS TO THE QUESTIONS.

From *Declaration of Sentiments*

Line When in the course of human events, it becomes necessary for one portion of the family of man to assume among the people of the earth a position
5 different from that which they have hitherto occupied, but one to which the laws of nature and nature's God entitle them, decent respect to the opinions of mankind requires that they should
10 declare the causes that impel them to such a course.

We hold these truths to be self-evident: that all men and women are created equal; that they are endowed
15 by their Creator with certain inalienable rights, that among these are life, liberty, and the pursuit of happiness; that to secure these rights governments are instituted, deriving their
20 just powers from the consent of the governed. When any form of government becomes destructive of these ends, it is the right of those who suffer from it to refuse allegiance to it, and to
25 insist upon the institution of a new government, laying its foundation on such principles, and organizing its powers in such form as to them shall seem most likely to effect their safety
30 and happiness. Prudence, indeed, will dictate that governments long established should not be changed for light and transient causes; accordingly, all experiences hath shown that mankind
35 are more disposed to suffer, while evils are sufferable, than to right themselves by abolishing the forms to which they are accustomed. But when a long train of abuses and usurpations, pursuing

40 invariably the same object evinces a design to reduce them under absolute despotism, it is their duty to throw off such government, and to provide new guards for their future security. Such
45 has been the patient sufferance of the women under this government, and such is now the necessity which constrains them to demand the equal station to which they are entitled.
50 The history of mankind is a history of repeated injuries and usurpations on the part of man toward women, having in direct object the establishment of an absolute tyranny over her. . . . [An
55 explanation of fifteen specific grievances follows this paragraph.]
He has endeavored, in every way that he could, to destroy her confidence in her own powers, to lessen her
60 self-respect, and to make her willing to lead a dependent and abject life. Now, in view of this entire disfranchisement of one-half the people of this country, their social and religious degradation,
65 — in view of the unjust laws above mentioned, and because women do feel themselves aggrieved, oppressed, and fraudulently deprived of their most sacred rights, we insist that they have
70 immediate admission to all the rights and privileges which belong to them as citizens of the United States. . . .

—Elizabeth Cady Stanton

1. At the end of the second paragraph, in the sentence beginning "Such has been the patient . . ." (lines 44–49), which of the following is the best meaning for the word "constrains"?

   (A) Restrains
   (B) Coerces
   (C) Encourages
   (D) Demands
   (E) Entitles

2. From your reading of this selection, what does the writer believe about the origin of women's rights?

   (A) They come from government.
   (B) They come from nature.
   (C) They come from God.
   (D) They come from society.
   (E) They come from men.

3. The syntax and organization of the passage serve to

   I. establish an extended analogy to the Declaration of Independence
   II. create a powerful argument supporting the writer's position
   III. point out the effects of disenfranchisement

   (A) I only
   (B) I and II only
   (C) II and III only
   (D) I and III only
   (E) I, II, and III

4. In the sentence beginning "He has endeavored . . ." (lines 57–61), the repetition of the infinitive phrases serves which of the following rhetorical functions?

   I. Provides parallel structure to intensify the message
   II. Details the list of grievances
   III. Creates an intellectual tone

   (A) I only
   (B) II only
   (C) III only
   (D) I and II only
   (E) II and III only

5. The writer emphasizes the evils experienced by women in order to further her argument for

   (A) abolishing all government
   (B) writing powerful statements
   (C) holding demonstrations
   (D) amending the Constitution
   (E) demanding equal rights

6. To what does the writer liken the plight of women in the United States?

   (A) To the universal plight of women
   (B) To the plight of wives
   (C) To the plight of all oppressed people
   (D) To America's plight as a colony
   (E) To the plight of slaves

7. Which of the following best describes the tone of this passage?

   (A) Inspiring, powerful
   (B) Serious, angry
   (C) Objective, informative
   (D) Emotional, pretentious
   (E) Dramatic, portentous

8. This passage is an example of which of the following modes of discourse?

   (A) Argument
   (B) Persuasion
   (C) Exposition
   (D) Narrative
   (E) Description

9. The passage as a whole can best be described as which of the following?

   (A) A commentary about women's suffrage
   (B) An indictment of men's tyranny over women
   (C) A declaration of independence for women
   (D) A feminist diatribe
   (E) A political lament

10. In the sentence beginning "We hold these truths to be self-evident: . . ." (lines 12–21), the best meaning for the word "inalienable" is

    (A) undeniable
    (B) fundamental
    (C) natural
    (D) God-given
    (E) not to be taken away

exercises

ANSWER KEY AND EXPLANATIONS

1. B	3. B	5. E	7. A	9. C
2. C	4. D	6. D	8. A	10. E

1. **The correct answer is (B).** This vocabulary question presents a challenge. All the choices, with the exception of choice (A), which is an antonym for *constrains* in this context, make sense in the sentence. You want the strongest choice because the sentence needs a word meaning "forces." Choices (C) and (E) are weaker than choices (D) and (B), so you can eliminate them. Choice (D) creates a repetition in the sentence ("which demands them to demand"), so it is not the best choice. Choice (B) remains as the strongest verb and best response.

2. **The correct answer is (C).** The question, which is rather easy, asks you to recall a detail and interpret it. The author, Elizabeth Cady Stanton writes, ". . . they are endowed by their Creator with certain inalienable rights." Ask yourself, what is the Creator? You know that the Creator is not the government, choice (A); society, choice (D); or men, choice (E). You might be able to make a case for nature, choice (B). However, nature is rarely if ever called the Creator, so that choice is not the most accurate.

3. **The correct answer is (B).** Don't be misled. Point III, a part of choices (C), (D), and (E), is a distracter. The effects of disenfranchisement are mentioned, but the question revolves around syntax and organization. Choice (B) is the correct answer because both I and II are used to support the syntax and organization of the passage.

4. **The correct answer is (D).** Point III is a distracter. The repetition of infinitive phrases provides both point I, parallel structure, and point II, a list of grievances, so choice (D) is the correct answer because it is the only answer that has both points I and II.

5. **The correct answer is (E).** This comprehension question asks for the main idea. Ask yourself, what point is the writer making? Stanton certainly does not advocate the overthrow of all governments; she wants the rules of the U.S. government to apply fairly to all citizens, so choice (A) is incorrect. The writer might feel that choices (B) and (C) are good methods for spotlighting the problem, but neither reflects the main purpose of the passage. Choice (D) would be required to gain equal rights, but that is implied in the passage and is not the main idea.

6. **The correct answer is (D).** This is a cultural question that relies on your knowledge of U.S. history. Just as the British colonists felt that they were denied their rights as citizens by the British, Stanton and her peers felt that U.S. women were denied their rights as citizens by the U.S. government. The remaining choices, (A), (B), (C), and (E), have little or no relationship to the Declaration of Independence.

7. **The correct answer is (A).** While the article has some elements of choices (B) and (E), neither choice is entirely correct. The document is serious but not necessarily angry, choice (B), and portentous but not necessarily dramatic, choice (E). The passage is argumentative, not objective, so choice (C) is not the answer. Although based on the Declaration of Independence, some readers of the Declaration of the Sentiments might have considered it emotional and pretentious, choice (D), but that is not the tone the author set out to create. That leaves choice (A) as the correct answer.

8. **The correct answer is (A).** You can immediately eliminate choices (C), (D), and (E) because the selection is not simply informative, does not tell a story, and does not describe a person, place, thing, event, or idea. The answer hinges on your understanding of the difference between persuasion and argumentation. Argumentation is a more powerful type of writing than persuasion. That eliminates choice (B), because this is a very strong piece of writing.

9. **The correct answer is (C).** If you remembered question 6, about the Declaration of Independence, you had a good idea about how to answer this question. The selection advocates female suffrage, not just comments on it, so choice (A) is incorrect. The writer discusses men's tyranny over women, but that is only part of the argument, so you can eliminate choice (B). You can eliminate choices (D) and (E) as inappropriate descriptions of this passage. The word *diatribe*, choice (D), has a negative connotation, and *lament* has a connotation of weakness.

10. **The correct answer is (E).** All the answers for this question make sense. You must pick the best one. While human rights may be undeniable, choice (A); fundamental, choice (B); natural, choice (C); and God-given, choice (D), the most important aspect is that they cannot be made alien; that is, they cannot be taken away, choice (E).

EXERCISE 4

Directions: This section consists of selections of literature and questions on their content, style, and form. After you have read each passage, choose the best response to each question.

QUESTIONS 1–10. READ THE PASSAGE CAREFULLY, AND THEN CHOOSE THE ANSWERS TO THE FOLLOWING QUESTIONS.

Line   Washington, April 14, 1865
Published in the *New York Herald*,
April 15, 1865

Washington was thrown into an
5   intense excitement a few minutes
before eleven o'clock this evening, by
the announcement that the President
and Secretary Seward had been
assassinated and were dead.
10   The wildest excitement prevailed in
all parts of the city. Men, women, and
children, old and young, rushed to and
fro, and the rumors were magnified
until we had nearly every member of
15   the Cabinet killed. Some time elapsed
before authentic data could be ascer-
tained in regard to the affair.
The President and Mrs. Lincoln
were at Ford's theatre, listening to the
20   performance of The American Cousin,
occupying a box in the second tier. At
the close of the third act a person
entered the box occupied by the
President, and shot Mr. Lincoln in the
25   head. The shot entered the back of his
head, and came out the temple.
The assassin then jumped from the
box upon the stage and ran across to
the other side, exhibiting a dagger in
30   his hand, flourishing it in a tragical
manner, shouting the same words
repeated by the desperado at Mr.
Seward's house, adding to it, "The
South is avenged," and then escaped
35   from the back entrance to the stage,
but in his passage dropped his pistol
and his hat.
Mr. Lincoln fell forward from his
seat, and Mrs. Lincoln fainted.
40   The moment the astonished audience could realize what happened, the

President was taken and carried to Mr.
Peterson's house, in Tenth street,
opposite the theatre. Medical aid was
45   immediately sent for, and the wound
was at first supposed to be fatal, and it
was announced that he could not live,
but at half-past twelve he is still alive,
though in a precarious condition.

1. This passage is an example of which of the following modes of discourse?

   (A) Description
   (B) Exposition
   (C) Narration
   (D) Persuasion
   (E) Argument

2. Which of the following best describes the tone of this passage?

   (A) Angry
   (B) Objective
   (C) Dramatic
   (D) Solemn
   (E) Emotional

3. The sentence from the second paragraph beginning "Men, women, and children, old and young, rushed to and fro. . . ." (lines 11–15) is an example of which of the following?

   (A) Parallelism
   (B) Simple sentence
   (C) Run-on sentence
   (D) Archaic English
   (E) Exaggeration

4. In the first two paragraphs, the writer's rhetoric and syntax combine to create an impression of

   I. excitement and chaos
   II. fear and tragedy
   III. terrible news and uncertainty

   (A) I only
   (B) II only
   (C) III only
   (D) I and II only
   (E) I and III only

5. In the fourth paragraph, what is the best meaning of the word "tragical" (line 30)?

   (A) Sorrowful
   (B) Dramatic
   (C) Terrible
   (D) Threatening
   (E) Deadly

6. In this passage, which of the following rhetorical devices is most evident?

   (A) Appealing to authority
   (B) Massing of factual information
   (C) Abstract generalizations
   (D) Emotional appeal
   (E) Anecdotal information

7. Which of the following best summarizes the purpose of the passage?

   (A) To discuss the reason for the city's excitement
   (B) To report the news of President Lincoln's death
   (C) To clarify the report of the assassination attempt on President Lincoln
   (D) To report that President Lincoln is still alive
   (E) To give an account of the events at Ford's Theatre

8. Reviewing the diction of the passage, which of the following best characterizes the writer's style?

   (A) Informal diction
   (B) Colloquial diction
   (C) Slang diction
   (D) Formal diction
   (E) Pretentious diction

9. In this selection, which of the following patterns of organization is most in evidence?

   (A) Development by details
   (B) Chronology
   (C) Cause and effect
   (D) Analysis
   (E) Synthesis

10. In the last sentence of the last paragraph (lines 44–49), what is the best meaning for the word "precarious"?

   (A) Risky
   (B) Dangerous
   (C) Vulnerable
   (D) Uncertain
   (E) Treacherous

exercises

ANSWER KEY AND EXPLANATIONS

1. B	3. A	5. B	7. C	9. B
2. B	4. E	6. E	8. D	10. D

1. **The correct answer is (B).** The passage explains what happened at Lincoln's assassination. A clue is offered in the introduction, where the selection is identified as a newspaper article. News articles almost always are expository, answering who, what, where, when, why, and how. There is no effort to persuade in the selection, so choices (D) and (E) can be eliminated. While there are some descriptive elements, the purpose is to inform, thus excluding choice (A). You might have thought twice about choice (C), but the factual nature of the piece eliminates narration, the telling of a story.

2. **The correct answer is (B).** To answer this question correctly, you need to identify the feeling that the article gives you, not the feeling of the event reported. That people were angry and emotional is true, but the tone is neither angry, choice (A), nor emotional, choice (E). The event is very dramatic, choice (C), yet the writer presents the situation in an informative and impersonal manner, making choice (C) incorrect. Consequent events were solemn, not this article, choice (D). That leaves choice (B) as the correct answer.

3. **The correct answer is (A).** You probably recognized several examples of parallel construction in the sentence. If not, you could discover the answer by the process of elimination. The sentence is a grammatically correct compound-complex sentence, so choices (B) and (C) are incorrect. This sentence is certainly not archaic English. To be so, it would read like *Beowulf* or *The Canterbury Tales*, making choice (D) invalid. There is no exaggeration in this factual reporting of a very distressing event. Thus, choice (E) is incorrect.

4. **The correct answer is (E).** The question is about rhetoric and its effect in creating an impression in the first two paragraphs. Don't be carried away by what you know about the historical event. Although the assassination of Lincoln was indeed a tragedy and undoubtedly generated fear (point II), that is not the sense that was related in the first two paragraphs. They talk about excitement and rumors and people rushing to and fro. These facts relate to points I and III. The only answer choice that includes both points is choice (E).

5. **The correct answer is (B).** Did you notice that several of these answers made sense in the sentence, but only one made sense in the context of the article? This is why in order to choose the correct answer, you need to read a few lines above and below the line that is identified. The assassin waved a dagger after he shot Lincoln. The gesture was dramatic, choice (B), more than terrible, choice (C), and not very threatening, choice (D), or deadly, choice (E). Choice (A), sorrowful, is illogical.

6. **The correct answer is (E).** This question may seem difficult, but you can eliminate the incorrect answers through logical thinking. Does the article appeal to authority? No, authorities are not cited, let alone addressed. Therefore, choice (A) is incorrect. Is there a mass of information? Yes, the article presents information, but it is not an overwhelming amount, so choice (B) is invalid. The article is a factual report, containing neither abstractions nor appeals to emotion, so choices (C) and (D) are incorrect.

7. **The correct answer is (C).** You may have found this main-idea question fairly easy. All responses except choice (B) are truthful. However, choices (A), (D), and (E) are support for the purpose of the article—to give the facts about the assassination attempt on the president.

8. **The correct answer is (D).** Several of the answers, choices (A), (B), and (C), are redundant, so you can conclude that these are incorrect. The article is not affected or ostentatious, which eliminates choice (E).

9. **The correct answer is (B).** Choices (C), (D), and (E) are easily ruled out because although they may be in evidence in parts of the article—cause and effect in the description of why rumors were flying—none of them predominates in the article. The selection offers details, but in terms of the pattern of organization, choice (B), chronology, is the most important feature.

10. **The correct answer is (D).** For vocabulary questions, substitute in the sentence each of the possible choices to see which is closest in meaning. Using this process, choices (A), (B), and (E) don't quite fit the context. Choice (C) is tempting, but the actual definition of the word precarious is "uncertain, insecure."

EXERCISE 5

Directions: This section consists of selections of literature and questions on their content, style, and form. After you have read each passage, choose the best response to each question.

QUESTIONS 1–10. READ THE PASSAGE CAREFULLY, AND THEN CHOOSE THE ANSWERS TO THE QUESTIONS.

From *Extinct Animals* written by L. H. Heller in 1908

Line   Many animals which inhabited the
earth in bygone periods have entirely
disappeared, leaving not even a
modern representative of their race.
5   Others, no doubt, were known to
pre-historic peoples, concerning which
no record has come down to us. But
within the period of recorded observation, many animals have lived and died
10   out; various causes contributing to
their extermination, not least among
these being in the presence of mankind. Man reconstructs the face of the
earth to suit his needs; he cuts down
15   forests, plows or burns over prairie
lands, changes the course of rivers,
drains the swamps, and thus destroys
the natural environment of many of
nature's wild children. Then, too, he
20   destroys creatures directly; he kills
them for food, for clothing, or for other
utilitarian purposes; he hunts them
because he fears them, as dangerous
foes to himself, or to his agricultural
25   pursuits; he destroys them for sport;
and finally he draws them from feral
conditions by domestication. Not only
thus does man directly injure by
exterminating influences, but his
30   coming accompanied by exterminating
influences, kills out certain other
creatures. These, when man has
destroyed their natural prey, practically die of starvation before they can
35   adapt themselves to changed conditions. Then the domestic dogs, cats,
etc. help on the work of slaughter in
certain ways, by preying upon wild life.

1. Which of the following best characterizes the tone of this passage?

    (A) Reproachful
    (B) Serious
    (C) Scholarly
    (D) Impassioned
    (E) Objective

2. What is the function of the first
sentence of the passage?

    I.   To state the main topic of
the selection
    II. To state the author's opinion
    III. To arouse interest in the thesis

    (A) I only
    (B) II only
    (C) III only
    (D) I and II only
    (E) I and III only

3. The mode of discourse for this
passage may best be characterized as

    (A) descriptive
    (B) narrative
    (C) expository
    (D) argumentative
    (E) persuasive

4. The best meaning for the word "feral"
(line 26) is

    (A) primitive
    (B) untamed
    (C) deadly
    (D) fierce
    (E) tricky

5. The first sentence of the passage (lines 1–4) contains all of the following EXCEPT a(n)

   (A) coordinating conjunction
   (B) negative adverb
   (C) prepositional phrase
   (D) participial phrase
   (E) intransitive verb

6. Which of the following best describes the theme of the passage?

   (A) Humankind as a destructive force in nature
   (B) The extinction of wild animals
   (C) Human beings' effect on wild animals
   (D) Humankind's responsibility for extinction of wild animals
   (E) Humankind's role in halting the extinction of wild animals

7. In this passage, which of the following rhetorical devices is most evident?

   (A) Stereotyping
   (B) Emotional appeal
   (C) Statement of facts
   (D) Causal relation
   (E) Simile

8. In the final sentence of the passage, which phrase(s) intensifies the mood of the selection?

   I. Domestic dogs, cats, etc.
   II. The work of slaughter
   III. Preying upon wild life

   (A) I only
   (B) II only
   (C) III only
   (D) I and II only
   (E) II and III only

9. In the sentence beginning "Not only thus does man . . ." (lines 27–32), to what does "thus" refer?

   (A) The direct and indirect actions of humans
   (B) Humankind's hunting of animals
   (C) The previous sentence
   (D) Humankind's fear of some animals
   (E) Humankind's alteration of the environment

10. In the clause "[man] destroys the natural environment of many of nature's wild children" (lines 17–19), "wild children" is an example of which of the following?

   (A) Simile
   (B) Metaphor
   (C) Personification
   (D) Analogy
   (E) Figurative language

exercises

ANSWER KEY AND EXPLANATIONS

1.	C	3.	D	5.	A	7.	D	9.	C
2.	D	4.	B	6.	D	8.	E	10.	C

1. **The correct answer is (C).** The key to this question is to sift through the choices to select the one that is best. Choice (E) is easily eliminated because the author examines only one side of the issue, people's negative effect on the environment. Choices (A), (B), and (D) are somewhat true, but choice (C) best characterizes the author's attitude and, therefore, most accurately reflects the tone of the passage.

2. **The correct answer is (D).** Evaluate the Roman numeral points first to see which one(s) may be true in relation to the question. Does the sentence state the main topic of the passage? Yes. Does it state the author's opinion? Yes. Does it arouse interest in the thesis? Not really. The rhetoric and style of this sentence is not exciting; it does not provide a "hook" to entice readers to read on. This means that you can eliminate any response with point III in it, choices (C) and (E). The sentence functions to state both the main topic and the author's view; therefore, choice (D), which includes both I and II, is the correct answer.

3. **The correct answer is (D).** This is a question about the mode of discourse of this selection. Using the process of elimination, choice (A) is wrong because the writer is not simply describing something. Choice (B) is incorrect because the author is not telling a story. You can eliminate choice (C) because the author is not simply telling or explaining something. Choice (E) may be tempting because the author does indeed want you to think as he does, but choice (D) is the best response because the author's primary purpose is to give the reader information from which to draw certain conclusions.

4. **The correct answer is (B).** This is a vocabulary question. Use the context of the sentence to help you make your choice. Reread the sentence in which the word appears, and then substitute each of the possible choices to see which is closest in meaning. In context, Choices (C), (D), and (E) are easily eliminated because they do not make sense in the context of the sentence. Choice (A) is incorrect because primitive can be applied to an animal or its condition only if the connotation is prehistoric. Choice (B) is the correct answer, given the context and the fact that it modifies *conditions*.

5. **The correct answer is (A).** This question tests your knowledge of English grammar. Sift through each of the grammatical applications in the sentence until you identify all that are present. There is a negative adverb, choice (B), "not even." There is a prepositional phrase, choice (C), "of their race." There is a participial phrase, choice (D), "leaving not even." There is an intransitive verb, choice (E), "have disappeared." What remains? Choice (A). There is no coordinating conjunction.

6. **The correct answer is (D).** This kind of question asks that you select the choice that best tells what the passage is about. Choice (E) is eliminated because the idea, although implied, is not actually stated in the passage. Choices (A), (B), and (C) are touched on in the passage, but choice (D) is the strongest message to the reader.

7. **The correct answer is (D).** The writer makes a number of statements as if they were factual, but they may actually be opinions, so choice (C) can be eliminated. In a simile, a writer says *something is like something else;* there is no evidence of that figure of speech in this piece, so choice (E) can also be eliminated. Depending on whether or not you agree with the author, you may see stereotyping in the passage, but that was not the author's intent, so cross off choice (A). The author is building his case on a series of reasons, so choice (B) is incorrect. That leaves causal relation, choice (D). Even though all the causes contributing to extinction may not be mentioned, the device is still causal relation.

8. **The correct answer is (E).** Point I, part of choices (A) and (D), contains no words that would intensify the mood. The words *slaughter* and *preying* in points II and III have emotional connotations that would intensify the mood of the sentence and assist the author in achieving his purpose. Only choice (E) has both points and is, therefore, the correct answer.

9. **The correct answer is (C).** The antecedent of *thus* refers to the previous sentence and all the actions of humankind described in it, choice (C). Choices (B) and (E) are too narrow. The remaining choices do not make sense in context.

10. **The correct answer is (C).** This is a language question that tests your knowledge of figures of speech. You can eliminate choices (A), (B), and (D) immediately because each refers to some kind of comparison, and there is no comparison in the clause. Figurative language, choice (E), a kind of vivid imagery, is generally true but not appropriate. This is a specific example of personification, the giving of human qualities to nonhumans, e.g., wild animals.

answers

exercises

SUMMING IT UP

- The questions in Section I ask you about passages from a variety of sources, rhetorical modes, historical eras, and literary periods and disciplines.

- Most of the questions assess how carefully you read, how well you interpret what you read, and how well you analyze literature. Some questions will ask you about grammar, mechanics, structure, organization, development, or footnotes.

- You will have approximately one minute to answer each multiple-choice question.

- You receive one point for each correct answer you give. You receive no points for each question you leave blank. If you answer incorrectly, one-quarter point is subtracted. This is the guessing penalty. Section I accounts for 45 percent of your final composite score.

- Scan the passages to decide the order in which you want to answer them. You do not have to answer the selections in the order presented. Then skim for an overall impression of the selection. Finally, read the selection carefully.

- You may find a multiple-choice question that asks you to determine the purpose of a footnote. These are fairly straightforward comprehension questions. A close reading of the footnote against the answer choices will help you determine the correct answer.

About the Free Response and Synthesis Essays

chapter 4

OVERVIEW

- **Basic information about section II**

- **Types of essays on the test**

- **Strategies for acing the essays**

- **The essay: a quick review**

- **A final word of advice on writing your essays**

- **Analyzing literature**

- **Practicing**

- **Self-evaluation rubric for the free response essays**

- **Self-evaluation rubric for the synthesis essays**

- **Summing it up**

Section II of the Advanced Placement test for English Language & Composition contains three essays asking you to analyze literary style, discuss rhetorical usage, and defend a position. There are several things to remember about the test. First, usually when you work on an essay, you have adequate time to brainstorm, prewrite, revise, and edit. On the AP test, your time is limited. Second, most of the essays you have written in English class involve literature you and your classmates have studied. On this test, you most likely have not seen the selections previously. Finally, you know your English teacher. You know what he or she thinks is important. You recognize your teacher's preferences in organization, mechanics, and sentence structure. You do not know the individuals who will score your AP essays, so you cannot write to the audience. If you are wondering how you are going to be successful, we can help.

This chapter lays out some basic information about the essay portion of the test and about good writing in general. In addition, this chapter will help you

TIP

Check the *Practice Plans for Studying for the AP English Language & Composition Test* on pp. 15–20.

to understand what the essay questions ask and how to answer each specific type of question. Now is the time to plan and practice, so you will have the self-confidence to excel, not panic.

You will explore the different types of essays on the AP test and have ample opportunities to practice writing sample essays. Use the rubrics and scoring guides to pinpoint your weaknesses and to improve as you write each subsequent essay.

Use the *Practice Tests* as tools to improve your writing, too. The techniques described in this chapter will help you to write each of your practice essays in 40 minutes. Give yourself the full 15-minute reading period to read, analyze, and make notes about the sources for the synthesis essay. When you have finished each test, turn to the *Answer Key and Explanations* section. Compare each essay to the list of suggested points that you might have developed in that essay. Score your essay against the *Self-Evaluation Rubrics*. Ask a reliable friend, an AP classmate, or a teacher to evaluate your essay holistically. Where are you weak? What can you improve? Take several of the points from the list and rework your essay with those points, strengthening the weak areas.

Reevaluate your essay. Again, compare the points you made with the ones we suggest. Did our suggestions help you to better understand what the question is asking? Is your rewritten essay more tightly focused on the question and more clearly developed as a result of incorporating some of our points? Still need work on your weak points? How much did you improve?

Now, stop. Do not keep working on the same essay to polish it to perfection. You won't have that opportunity during the test. The purpose of reworking your essay is to help you pinpoint what the question is really asking and how you can best answer it with a clear, coherent, and unified essay. Keep in mind what you learned on your first try and go on to the next essay.

BASIC INFORMATION ABOUT SECTION II

❶ Section II has three essay questions. They probably will ask you to analyze literary style, discuss rhetorical usage, and defend a position.

NOTE

You will need a pen to write your essays. Be safe: take at least two.

❷ One of the three essay questions will include several sources. In writing your essay, you must synthesize the information in at least three of those sources to support your argument.

❸ You will have 2 hours to write the essays and 15 minutes to read the sources for the synthesis essay. The College Board suggests you allot approximately 40 minutes to write each essay.

❹ Each essay is scored from 0 to 9, with 9 being the highest.

⑤ A different reader with knowledge of the literary work that you discuss will read each of your essays.

⑥ The essays together account for 55 percent of your final composite score.

What does all this mean? It means that you need to do some planning and practicing.

If you have 2 hours—120 minutes—to write all three essays, you cannot spend 90 minutes on one and 15 minutes apiece on the other two. When you practice, take 5 or so minutes for each of the nonsynthesis essays to read each question and selection and to plan what you will say. Use the remaining time—35 minutes each—to write and revise those two essays. You will have 15 minutes to read the sources for the synthesis essay.

Skim the three questions and then put them in the order in which you want to answer them. Begin with the easiest, then move to the next hardest, and finally, write the most difficult.

Because your three essays will be read by three different people, you don't have to worry that one weaker essay will pull down the scores for the other two essays. Instead, you can be confident that your clear, coherent, unified—and neatly written—essays will brighten each grader's pile of vague, incoherent, fragmented, and illegible essays.

You are probably thinking that our mentioning a neatly written paper is a bit fatuous. While neatness does not count, it does matter. Why? Neatness affects legibility. You cannot expect a reader faced with hundreds of papers to score to take time to puzzle over your handwriting. Write as neatly as you can. If your cursive style is tiny and cramped or large and ill-defined, try printing. You will not have time for much revision, but if you do revise, do it neatly and clearly.

TYPES OF ESSAYS ON THE TEST

There are two types of essays on the AP English Language & Composition Test: free response and synthesis. Typically, the synthesis essay will ask you to take a position and support it by synthesizing information from several sources. The purpose is to convince the reader of your position on an issue. The free response essays are typically expository or persuasive. The purpose of expository essays is to inform the reader of something, whereas the purpose of persuasive writing is to influence the reader's opinion and to lead your reader to act in a certain way. Knowing the elements of each mode of writing ensures that you can work effectively in that manner.

Guidelines for Exposition
1. Limit your main point, so it can be developed in the 40-minute time period.
2. Be sure that your main point lends itself to a factual treatment.
3. Brainstorm supporting information that you will need in order to explain your main idea thoroughly to your reader.
4. Develop a thesis statement and break it down into several subtopics.
5. Organize the subtopics and their supporting information for clarity.
6. Concentrate on explaining as you write.

Expository Essays

NOTE

Review literary and rhetorical terms in Appendix B.

If the essay prompt asks you to present information, to explain style, to define a concept or idea, or to analyze rhetoric, you are being asked to write an expository essay. Expository essays are usually objective and straightforward. The distinguishing characteristics of exposition are an explanatory purpose and an informative tone, because expository essays are intended to communicate factual material.

An expository essay should follow the standard three-part essay structure. However, the essay's thesis statement should be clearly explanatory, presenting a factual statement that the body of the essay elaborates upon, clarifies, and explains.

The supporting information furthers the explanatory purpose by providing sufficient examples and details to give your reader an understanding of your main point. Such information should be verifiable, so avoid controversial statements. Your support should be organized logically in subtopics that develop important elements of your main point. These guidelines will help you plan, write, and revise an expository essay.

As you write your expository essay, focus on explaining your topic to the audience. Move logically through the steps of the process or through the supporting details for a concept by providing all the information a reader needs to understand what you are presenting. Be sure to use transitions to assist your audience in following your explanation. If time remains, revise your essay, checking for unity and coherence. Review your word choices to ensure an objective, informative tone.

Argument and Persuasion

An essay that asks you to defend, challenge, or qualify a claim is argumentation. The formal definition of argument is writing that attempts "to convince the reader of the truth or falsity of a given proposition or thesis." In writing an argument, you set out a thesis, or opinion, of your own and proceed to defend it.

If you are asked to write an essay that analyzes which is the more persuasive argument between two positions or to consider opposing positions on an issue and develop a solution, you are being asked to write a persuasive essay. The purpose is to influence the reader to take an action that agrees with your thesis. This is one step past argument. You are attempting to persuade the reader to adopt your point of view and then to do something about it. Argument stops at the attempt to change the reader's mind about an issue.

Both modes of writing are often subjective. However, you must include in both types logical reasoning and convincing factual information in order to defend your opinion effectively. Both modes of writing differ from other kinds of essays in tone and in the requirement that they include supporting evidence. However, both modes of writing are similar to expository essays in that they use the same three-part essay format—introduction, body, conclusion. The thesis statement should present your position in a reasonable tone. You may not be able to convince every reader of the validity of your opinion, but your essay should demonstrate that you thought carefully, critically, and logically about the issue.

In writing both persuasive and argument essays, you must include supporting material that provides convincing evidence for your thesis statement. Support must consist of logical reasons or examples, facts, and details. Your supporting information should never be based on unsubstantiated opinions. Your evidence should be solid, authoritative, rational, and believable, appealing even to those readers who disagree with you. You want to show your readers that you are well informed and have thought about opposing arguments.

For the free-response persuasive essays on the AP English Language and Composition Test, you will have to rely on your own experience and reading and whatever information you may find in the relatively brief selection. Or the free response essay prompt may be only a quotation that you must support from your own experience and reading.

The synthesis question will provide a number of sources that you are to draw upon to find support for your position. All of your support must defend your position. In addition to the sources, you may include ideas from your own experience and reading. However, all the information that you use from the sources along with your own ideas must be synthesized to create a coherent, unified essay. The stronger the link between your argument and your sources, the higher your score will be on the exam. Also, remember that in using information from a source, you must cite the source—whether you quote directly from it or just restate ideas or information from it in your own words.

Your tone should be persuasive but reasonable, forceful but respectful of opposing viewpoints. In writing either a persuasive or argument paper for class, you would adjust your tone to your audience and take into consideration whether your audience might be sympathetic, apathetic, or strongly opposed to your position. You might choose a humorous, lighthearted approach or a serious, academic tone. Depending on the topic, the latter is probably the better tone for

TIP

Vary your sentence structure by:

- Beginning with a prepositional phrase
- Using adverbs and adverbial phrases
- Starting with dependent clauses
- Using various conjunctions—*not only, either, yet, so*
- Including infinitives and participles
- Beginning with adjectives and adjective phrases
- Employing inversions

both the persuasive and argument essays. Be sure to maintain whatever tone you choose throughout the essay.

When you advocate a highly controversial opinion, an effective method for developing supporting information is to list the principal arguments for your position and then marshal the strongest arguments against your viewpoint. After each opposing argument, present counterarguments for your side.

The following eleven guidelines will help you with writing both argument and persuasion essays:

TIP

Use transitions to create a roadmap for your argument.

1. Use your knowledge and beliefs to choose an opinion/topic that you can support.

2. Decide how persuasive you must be to make your points—the intensity of your purpose and tone.

3. Determine your readers' probable response to your position.

4. Brainstorm for specific examples, facts, details, reasons, and events that support your thesis statement.

5. If your opinion is controversial, consider the opposing arguments and list evidence for and against your position.

6. State your opinion in a thesis statement that is direct, significant, and supportable.

7. Organize your support in order of importance.

8. Consider conceding one or two points to the other side if your main point is highly controversial.

9. Use concrete, specific words. Be sure your language is reasonable but compelling. Don't be emotional

10. Employ smooth, logical transitions.

11. Revise your paper by examining your word choices to ensure a balanced, forceful, and consistent tone.

A WORD ABOUT THE SYNTHESIS ESSAY

The following tips will help you specifically with planning and writing the synthesis essay:

- Use at least the minimum number of sources to support your argument. You do not want to lower the score of a well-written essay because you failed to follow instructions.

- Incorporate the sources in your argument, but be careful to ensure that your *argument* is the focus of the essay, not the sources. Your arguments and sources should support your thesis, not the other way around.

- Do not simply summarize or restate the information provided in the sources.

- Show an understanding of the sources and successfully develop your position.

A WORD ABOUT LOGIC

When you write persuasively or argumentatively, you must think critically. First, you must analyze and evaluate the information so you can decide if it is reliable. Second, you must distinguish between valid and invalid forms of reasoning to determine if a position holds up under scrutiny.

To determine if material is reliable, you must distinguish fact from opinion. A fact, of course, is a statement that can be verified by objective means. An opinion is subjective and should be supported by relevant facts before it is considered valid. An opinion may express personal feelings about an idea or condition, or it may reflect a judgment or prediction based on facts. No matter which, an opinion is not valid if the facts supporting it are insufficient.

After you have verified facts and determined that the opinions are valid, you must analyze how the information is presented. To draw valid conclusions, you must think logically and reasonably about the material. There are two types of formal reasoning: inductive and deductive. Each produces valid conclusions when used properly, but each can lead to invalid conclusions when used incorrectly.

Inductive reasoning moves from specific facts to a conclusion, or a generalization, based on those facts. A valid generalization is supported by evidence and holds true in a majority of circumstances. If the reasoning is illogical, the result is a logical fallacy. Errors in logic can take the form of the following:

- A hasty generalization or statement that is made about a large number of cases or a whole group on the basis of a few examples, without taking into account qualifying factors.

  Example: Teenage drivers have poor skills; therefore, they cause most of the automobile accidents.

- A non sequitur is an idea or conclusion that does not follow logically from the preceding idea.

  Example: Vladimir would be a great history teacher because he was born in Europe and has traveled extensively on three continents.

Deductive reasoning moves from the generality that is assumed to be true to specific cases. Logical fallacies occur when deduction is used incorrectly.

- "Begging the question" occurs when a general statement is restated without supporting evidence or facts, assuming as true something that needs to be proved or explained.

NOTE

Applying logic can help you with the multiple-choice section as well as the essay questions.

Example: The lawyer said he is qualified to try the case because he has tried other cases.

In addition to inductive and deductive reasoning, two other forms of reasoning can be used to reach valid conclusions: cause and effect and analogy. A cause-and-effect sequence is one in which something is affected by one or more events that occurred before it.

- A false cause results when one thing preceding another is assumed to have caused a second event.

Example: If I sleep 8 hours tonight, I can run 5 five miles in the morning.

An analogy is a comparison between two things that are similar in some ways but are essentially dissimilar.

- A false analogy is one that overlooks essential dissimilarities between two things being compared.

Example: Debbie is like her sister because they both have freckles.

When you apply logic to an analysis or to your own writing, use these questions to examine an author's logic.

Questions for Valid Reasoning

Generalizations

1. What facts are being presented as evidence to support the general statement?

2. Are there any exceptions to the statement?

3. Are enough cases or examples presented to lead you to a solid conclusion, or does the material lead you to jump to hasty generalizations?

Cause and Effect

1. What evidence is there that the first event or situation could have caused the second, or does the cause-and-effect sequence reveal a non sequitur?

2. What other events might have caused the second event?

3. Could the second event have occurred without the first?

Analogies

1. How are the two things compared essentially different?

2. How are the things similar? Is the comparison logical or does it lead to a false analogy?

3. What is the truth that the comparison tries to show?

NOTE: These questions are general. You will need to adapt them to the type of prose you are reading. Some questions may be more appropriate for fiction, while others work better with nonfiction. By using them throughout this chapter, you will know automatically which ones are appropriate to use with a given prose passage.

STRATEGIES FOR ACING THE ESSAYS

Analyzing and evaluating literature requires skill and thoughtfulness. It is important to read the material carefully. You also must make the effort to understand the writers and be sensitive to their meaning. Writing good essays about language and literature requires the realization that your reader and evaluator can only receive what you place on your paper, not your unstated ideas. If your thesis is clear in your mind, you can state it clearly on paper. If you fully support that thesis with interesting, apt, and logical information that is well-organized, fully developed, coherent, and unified, your reader has a far better chance of understanding your message. If you also include good word choice and tone, you will ace the essay questions.

This section sets out two customized plans of attack for writing the two types of essays. You will not that many of the strategies are the same.

Plan of Attack for the Free Response Essays

STEP 1: READ THE MATERIAL

The mistake that students often make is writing an essay about something other than the question they are asked to answer. It may be a fabulous "9" essay in all other ways, but if it does not answer the question, it will earn you a low score.

First, identify the type of essay question you are being asked to answer. Is it asking you for interpretation, analysis, and/or evaluation of the selection?

Underline the important points or key words in the question. Are you being asked to explain how the writer's use of a motif affects the mood? Underline *explain*, *motif*, and *mood*. You now know that one of the things you will need to look for as you read is a motif.

Restate the question to yourself—paraphrase it—to be sure you understand what you are being asked to do.

Once you know what you will need to write about, you are ready to read the selection, and you will need to read it several times. Remember, you have about 5 minutes to read and plan, but the selections are short. Follow these steps to get the most out of each reading:

- Regardless of what the question is asking, you need to determine the theme or meaning of the piece first. In order to talk about elements of the selection, you need to know what the piece is about.

- The first time you read, skim the passage.

- The second time, read carefully.

- Be aware of language and diction, person, tone, the writer's intentions and purpose, the selection's impact, and special techniques.

NOTE

Remember to use present tense when you analyze writing.

NOTE

Write the essay that you feel most confident about first. Save the most difficult for last.

NOTE

You will be given paper for your essay, and you will be able to use your test booklet for scratch paper.

- As you read, underline words and sentences that seem significant and that you might want to quote in your essay. Jot down notes. However, do not spend a lot of time doing this.

STEP 2: PLAN AND WRITE YOUR ESSAY

- After you have completed your reading, take a few minutes to plan what you will write. Brainstorm or list ideas and thoughts, but do not outline. Outlining wastes time. What you want to do is analyze the passage. List how each literary element enhances the communication in the passage. Make another list of examples and supporting evidence from the passage. Review anything you underlined in the passage to include in the lists.

- Check through your notes and lists and develop your thesis.

- Organize your ideas and begin writing.

- Periodically reread your introductory paragraph to be sure you stay on track to prove your thesis. Do more than summarize. Include your insights, reactions, and emotions.

- Be sure to include examples from the selection to support your points. However, don't try to use copious quotations to fill up the sheets. You don't need to use complete sentences; you can use ellipses.

- Write an effective concluding paragraph. Restate your thesis and summarize how your essay supports it.

NOTE

Time yourself as
you plan and
write your
practice essays.
That way you will
become
comfortable with
the time limits on
the actual
AP test.

The chart "Analyzing Literature" on pp. 122–123 suggests questions to ask yourself to help you analyze literary elements to find the meaning in what you read. Use this chart to prepare the practice essay questions in this chapter. Try it for the essays you have to write about prose selections in school, too, and see how much easier it is to organize and develop your thoughts.

STEP 3: REVISE YOUR ESSAY

Pace yourself so that you have at least 2 minutes to reread your essay for proofreading and revision. Cross out any irrelevant ideas or words and make any additions—neatly. If you have been following your informal plan to develop your thesis, you can use this time to make sure your grammar and mechanics are correct and your handwriting is legible.

Plan of Attack for the Synthesis Essays

STEP 1: READ THE MATERIAL

As in writing the free response essays, students make the mistake of not reading the question carefully and thoughtfully.

- Read the Introduction carefully. Consider what you think about the topic.

- Underline the important points or key words in the Assignment. These are the things that you will need to look for as you read the sources.

- When you read the claim made in the Assignment, decide if you want to challenge, defend, or qualify the claim. Whatever you decide, keep your decision in mind as you read the sources. Note that reading the sources may change your mind about how to approach the claim, so it is important to keep an open mind at this point.

- Restate the question to yourself—paraphrase it—to be sure that you understand what you are being asked to write about.

You now have slightly fewer than 15 minutes to read and analyze the sources. The Assignment will give you a minimum number of sources to cite in your essay. For example, if there are six sources, you may be asked to use a minimum of three sources to support your argument. Regardless of the type of essay you have to write, you first have to determine the theme or meaning of the selection. You will need to read each selection or source several times.

- The first time you read each source, skim.

- The second time, read carefully.

- Be aware of the theme, the writer's purpose, the intended audience, the source's impact, any rhetorical devices, and any bias or propaganda elements in each piece.

- Note how the sources are identified. As part of the prompt, you will be given two ways to refer to the sources—either by letter (Source A, Source B, etc.) or by a designated name provided in parentheses next to the source letter. Choose now which identifying system you want to use, so that you don't confuse yourself or your reader. The letter system is faster. Begin to use the identifier as soon as you begin to make notes.

- As you read, underline words and sentences that seem significant and that you might want to quote in your essay. Jot down notes. However, do not spend a great deal of time doing this. Remember also that quoting sources is not the same as internalizing the information from sources and producing a synthesis of ideas.

STEP 2: PLAN AND WRITE YOUR SYNTHESIS ESSAY

- After you have completed reading the sources, go back to the Introduction to the question and ask yourself if you have changed your mind about what you think about the topic.

- Reread the Assignment and make the final decision about whether you are going to challenge, defend, or qualify the claim.

- Once you have decided, review the sources and your notes and choose *at least* the minimum number of sources to use in your essay.

- Brainstorm or list information from the sources and your own knowledge and opinions that relate to the topic and the position you are taking. Do not create a formal outline. List points that you want to make and list information that supports those points.

- Using your notes, formulate a thesis statement.

- Organize your ideas by numbering them in the order you want to use them. Begin writing.

- Periodically reread your introduction to be sure you stay on track to prove your thesis. Include your own ideas with the information from the sources. Do not summarize or just paraphrase the sources. Integrate the information in the sources to create convincing support for your argument.

- Write an effective conclusion. Restate your thesis and summarize your support.

STEP 3: REVISE YOUR ESSAY

Pace yourself so that you have at least 2 minutes to reread your essay for proofreading and revision. Cross out any irrelevant ideas or words and make any additions—neatly. This is the time to make sure that you have given attribution to every idea that you have used from the sources. The directions state you are "to attribute both direct and indirect citations." Students tend to overlook the need to provide citations for ideas that come from sources. This is also the time to check for errors in grammar, usage, and mechanics. Check your handwriting for legibility, too.

THE ESSAY: A QUICK REVIEW

NOTE

An intriguing, informative introductory paragraph will make a good impression on your readers.

You will recall that an essay is a group of paragraphs that work together to present a main point, or thesis. An essay contains an introductory paragraph, separate paragraphs that develop the thesis, and a concluding paragraph. You can see the parts of a five-paragraph essay—the beginning, called the introduction; the middle, called the body; and the ending, called the conclusion—diagrammed on the next page.

To communicate clearly and precisely, you must determine who your audience is, what your purpose is, and what the appropriate tone is. Your writing must be clear and coherent. For the AP essays, consider the following suggestions.

Audience

You have an audience of one—a College Board–trained reader who teaches high school or college English and who will be reading hundreds of similar papers. She or he has knowledge of the literary work you have written about and will have a scoring guide or rubric to evaluate your paper. He or she will score your essay holistically, i.e., there is no single score for things like grammar and punctuation. The reader will consider every aspect of writing for its impact

INTRODUCTION
Interesting Material and Background Information on Topic

Thesis Statement

The introduction should catch the reader's attention, establish the purpose and tone, and present the thesis statement or the main idea.

Body Paragraph 1
Supporting Information

Each paragraph within the body of the essay should develop a subtopic of the main point by providing strong supporting information.

Body Paragraph 2
Supporting Information

Each paragraph within the body of the essay should develop a subtopic of the main point by providing strong supporting information.

Body Paragraph 3
Supporting Information

Each paragraph within the body of the essay should develop a subtopic of the main point by providing strong supporting information.

CONCLUSION
Reminder of Thesis Statement

Summary or Final Remarks

The conclusion of an essay should bring the essay to a satisfactory close and remind the reader of the main point.

on the overall impression of your essay. (Our rubric singles out the various descriptors so you can pinpoint your weaknesses to work on and increase your overall score.)

Purpose

Your purpose is to get a score of 5 or better. To do that, you need to write a unified, coherent, and consistent essay that answers the question. A well-written essay that misses the point of the question will not get you a good score.

Tone

Your tone is the reflection of your attitude toward the subject of the essay. A writer's tone, for example, may be lighthearted, brusque, or serious. The safest tone to adopt is formal and subjective, since you are being asked your opinion. You do not want to be stuffy and pretentious by using phrases such as "one understands" or "we can surmise." On the other hand, do not be too casual either by writing things like "you know what I mean." Most students, however, err on the side of "faux" erudition, using big words and convoluted constructions. When is doubt, write what you mean simply and directly.

How do you develop the proper tone? Through style. Your style should be your own natural style that you use for school essays. That means:

- Using proper grammar and punctuation.

- Choosing words that convey your meaning in an interesting rather than a pedestrian or vague way: "The author created a dynamic personality in Tom Jones" versus "The main character is interesting."

- Avoiding the use of several words when one will do: "There are a number of aspects to the character that are dynamic such as . . ." versus "Jones is both a rascal and . . ."

- Avoiding hackneyed phrases and clichés such as "The writer was on cloud nine" versus "The writer's tone showed her enthusiasm."

TIP

Whenever possible, write in the active voice. Your essay will seem stronger.

Your style adds interest to the paper. Interesting words and phrasing, as much as a unique point of view about a subject, can make a paper interesting to read.

Unity

Unity is another word for clarity. All of your essay's ideas and information must belong together and be essential to the development of the thesis. The parts of the essay—the introduction, the body, and the conclusion—should all focus on the main idea. Each paragraph must relate to every other, and every paragraph must support the overall thesis. In addition, each paragraph within the essay must be unified. Each paragraph must have a topic sentence, and every sentence in the paragraph must relate to every other and add to the development of the topic sentence. In other words, a unified paper is one that is clearly developed. The introduction and the conclusion work together to create unity. The introduction establishes the main point. Then the conclusion echoes the ideas or key words of the introduction.

Perhaps the most important element creating unity in an essay is the clarity of the thesis statement. Remember that your thesis statement contains the central idea that you have developed from brainstorming ideas to respond to the essay prompt. As the *Harbrace College Handbook,* that venerable college English manual, states: "[Your thesis statement] is basically a claim statement, that is, it indicates what you claim to be true, interesting, or valuable about your subject."

If the thesis statement is focused and clear, it outlines the scope of the essay and the boundaries separating the relevant from the irrelevant. In the same way, the subtopics must logically grow out of the thesis. When the subtopics represent significant aspects of the main point and relate to each other, in all probability you will write a unified essay.

Although you can place your thesis statement anywhere in your essay, it is probably safest to put it in the introduction, even as the first sentence, so you can refer to it as you write to be sure that everything you are writing develops and supports it. Putting the thesis first also gets you started writing.

Coherence

In a coherent essay, a reader can move smoothly and logically from one thought to another. A coherent essay is one in which the ideas within each paragraph and within the essay as a whole are in logical order and their connections flow. Coherence depends on clear, relevant ordering of ideas and the introduction of transitional words and phrases. Many methods exist for organizing ideas logically. The following chart offers five methods for organizing your work.

Organization of Supporting Information	
Chronological order	Information arranged in time sequence
Spatial order	Information arranged according to space relationships
Order of importance	Information arranged from least important to most important or vice versa
Compare and contrast	Information arranged according to similarities and differences between two or more subjects
Developmental order	Information arranged so that one point leads logically to another

Transitions

In addition to being logically organized, a coherent essay moves smoothly from one thought to the next because its ideas are connected by transitions, repetition of key words, synonyms, and pronouns. Transitions indicate how one idea relates to another, while repetition of words ties ideas together. The following are some transitions that help establish logical order.

Time Relationship		
after	finally	later
before	first	meanwhile
during	second	next
earlier	third	then
Spatial Relationship		
above	beneath	near
ahead	beyond	outside
before	here	over there
behind	inside	
Comparison or Contrast		
although	indeed	nonetheless
conversely	in like manner	similarly
however	instead	whereas
in contrast	likewise	yet
Cause and Effect		
accordingly	inevitably	then
as a result	on account of	therefore
because of	since	thus
consequently		
Addition		
also	furthermore	not only
as well	in addition	too
besides	moreover	
Emphasis		
indeed	in other words	
in fact	most of all	most significantly
Examples		
also	for example	specifically
as an illustration	in particular	that is
for instance	namely	

Adequate Development

What is an "adequate development"? You have approximately 40 minutes to read, plan, and develop your ideas—neatly. In addition to the thesis statement, your essay must contain enough specific information to explain your main idea. Support consists of examples, details, facts, reasons, or events. The following chart presents five types of supporting information that you can use to develop your thesis.

Kinds of Support		
Type of Support	**Definition**	**Example**
Examples	Particular instances of a general idea or principle	An essay about the best movies of the year might include a discussion of three or four films.
Details	Small items or pieces of information that make up something larger	An essay about an author might describe details about his or her career.
Facts	Specific pieces of information that can be verified	An essay about the tone and style of a selection might include quotations.
Reasons	Explanations, justifications, or causes, often answering the question *why?* about the main idea	An essay advocating gun control might include an explanation of ineffective current laws.
Events	Incidents or happenings	An essay about a travel memoir might include one or two amusing anecdotes.

A well-developed essay must contain enough support to meet the expectations established by your introduction and thesis statement. In addition, the supporting information must make the essay seem complete. The five types of support will work with both synthesis and nonsynthesis essays.

A FINAL WORD OF ADVICE ON WRITING YOUR ESSAYS

The following are some suggestions to help you write clear, well-organized, well-reasoned, coherent, and interesting essays. If you keep these suggestions in mind as you write your practice essays, these steps will come naturally to you on the day of the test.

- Begin writing your first paragraph by stating the thesis clearly. Take a full 5 minutes to be sure that you are writing a clearly stated and interesting introduction.

- At the end of the first paragraph, read it to be sure that your ideas are logically following each other and supporting the thesis.

- Write a transition into the second paragraph. Check your list of ideas.

NOTE

Do not forget the simple things such as capitalization, punctuation, and spelling. See Chapter 5 for a quick review.

ANALYZING LITERATURE

IDENTIFICATION
Genre/Mode of Discourse
1. What type of prose is it—fiction or nonfiction? Exposition, persuasion, argument, description, narrative, or drama?
2. Are points developed by definitions, examples, facts, events, or quotations and citations?

Author
1. Who is the author?
2. What do you know about the writer?
3. What do you know about the time period or literary period in which the passage was written?

Title
1. If there is a title, what does it tell you?
2. What does it suggest about the subject or the theme (meaning) of the passage?

Subject
1. What is the subject of the passage?
2. What is this selection about?

Theme/Thesis
1. What is the theme, or central idea, of the selection?
2. How is the theme conveyed?

LITERARY ELEMENTS
Setting
1. Where and when does the selection take place?
2. What details does the writer use to create the setting?
3. Does the setting create a mood or feeling?
4. Is the setting a symbol for an important idea the writer wants to convey?
5. Does the setting play a role in the central conflict?

Point of View
1. Is the passage told from the first-person or from the third-person point of view?
2. Is the narrator limited or omniscient?
3. What effect does the point of view have on the way you experience the selection?

Central Conflict
1. In what struggle is the protagonist involved?
2. Is the central conflict internal, within the main character's mind, or external, with another character, society, or nature?
3. How is the conflict resolved?

Development
1. What events take place in the selection?
2. Does the piece have an introduction?
3. If so, what does the reader learn in the introduction?

4. What is the inciting incident?
5. What happens during the development?
6. When does the climax occur?
7. What events mark the resolution?
8. Does the selection have a denouement?
9. Are there special plot devices, such as a surprise ending, foreshadowing, or flashbacks?

Characterization
1. Who is the protagonist or speaker?
2. Who are the other major and minor characters?
3. Is there conflict among characters?
4. How does the writer develop each of the characters or the speaker?
5. Which characters change and which are flat?

LANGUAGE AND STYLE
Rhetorical Elements
1. What words does the writer choose?
2. Are there denotative words, connotative words, abstract words, or inclusive words?
3. What is the tone?

Organization and Structure
1. What kinds of sentence structure are present?
2. Is there sentence variety?
3. Does sentence length vary?
4. How is the passage organized?
5. What type of structure did the writer use?

Literary Devices and Figures of Speech
1. Does the writer make use of devices such as euphony or alliteration?
2. Does the passage contain any examples of figurative language, such as hyperbole, metaphor, or simile?
3. Is there symbolism? What is it?

Diction
1. Is there a specialized vocabulary?
2. Does the writer employ irony to communicate meaning?
3. Are overstatement or understatement used?
4. Is the language inflated by scholarly, technical, or scientific words or overly long phrases?
5. Does the selection contain jargon or euphemisms?
6. What are some of the writer's best-worded phrases?
7. Is the word choice colloquial, idiomatic, scientific, formal, informal, or concrete?

NOTE: These questions are general. You will need to adapt them to the type of prose you are reading. Some questions are more appropriate for fiction, while others work better with nonfiction. By using them throughout the chapter, you will become so familiar with the questions that you will know automatically which ones to use with each prose passage on the test.

- Do more than summarize. Include your insights, reactions, and emotions.

- Keep writing until you have used all the RELEVANT ideas on your list. If a new idea comes from the flow of your writing, use it if it fits.

- Use transitions.

- Periodically reread your introductory paragraph to be sure you are staying on track to prove your thesis. If you must change something, cross it out neatly.

- Do not be concerned about perfection. No essay can be perfect in just 40 minutes.

- Allow time to write a solid concluding paragraph. There are several ways to approach the conclusion: rephrasing the thesis, summarizing the main points, or referring in some way back to your opening paragraph. Do not leave the reader wondering, "So what?"

PRACTICING

The following questions and selections are very similar to those that you will find on the actual AP test. Apply the suggestions and strategies you have just read and write about the excerpt from Ralph Waldo Emerson's *Self-Reliance*. Then check your essay by reading the suggested points of discussion that follow. Evaluate yourself by using the *Self-Evaluation Rubric for the Free Response Essays* on p. 140.

EXERCISE 1

SUGGESTED TIME—40 MINUTES

Directions: Read the following passage carefully. It was written by Ralph Waldo Emerson, one of the most influential of the Transcendentalists. Discuss how the author's style contributes to his arguments espousing transcendental ideas. Consider such elements as literary devices, tone, and rhetoric.

From *Self-Reliance*

Line There is a time in every man's education when he arrives at the conviction that envy is ignorance; that imitation is suicide; that he must take himself
5 for better, for worse, as his portion; that though the wide universe is full of good, no kernel of nourishing corn can come to him but through his toil bestowed on that plot of ground which
10 is given to him to till. The power which resides in him is new in nature, and none but he knows what that is which he can do, nor does he know until he has tried. Not for nothing one face, one
15 character, one fact makes much impression on him, and another none. This sculpture in the memory is not without preestablished harmony. The eye was placed where one ray should
20 fall, that it might testify of that particular ray. We but half express ourselves, and are ashamed of that divine idea which each of us represents. It may be safely trusted as
25 proportionate and of good issues, so it be faithfully imparted, but God will not have his work made manifest by cowards. A man is relieved and gay when he has put his heart into his
30 work and done his best; but what he has said or done otherwise, shall give him no peace. It is a deliverance which does not deliver. In the attempt his genius deserts him; no muse befriends;
35 no invention, no hope.

Trust thyself: every heart vibrates to that iron string. Accept the place the divine providence has found for you; the society of your contemporaries, the
40 connection of events. Great men have always done so and confided themselves childlike to the genius of the age, betraying their perception that the absolutely trustworthy was stirring at
45 their heart, working through their hands, predominating in all their being. And we are now men, and must accept in the highest mind the same transcendent destiny; and not minors
50 and invalids in a protected corner, but guides, redeemers, and benefactors, obeying the Almighty effort and advancing on Chaos and the Dark. . . .

Society everywhere is in conspiracy
55 against the manhood of every one of its members. Society is a joint-stock company in which the members agree for the better securing of his bread to each shareholder, to surrender the
60 liberty and culture of the eater. The virtue in most request is conformity. Self-reliance is its aversion. It loves not realities and creators, but names and customs.
65 Whoso would be a man must be a nonconformist. He who would gather immortal palms must not be hindered by the name of goodness, but must explore if it be goodness. Nothing is at
70 last sacred but the integrity of our own mind. Absolve you to yourself, and you shall have the suffrage of the world. . . .

A foolish consistency is the hobgob-
75 lin of little minds, adored by little statesmen and philosophers and divines. With consistency a great soul has simply nothing to do. He may as well concern himself with his shadow
80 on the wall. Speak what you think now in hard words and tomorrow speak what tomorrow thinks in hard words

again, though it contradict everything
you said today. "Ah, so you shall be
85 sure to be misunderstood?"—Is it so
bad, then, to be misunderstood?
Pythagoras was misunderstood, and
Socrates, and Jesus, and Luther, and

90 Copernicus, and Galileo, and Newton,
and every pure and wise spirit that
ever took flesh. To be great is to be
misunderstood. . . .

—Ralph Waldo Emerson

Before you turn the page and read our suggestions for an essay on this selection, score
your essay using the *Self-Evaluation Rubric for the Free Response Essays* on p. 140.

SUGGESTIONS FOR EXERCISE 1

The following are points that you might have chosen to include in your essay on a passage from *Self-Reliance*. Consider them as you perform your self-evaluation. You will notice that we discuss elements of literature that are not called for in the essay question. However, by identifying the author, naming the type of literature, and writing the title you have a place to begin and you give yourself an opportunity to include information that should impress your readers.

Mode of Discourse

This selection is a persuasive essay, a piece of nonfiction. While you were not asked about this point directly in the question, by being specific about what type of literature you read, you appear to know literature.

Author

A philosopher, poet, orator, and writer, Ralph Waldo Emerson became the most influential member of the Transcendentalists, a group of Massachusetts intellectuals of the mid-nineteenth century. The Transcendental philosophy is one of responsible individualism. Adherents believed that all forms of being are united through a shared universal soul. They believed that God and the human spirit were reflected in nature. By studying nature, Transcendentalists thought they would come to know themselves and discover universal truths. The Transcendentalists valued intuition, individuality, and self-reliance.

Of course, you cannot find this in the selection, but you might remember some of this from your study of American literature. The information may help you understand the selection better.

Title

This selection is excerpted from *Self-Reliance*. The title speaks to one of Emerson's core beliefs, the importance of self-reliance, which, along with intuition and individuality, form the heart of the philosophical system known as Transcendentalism.

Subject

The subject, obviously, is self-reliance, Emerson's profound conviction that each person must count one's self, count for one's self, account to one's self, and nurture the seeds of greatness to be found within. Emerson advises each person to trust one's self, to accept one's self and one's place in life, to resist conformity, and to think little of society's regard; in fact, many great and wise spirits were misunderstood.

Literary Devices and Figures of Speech

In the first paragraph, Emerson uses an analogy, "kernel of . . . corn," comparing the effort needed to produce corn to the effort people must make to reach their potential. He uses imagery when he says "every heart vibrates to that iron string." He employs a number of metaphors—"Society is a joint-stock company," "immortal palms," and "a foolish consistency is the hobgoblin." Emerson makes reference to individuals who made important contributions in the fields of mathematics, philosophy, religion, and science and who were also nonconformists and misunderstood. They were great spirits and self-reliant, as we must be.

Themes and Theses

Emerson's thesis is that people (and, therefore, society) would be better served by espousing a creed of responsible individualism. He has immense faith in human potential, and he advocates that one must obey internal dictates only and that one must resist the pressures of society to conform. He conveys these beliefs directly and clearly throughout the essay.

Style

The author's tone is one of heartfelt emotion, and yet at the same time he writes in a logical and erudite manner, with an educated diction. He develops his ideas point by point, in order of importance. He uses a positive denotation for words proposing self-reliance (*nourishing*, *harmony*, *trust*) and negative ones for words describing conformity (*dark*, *conspiracy*, *foolish*). He uses a variety of sentence structures and employs a rhetorical question in the conclusion of the last paragraph.

Your Style

You have just read some important points that you might have included in your essay. Now review your introductory paragraph. If it seems a little dry, consider trying one of these types of openings to punch it up: more forceful or vivid language, a quotation, a rhetorical question, an anecdote, or perhaps one of Emerson's images. But whatever you add has to relate to your thesis.

Look at your concluding paragraph. A simple summary of your major points creates an effective conclusion. You can also end an essay with a relevant quote. A specific suggestion works well in a persuasive essay. If you have organized your writing around a problem/solution, consider a vivid image of the consequences.

Once you have evaluated your essay with the *Self-Evaluation Rubric* on p. 140 and reviewed our points, you may choose to revise your essay using the points suggested here. However, do not spend a great deal of time trying to make it perfect. Revise it simply to see how adding some of our points may make it stronger. Whether you revise or not, ask a classmate or your teacher to evaluate your essay for you using the *Self-Evaluation Rubric*. How does your own evaluation match with a more objective view? Keep the differences in mind as you write and score more essays.

Now that you have a sense of the logic involved in acing the free response essay questions of Section II, try *Exercise 2*. Study the points for evaluation and use the *Self-Evaluation Rubric*. If you are still unsure about writing free response essays, continue with *Exercises 3* and *4*.

EXERCISE 2

SUGGESTED TIME—40 MINUTES

Directions: James Boswell stated: "to write, not his panegyrick, which must be all praise, but his Life; which, great and good as he was, must not be supposed to be entirely perfect . . . in every picture there should be shade and light." Read the following passage carefully. Write an essay analyzing how Boswell's style contributed to success or failure in achieving his goal. Consider such literary and rhetorical elements as diction, point of view, and tone.

From *The Life of Samuel Johnson*, "Feelings"

Line [Said Johnson:] "Pity is not natural to man. Children are always cruel. Savages are always cruel. Pity is acquired and improved by the cultiva-
5   tion of reason. We may have uneasy sensations from seeing a creature in distress, without pity; for we have not pity unless we wish to relieve them. When I am on my way to dine with a
10 friend, and finding it late, have bid the coachman make haste, if I happen to attend when he whips his horses, I may feel unpleasantly that the animals are put to pain, but I do not wish him
15 to desist. No, sir, I wish him to drive on."

Johnson's love of little children, which he discovered upon all occasions, calling them "pretty dears," and giving
20 them sweetmeats, was an undoubted proof of the real humanity and gentle-ness of his disposition.

His uncommon kindness to his servants, and serious concern, not only
25 for their comfort in this world, but their happiness in the next, was another unquestionable evidence of what all, who were intimately ac-quainted with him, knew to be true.
30 Nor would it be just, under this head, to omit the fondness which he showed for animals which he had

taken under his protection. I never shall forget the indulgence with which
35 he treated Hodge, his cat; for whom he himself used to go out and buy oysters, lest the servants, having that trouble, should take a dislike to the poor creature. I am, unluckily, one of those
40 who have an antipathy to a cat, so that I am uneasy when in the room with one; and I own I frequently suffered a good deal from the presence of this same Hodge. I recollect him one day
45 scrambling up Dr. Johnson's breast, apparently with much satisfaction, while my friend, smiling and half-whistling, rubbed down his back and pulled him by the tail; and when I
50 observed he was a fine cat, saying, "Why, yes, sir, but I have had cats whom I liked better than this;" and then, as if perceiving Hodge to be out of countenance, adding, "but he is a
55 very fine cat, a very fine cat indeed."

This reminds me of the ludicrous account which he gave Mr. Langton of the despicable state of a young gentle-man of good family. "Sir, when I heard
60 of him last, he was running about town shooting cats." And then, in a sort of kindly reverie, he bethought himself of his own favorite cat, and said, "But Hodge shan't be shot; no, no, Hodge
65 shall not be shot."

—James Boswell

Use the *Self-Evaluation Rubric for the Free Response Essays* on p. 140 to help you assess your progress in writing your essays.

exercises

SUGGESTIONS FOR EXERCISE 2

Background Information

- Mode: nonfiction; excerpt from biography

- Author: James Boswell, mid- to late 1700s

- Title: a biography, one of the fullest records of a man's life ever written; character of Johnson revealed

- Subject: attitude toward animals, characterization of Johnson

Point of View

- First person

- Author as narrator

- Personal knowledge and experience

- Accounts of personal dialogues

Characterization

- Two characters: Johnson and Boswell

- Boswell: admiration of Johnson, respect, almost idolatry, conscientious record, frank

- Examples: allergy to cats, story of Langton

- Johnson: fondness for animals, kind feelings, humor, idiosyncratic

- Examples: getting oysters himself, thinking Hodge could understand language

Theme or Thesis

- People are made of contradictory qualities. A man as great as Johnson has quirks and idiosyncracies just as others do.

- Johnson is a man to be admired.

Style

- Most biographers are objective; Boswell is not.

- Diction shows admiration: fondness, indulgence, kindly reverie.

- Tone: admiration, respect, approval, amusement

- Sentences: direct quotes from conversation, varied, complex, but clear

- Examples: "But Hodge shan't be shot; no, no, Hodge shall not be shot."

- Use of specific details: pulling Hodge's tail, half-whistling

- Organization: anecdotal

exercises

EXERCISE 3

SUGGESTED TIME—40 MINUTES

Directions: Read the following work carefully. Then write a well-organized essay in which you discuss how the selection uses humor to comment on human nature and human conduct. Consider such literary elements as diction, narrative pace, satire, and point of view.

From "Advice to Little Girls"

Line Good little girls ought not to make mouths at their teachers for every trifling offense. This retaliation should only be resorted to under peculiarly
5 aggravated circumstances.

If you have nothing but a rag-doll stuffed with sawdust, while one of your more fortunate little playmates has a costly China one, you should treat her
10 with a show of kindness nevertheless. And you ought not to attempt to make a forcible swap with her unless your conscience would justify you in it, and you know you are able to do it.
15 You ought never to take your little brother's "chewing-gum" away from him by main force; it is better to rope him in with the promise of the first two dollars and a half you find floating
20 down the river on a grindstone. In the artless simplicity natural to his time of life, he will regard it as a perfectly fair transaction. In all ages of the world this eminently plausible fiction has
25 lured the obtuse infant to financial ruin and disaster.

If at any time you find it necessary to correct your brother, do not correct him with mud—never, on any account,
30 throw mud at him, because it will spoil

his clothes. It is better to scald him a little, for then you obtain desirable results. You secure his immediate attention to the lessons you are
35 inculcating, and at the same time your hot water will have a tendency to move impurities from his person, and possibly the skin, in spots.

If your mother tells you to do a
40 thing, it is wrong to reply that you won't. It is better and more becoming to intimate that you will do as she bids you, and then afterward act quietly in the matter according to the dictates of
45 your best judgment.

You should ever bear in mind that it is to your kind parents that you are indebted for your food, and your nice bed, and for your beautiful clothes, and
50 for the privilege of staying home from school when you let on that you are sick. Therefore you ought to respect their little prejudices, and humor their little foibles until they get to crowding
55 you too much.

Good little girls always show marked deference for the aged. You ought never to "sass" old people unless they "sass" you first.

—Mark Twain

Use the *Self-Evaluation Rubric for the Free Response Essays* on p. 140 to help you assess your progress in writing your essays.

SUGGESTIONS FOR EXERCISE 3

The following are points you might have chosen to include in your essay on Mark Twain's "Advice to Little Girls." Consider them as you perform your self-evaluation. Revise your essay using points from this list to strengthen it.

Form or Mode
- Humorous essay

Theme
- Facetious advice telling girls how to behave

Characters
- Narrator, Mark Twain
- Addressing girls in general

Dialogue
- No specific dialogue
- Chatty and familiar style

Conflict
- Girls versus convention

Plot/Development
- Basically, advice on how girls can actually do what they want while appearing to be ever so proper

Setting
- Mid-1800s

Point of View
- Written to the second person

Diction
- Very informal
- Much humor
- "And you ought not to attempt to make a forcible swap with her unless your conscience would justify you in it, and you know you are able to do it."
- Tone: tongue in cheek
- Folksy language

EXERCISE 4

SUGGESTED TIME—40 MINUTES

Directions: Write a persuasive essay that either qualifies, agrees with, or disagrees with these social scientists' assertion.

Many behavioral scientists and psychologists have come to believe that success in school, in the workplace, on the playing field, and elsewhere in life is not so much determined by intellect but by social intelligence—the ability to work with others, lead and motivate others, and inspire team spirit.

SUGGESTIONS FOR EXERCISE 4

The following are some of the points you might have chosen to include in your persuasive essay. Consider them as you perform your self-evaluation. Did you fall into any of the traps of illogical reasoning? Revise your essay using points from this list to strengthen it.

- A thesis that states your stand or point of view on the reasons for success. It must be supported by valid evidence.

- Evidence that the reader should be willing to accept as true without further proof

- Evidence comprising a major portion of the essay, especially if you have created a controversial or complex thesis. Bear in mind that the more commonly acknowledged or the more widely shared an experience, the fewer examples you need.

- Evidence in the form of statistics, illustrations, specific examples, personal experience, occurrences reported by authorities

- Perhaps demonstration of proof, showing the connection between the truth of the supporting evidence and the truth of the assertion; often signaled by words *because* or *as well*

- Definition of any term whose exact meaning is essential to clearly communicating your position

- Soundly reasoned with no distortions of evidence

- Answers to objections from the opposition

- Matching of structure to your audience and goal

EXERCISE 5

SUGGESTED TIME—15 MINUTES FOR READING AND 40 MINUTES FOR WRITING

Directions: The following prompt is based on the following three sources. This assignment requires that you synthesize a number of sources into a coherent, well-written essay. For this practice exercise, use all three sources in your answer. Refer to the sources to support your position. Do not simply paraphrase or summarize the sources. Your argument should be the focus of your essay and the sources should support this argument. Remember to attribute both direct and indirect citations.

Introduction: Beginning in the 1990s, television stations have increasingly turned to reality TV shows and away from scripted shows in an effort to gain higher view ratings. Reality TV shows are inexpensive to produce compared to scripted shows, which translates to increased profits for many stations. Because they are inexpensive to produce and highly popular with viewers, some people believe that reality TV might replace scripted TV in the future.

Assignment: Read the following sources (including any introductory information) carefully. **Then, in an essay that synthesizes all three of the sources for support, take a position that defends or challenges the claim that reality TV will replace scripted TV because reality TV is more popular with television viewers today.**

You may refer to the sources by their titles (Source A, Source B, etc.) or by the descriptions in parentheses.

Source A (TPN press release)

Source B (Chart)

Source C (Tolly)

SOURCE A

Press Release, The Popular Network (TPN), September 2006

The Popular Network (TPN) would like to announce an exciting new change in our programming format. Due to the recent success of "The Jones Family," "Creating the Band," "Castaways," and "College Dorm Days," we have decided to deliver to viewers even more reality television. Beginning in October, Tuesday nights on TPN will be "Real TV Nite," an exciting new format in which all shows aired from 7 p.m. to 11 p.m. will be unscripted, real-life shows. In addition to our already popular shows mentioned previously, we will be adding four brand-new, hour-long reality TV shows, beginning at 7 p.m. These hour-long shows have been created in response to viewer-enjoyment surveys taken over the past year, in which the chief request of viewers was additional longer-format reality shows. The new shows are "Race from Coast to Coast," "Dr. Dana's Advice Hour," "Becoming a Music Star," and "Finding True Love." Three of these shows are competitions; survey responses indicated that viewers wanted to see more contests, and here at TPN, we strive to please the viewers. We also strive to please our shareholders and, due to lower production costs of reality TV, our shareholders will notice a significant increase in profit. Real TV Nite will revolutionize the television industry, so stay tuned for the exciting developments!

SOURCE B

Selected results from the NETWORK RATINGS SYSTEM for June 22, 2006.

Shows/Designation*	Time Slot	Number of Viewers
Pals (S)	8–8:30 p.m.	1 million
The Beach (R)	8–8:30 p.m.	1.5 million
Singing Star (R)	8–8:30 p.m.	500,000
For the Defense (S)	9–10 p.m.	3 million
My Nanny (R)	9–10 p.m.	2 million
Doctors in Love (S)	9–10 p.m.	1 million
Finding the Truth (S)	10–11 p.m.	2 million
Looking for "The One" (R)	10–11 p.m.	3 million
Who Did It? (R)	10–11 p.m.	2.5 million

* (R) denotes a reality television show. (S) denotes a scripted show.

SOURCE C

Tolly, Jennifer. "What do teenagers want to watch?" *Parents Television Guide Monthly,* April 2006.

What do teenagers want to watch? This is a question that perhaps many teenagers and their parents could easily answer, but the answer is not so apparent to many television networks. It is a fact that teenagers today watch much more television than their parents ever did and, because of this, teenagers have become the new "target market" for networks. And what have the networks decided? They have decided that what teens want is reality TV. The question is: are they correct, or is this an error in judgment that will cost many networks a whole lot of money?

The reality obsession began with shows on a popular music video network, MMV. MMV began airing reality shows that involve teenagers and college kids in a variety of formats. Many of these shows were meant to be informative, such as "A Day in the Life," which attempts to show how teenagers throughout the U.S. are both similar and different, from small town kids to city kids. Other reality shows on the network seemed to be less educational or informative, such as dating shows and make-over shows. However, whether parents liked the shows or not, teenagers were watching them, and network television took notice. Beginning last year, many network stations began airing more and more reality TV shows. According to the networks, their ratings soared. Networks seemed to believe that they finally captured the attention of today's teenagers. However, many parents and industry professionals now believe that the spike in network-based (as opposed to cable-based) ratings among teenagers will be short lived and is only a result of the fact that this type of programming is new and novel. The fear that many networks should have, if they do not already, is that the novelty of reality TV will wear off if reality TV is all that is available. Networks should not discount the fact that variety in programming is a good thing, and ever-fickle teens can quickly change their mind—reality TV can become un-cool as quickly as it became cool.

SUGGESTIONS FOR EXERCISE 5

This question asks for a synthesis essay that supports, qualifies, or disputes the argument that reality TV will replace scripted TV because reality TV is more popular with television viewers today. It does not matter which position you take as long as you provide adequate support for your argument using your own opinions along with information from the sources. You may argue that reality TV will replace scripted TV for reasons other than popularity with viewers, as long as you can support this claim. Consider the following as you complete your self-evaluation. Revise your essay using points from the list to strengthen it if necessary. Remember to proofread your response and make sure your grammar, syntax, and spelling are correct.

Thesis statement/introduction

- Clear definition of the issue—in this case, reality TV programming replacing scripted TV

- Clear statement of your position on the issue: statement of the reason you agree or disagree with the statement that reality TV will replace scripted TV because reality TV is more popular with viewers

Supporting details

- Support is based on your own opinions about the position you take but information in the sources should also be used

- Show a clear connection between the sources you cite

- Sources are seamlessly integrated with appropriate transitions

- All three sources are used

- Explain the logic of how you arrived at the conclusion you did, based on the information provided in the sources

- Acknowledge opposing arguments and refute them

- Attribute both direct and indirect citations

Conclusion

- Include a restatement of your thesis tied into the supporting evidence you used. (ex: In sum, there can be no other conclusion drawn from the evidence except to say that in the future people will demand even more reality TV than they do today.)

- Conclusion neatly sums up your argument.

SELF-EVALUATION RUBRIC FOR THE FREE RESPONSE ESSAYS

	8–9	6–7	5	3–4	1–2	0
Overall Impression	Demonstrates excellent control of the literature and outstanding writing competence; thorough and effective; incisive	Demonstrates good control of the literature and good writing competence; less thorough and incisive than the highest papers	Reveals simplistic thinking and/or immature writing; adequate skills	Incomplete thinking; fails to respond adequately to part or parts of the question; may paraphrase rather than analyze	Unacceptably brief; fails to respond to the question; little clarity	Lacking skill and competence
Understanding of the Text	Excellent understanding of the text; exhibits perception and clarity; original or unique approach; includes apt and specific references	Good understanding of the text; exhibits perception and clarity; includes specific references	Superficial understanding of the text; elements of literature vague, mechanical, overgeneralized	Misreadings and lack of persuasive evidence from the text; meager and unconvincing treatment of literary elements	Serious misreadings and little supporting evidence from the text; erroneous treatment of literary elements	A response with no more than a reference to the literature; blank response, or one completely off the topic
Organization and Development	Meticulously organized and thoroughly developed; coherent and unified	Well organized and developed; coherent and unified	Reasonably organized and developed; mostly coherent and unified	Somewhat organized and developed; some incoherence and lack of unity	Little or no organization and development; incoherent and void of unity	No apparent organization or development; incoherent
Use of Sentences	Effectively varied and engaging; virtually error free	Varied and interesting; a few errors	Adequately varied; some errors	Somewhat varied and marginally interesting; one or more major errors	Little or no variation; dull and uninteresting; some major errors	Numerous major errors
Word Choice	Interesting and effective; virtually error free	Generally interesting and effective; a few errors	Occasionally interesting and effective; several errors	Somewhat dull and ordinary; some errors in diction	Mostly dull and conventional; numerous errors	Numerous major errors; extremely immature
Grammar and Usage	Virtually error free	Occasional minor errors	Several minor errors	Some major errors	Severely flawed; frequent major errors	Extremely flawed

SELF-EVALUATION RUBRIC FOR THE SYNTHESIS ESSAYS

	8–9	6–7	5	3–4	1–2	0
Overall Impression	Demonstrates excellent control of effective writing techniques, sophisticated argumentation, and well integrated synthesis of source information; uses citations convincingly	Demonstrates good control of effective writing techniques; somewhat thorough and incisive; uses citations appropriately	Demonstrates general competence in stating and defending a position; some inconsistencies and weaknesses in argumentation	Demonstrates some skill but lacks understanding of question and sources	Demonstrates little skill in taking a coherent position and defending it or in using sources	Lacks skill and competence
Understanding of the Text	Takes a clear position that defends, challenges, or qualifies the question accurately	Demonstrates a somewhat superficial understanding of the sources	Displays some misreading of the sources or some stretching of information to support the chosen position	Takes a position that may misread or simplify the sources; may present overly simple argument	Misreads sources, or lacks an argument, or summarizes the sources rather than using them to support a position	Position does not accurately reflect the sources; no more than a listing of the sources
Organization and Development	Clearly states a position; uses at least three sources to support that position convincingly and effectively; coherent and unified	Clearly states a position; uses at least three sources to support that position; adequate development of ideas but less convincing; coherent and unified	Generally clearly stated position and links between position and cited sources; some weaknesses in logic; cites three sources	Creates weak connections between argument and cited sources; cites only two sources	Lacks coherent development or organization; cites one or no sources	No apparent organization or development; incoherent; cites no sources
Use of Sentences	Effectively varied and engaging; close to error free	Varied and interesting; a few errors	Adequately varied; some errors	Somewhat varied and marginally interesting; one or more major errors	Little or no variation; dull and uninteresting; some major errors	Numerous major errors
Word Choice	Uses the vocabulary of the topic as evident in the sources; interesting and effective; virtually error free	Demonstrates ease in using vocabulary from the sources	Occasional use of vocabulary from the sources; occasionally interesting and effective	Somewhat dull and ordinary; some errors in diction; no attempt to integrate vocabulary from the sources	Mostly dull and conventional; no attempt to integrate vocabulary from the sources	Numerous major errors; extremely immature
Grammar and Usage	Virtually error free	Occasional minor errors	Several minor errors	Some major errors	Severely flawed; frequent major errors	Extremely flawed

Using the rubrics on the previous pages, rate yourself in each of the categories below for each exercise. Enter on the lines below the number from the rubric that most accurately reflects your performance in each category. Then calculate the average of the six numbers to determine your final score. It is difficult to score yourself objectively, so you may wish to ask a respected friend or teacher to assess your writing for a more accurate reflection of its strengths and weaknesses. On the AP test itself, a reader will rate your essay on a scale of 0 to 9, with 9 being the highest.

Rate each category from 9 (high) to 0 (low).

Exercise 1

SELF-EVALUATION		OBJECTIVE EVALUATION	
Overall Impression	_____	**Overall Impression**	_____
Understanding of the Text	_____	**Understanding of the Text**	_____
Organization and Development	_____	**Organization and Development**	_____
Use of Sentences	_____	**Use of Sentences**	_____
Word Choice (Diction)	_____	**Word Choice (Diction)**	_____
Grammar and Usage	_____	**Grammar and Usage**	_____
TOTAL	_____	**TOTAL**	_____
Divide by 6 for final score	_____	Divide by 6 for final score	_____

Exercise 2

SELF-EVALUATION		OBJECTIVE EVALUATION	
Overall Impression	_____	**Overall Impression**	_____
Understanding of the Text	_____	**Understanding of the Text**	_____
Organization and Development	_____	**Organization and Development**	_____
Use of Sentences	_____	**Use of Sentences**	_____
Word Choice (Diction)	_____	**Word Choice (Diction)**	_____
Grammar and Usage	_____	**Grammar and Usage**	_____
TOTAL	_____	**TOTAL**	_____
Divide by 6 for final score	_____	Divide by 6 for final score	_____

Exercise 3

SELF-EVALUATION		OBJECTIVE EVALUATION	
Overall Impression	_____	**Overall Impression**	_____
Understanding of the Text	_____	**Understanding of the Text**	_____
Organization and Development	_____	**Organization and Development**	_____
Use of Sentences	_____	**Use of Sentences**	_____
Word Choice (Diction)	_____	**Word Choice (Diction)**	_____
Grammar and Usage	_____	**Grammar and Usage**	_____
TOTAL	_____	**TOTAL**	_____
Divide by 6 for final score	_____	Divide by 6 for final score	_____

Exercise 4

SELF-EVALUATION

Overall Impression _____
Understanding of the Text _____
Organization and Development _____
Use of Sentences _____
Word Choice (Diction) _____
Grammar and Usage _____

TOTAL _____
Divide by 6 for final score _____

OBJECTIVE EVALUATION

Overall Impression _____
Understanding of the Text _____
Organization and Development _____
Use of Sentences _____
Word Choice (Diction) _____
Grammar and Usage _____

TOTAL _____
Divide by 6 for final score _____

Exercise 5

SELF-EVALUATION

Overall Impression _____
Understanding of the Text _____
Organization and Development _____
Use of Sentences _____
Word Choice (Diction) _____
Grammar and Usage _____

TOTAL _____
Divide by 6 for final score _____

OBJECTIVE EVALUATION

Overall Impression _____
Understanding of the Text _____
Organization and Development _____
Use of Sentences _____
Word Choice (Diction) _____
Grammar and Usage _____

TOTAL _____
Divide by 6 for final score _____

SUMMING IT UP

- Section II contains three essays asking you to analyze literary style, discuss rhetorical usage, and defend a position.

- You will have 2 hours to write the essays and fifteen minutes to read the sources for the synthesis essay.

- One of the three essay questions will include several sources. In writing your essay, you must synthesize the information in at least three of those sources to support your argument.

- Each essay is scored from 0 to 9, with 9 being the highest score.

- The essays together account for 55 percent of your final composite score.

- Because your three essays will be read by three different people, you don't have to worry that one weaker essay will pull down the scores for the other two essays. Write the essay that you feel most confident about first. Save the most difficult for last.

- Whenever possible, write in the active voice. Your essay will seem stronger.

- Do more than summarize. Include your insights, reactions, and emotions.

PART IV

ENGLISH USAGE AND GRAMMAR REVIEW

CHAPTER 5 · Grammar, Mechanics, and Usage Review

Grammar, Mechanics, and Usage Review

OVERVIEW

- **Grammar for the multiple-choice questions**
- **More practical advice on writing your essays**
- **98 common usage problems**
- **Summing it up**

This chapter has three parts: (1) a quick review of parts of speech for the multiple-choice section, (2) an overview of the mechanics and punctuation that you will need in order to write a grammatically correct essay, as well as some recommendations for refining your diction, and (3) suggestions for avoiding the top 98 usage problems.

GRAMMAR FOR THE MULTIPLE-CHOICE QUESTIONS

Any grammar questions on the AP English Language & Composition Test are really disguised comprehension questions. They will ask you to identify one of the parts of speech—nouns, verbs, adjectives, adverbs, prepositions, conjunctions, and interjections—or they will ask you to classify parts of a sentence—subjects, predicates, complements, modifiers, or antecedents. To answer questions in the multiple-choice section, remember:

Functions of Nouns and Pronouns

- For the subject, look for nouns, pronouns, or word groups (gerunds, participial phrases, or clauses) acting as essential nouns that tell you *who* or *what* the sentence is about.

    "What I have described in the Frenchman was merely the result of an excited, or perhaps of a diseased, intelligence."

    —*The Murders in the Rue Morgue*, Edgar Allan Poe

Note: The subject will not be stated if the sentence or clause is imperative.

"Do talk to me as if I were one," said Lord Warburton.

—*The Portrait of a Lady*, Henry James

- A gerund is a verbal that ends in *-ing* and serves as a noun. It may take objects, complements, and modifiers.

  Describing the Frenchman was a tour de force for Poe.

- A participle is a verb that ends in either *-ing* or *-ed* and modifies a noun or pronoun. A participle in a participial phrase may have objects, complements, and modifiers of its own.

  "What I have described in the Frenchman was merely the result **of an excited**, or perhaps of a diseased, **intelligence.**"

  —*The Murders in the Rue Morgue*, Edgar Allan Poe

- The direct object is a noun, pronoun, or group of words acting as a noun that receives the action of a transitive verb, the person or thing acted on. To find a direct object, rephrase the sentence by changing it into a *whom* or *what* question.

  "I believe that I have omitted **mentioning** that in my first voyage from Boston to Philadelphia, being becalmed off Block Island, our crew employed themselves catching cod and hauled up a great number."

  —*The Autobiography of Benjamin Franklin*, Benjamin Franklin

  Rephrased: I have omitted whom or what? The direct object is *mentioning*.

- An indirect object is a noun or pronoun that appears with a direct object and names the person or thing that something is given to or done for.

  "Whichever way I turn, O I think you could give **me** my mate back again if you only would."

  —"Sea-Drift," Walt Whitman

- A sentence can have both an object and an indirect object.

  "Whichever way I turn, O I think you could give **me** my **mate** back again if you only would."

  —"Sea-Drift," Walt Whitman

- An antecedent is a noun or words taking the place of nouns for which a pronoun stands.

  "No good novel will ever proceed from a superficial mind; that seems to me an **axiom** which, for the artist in fiction, will cover all needful moral ground: if the youthful aspirant take it to heart it will illuminate for him many of the mysteries of 'purpose.'"

  —"The Art of Fiction," Henry James

Functions of Verbs

- Verbs express action, occurrence (*appear, become, continue, feel, grow, look, remain, seen, sound,* and *taste*), or state of being (the verb *to be*).

  Ye Angells bright, **pluck** from your Wings a Quill;
  Make me a pen thereof that best **will write**:
  Lende me your fancy and Angellick skill
  To **treate** this Theme, more rich than Rubies bright.

  —"Meditation Sixty: Second Series,"
  Edward Taylor

- Verbs that express occurrence or state of being, also known as linking verbs, are intransitive verbs and have no objects.

  The first time that the sun rose on thine oath
  To love me, I **looked** forward to the moon
  To slacken all those bonds which seemed too soon
  And quickly tied to make a lasting troth.

  —*Sonnets from the Portuguese,*
  Elizabeth Barrett Browning

  Looked is an intransitive verb and, therefore, has no object. *Forward* is an adverb that answers the question "where," and the adverbial phrase "the first time" answers the question "when."

- Linking verbs may have predicate adjectives or predicate nominatives, also known as predicate nouns.

  "Of all historical problems, the nature of a national character **is the most difficult and the most important.**"

  —"American Ideals," Henry Adams

Verb Tenses

It would also be useful to review the tenses and forms of verbs, not necessarily because you may find multiple-choice questions about them but because the review will help you when you write your own essays. Verbs have six tenses to reveal the time of an action or condition. Each tense has a basic, progressive, and emphatic form.

TENSES AND FORMS OF VERBS			
	Basic Form	**Progressive Form**	**Emphatic Form**
Present	I talk a lot.	I am talking about it now.	I do talk more than most students.
Past	I talked with the group.	I was talking when you interrupted.	I did talk with you about that.
Future	I will talk to you Sunday.	I will be talking at the conference.	
Present Perfect	I have talked for almost an hour.	I have been talking too much.	
Past Perfect	I had talked to him a year ago.	I had been talking with you when he arrived.	
Future Perfect	I will have talked to the recruiter by the end of the week.	I will have been talking about this project for a month before I get approval.	

MORE PRACTICAL ADVICE ON WRITING YOUR ESSAYS

The basic grammar and punctuation we are talking about here will help you with writing. Review the following rules and tips before you write a practice essay, and then evaluate your finished essay against them. As you write your next essay, keep in mind any rules with which you had trouble. If necessary, focus on one rule at a time. It is important that you are comfortable with the rules of grammar and punctuation; that way, they flow naturally as you write, and you don't spend time thinking about where the commas should go.

Sentence Structure

Good writing has a variety of sentence structures: simple, compound, complex, and compound-complex. Sentence combining is one way to be sure you have a varied sentence pattern that adds to the interest of your writing. Consider the following examples as possibilities that you have to choose from, and note the correct punctuation for each. All quotations are from Henry Adams's "American Ideals."

SIMPLE SENTENCE

Of all historical problems, the nature of a national character is the most difficult and the most important.

Ralph Waldo Emerson, a more distinct idealist, was born in 1780.

COMPOUND SENTENCE

After the downfall of the French republic, they (Americans) had no right to expect a kind word from Europe, **and** during the next twenty years, they rarely received one.

Probably Jefferson came nearest to the mark, **for** he represented the hopes of science as well as the prejudices of Virginia.

COMPLEX SENTENCE

Lincoln was born in 1809, the moment **when** American character stood in lowest esteem.

Jefferson, the literary representative of his class, spoke chiefly for Virginians, and dreaded so greatly his own reputation as a visionary **that** he seldom or never uttered his whole thought.

COMPOUND-COMPLEX SENTENCES

Benjamin Franklin had raised high the reputation of American printers, **and** the actual President of the United States, **who** signed with Franklin the treaty of peace with Great Britain, was the son of a farmer, and had himself kept a school in his youth.

In the year 1800 Eli Terry, another Connecticut Yankee of the same class, took into his employ two young men **to help** him make wooden clocks, **and** this was the capital **on which** the greatest clock-manufactory in the world began its operation.

PARALLEL CONSTRUCTION

In addition to using dependent and independent clauses to add variety, try using words, phrases, and clauses in parallel constructions. Parallelism reinforces equal ideas, contributes to ease in reading, and, most importantly, adds clarity and rhythm to your ideas. The most simple parallelism employs comparisons and contrasts.

> Eli Whitney was **better** educated than Fitch, but had **neither wealth, social influence, nor patron to back his ingenuity.**

Review your own essays, and underline sentences that you could combine. Then try combining them on a separate sheet of paper. This is a good exercise to get you accustomed to varying your sentence structures as you write. But do not try for variety for the first time during the real test.

When combining sentences, do not fall prey to run-on sentences, sentence fragments, or comma splices.

NOTE

Remember to use present tense when writing about the author's intention in literary works.

NOTE

Writing timed essays, evaluating them, and then working to improve the weaknesses you identify is the best way to prepare for the test.

RUN-ON SENTENCES

A run-on sentence is a compound or compound-complex sentence in which neither a conjunction nor punctuation separates two or more independent clauses. You can fix a run-on sentence by using:

1. A coordinating conjunction, if you are writing a compound sentence

2. A coordinating adverb

3. A transitional phrase

4. And/or a semicolon in a complex or compound-complex sentence

The following examples are taken, with our apologies, from "Milton" by John Babington Macaulay.

1. Milton was, like Dante, a statesman and a lover**, and,** like Dante, he had been unfortunate in ambition and in love.

2. Milton was, like Dante, a statesman and a lover**; moreover,** like Dante, he had been unfortunate in ambition and in love.

3. Milton was, like Dante, a statesman and a lover**; in addition,** like Dante, he had been unfortunate in ambition and in love.

4. Milton was, like Dante, a statesman and a lover; like Dante, he had been unfortunate in ambition and in love.
   (Macaulay's choice)

Did you notice that these sentences are also examples of both comparison and the use of independent clauses as parallelism?

SENTENCE FRAGMENTS

A sentence fragment is just that—part of a sentence, a group of words that does not express a complete thought. If it has a verb form—a verbal such as a participle—it may look like a sentence, but it is not a sentence. You can avoid sentence fragments by always making sure that:

- The verb is a verb—not a participial form (-*ing* or -*ed*) without its auxiliary (some form of *have* or *be*) or an infinitive (*to* plus a verb).

   Such as it was. When, on the eve of great events, he [Milton] returned from his travels, in the prime of health and manly beauty. Loaded with literary distinctions, and glowing with patriotic hopes. . . .

- There is a subject. If there is none, add one or attach the fragment to a sentence.

   Such as it was. When, on the eve of great events, he [Milton] returned from his travels, in the prime of health and manly beauty, **loaded** with literary distinctions, and glowing with patriotic hopes. . . .

- You remove any incorrectly used subordinating conjunctions, or you combine the fragment so it becomes a sentence.

   Such as it was. When, on the eve of great events, he [Milton] returned from his travels, in the prime of health and manly beauty. **He was** loaded with literary distinctions, and glowing with patriotic hopes. . . .

The following is Macaulay's choice:

   Such as it was **when**, on the eve of great events, he [Milton] returned from his travels, in the prime of health and manly beauty, **loaded** with literary distinctions, and glowing with patriotic hopes. . . .

CONJUNCTIVE ADVERBS		TRANSITIONAL PHRASES
also	meanwhile	after all
anyhow	moreover	as a consequence
anyway	nevertheless	as a result
besides	next	at any rate
consequently	nonetheless	at the same time
finally	now	by the way
furthermore	otherwise	even so
hence	similarly	for example
however	still	in addition
incidentally	then	in fact
indeed	therefore	in other words
likewise	thus	in the second place
		on the contrary
		on the other hand

COMMA SPLICES

Comma splices occur when two or more independent clauses are joined by a comma (1) when some other punctuation or (2) a coordinating conjunction or (3) subordinating conjunction should have been used. The following is an example of a comma splice.

   Euripedes attempted to carry the reform further, it was a task beyond his powers, perhaps beyond any powers.

You could correct it by any of the following:

1. Euripedes attempted to carry the reform further; it was a task beyond his powers, perhaps beyond any powers.
    (Macaulay's choice)

2. Euripedes attempted to carry the reform further, **but** it was a task beyond his powers, perhaps beyond any powers.

3. **While** Euripedes attempted to carry the reform further, the task was beyond his powers, perhaps beyond any powers.

COORDINATING CONJUNCTIONS	SUBORDINATING CONJUNCTIONS	
and	after	no matter how
but	although	now that
or	as far as	once
for	as soon as	provided that
nor	as if	since
so	as though	so that
yet	because	supposing that
	before	than
	even if	though
	even though	till, until
	how	unless
	if	when, whenever
	inasmuch as	where, wherever
	in case that	whether
	insofar as	while
	in that	why

RELATIVE PRONOUNS
(used to introduce subordinate clauses that function as nouns)

that	who, whoever
what	whom, whomever
which	whose

You can also use subordinating conjunctions, conjunctive adverbs, and transitional phrases to link ideas between sentences and even paragraphs.

Now let us compare with the exact detail . . .
Once more, compare . . .
We venture to say, **on the contrary,** . . .

—"Milton," John Babington Macaulay

Mechanics and Punctuation

What do you need to know about mechanics and punctuation for the AP English Language & Composition Test? Enough to be able to write and punctuate grammatically correct sentences. (This, by the way, is a sentence fragment. In your own writing, an occasional sentence fragment works, but do not take the chance in your essays. The reader may not understand that you wrote a sentence fragment for a purpose, not as a mistake.)

If you find any of the rules in the following brief review unfamiliar, go back to your English composition text and review the appropriate section in more depth. Do some of the practice exercises that the text undoubtedly has.

The test evaluators may not expect you to write a flawless essay, but you want to make sure that your mechanics and punctuation are as correct as possible. Everything you do well adds to the favorable impression necessary for a high score. The same is true about punctuation. Using the correct punctuation makes a good impression on the readers. Remember, too, that errors in punctuation may interfere with clarity.

CAPITALIZATION

You have studied capitalization throughout your school years. The following list recaps the rules for capitalization you have learned.

Nouns

- Capitalize the first word in interjections and incomplete questions.

- Capitalize the first word in a quotation if the quotation is a complete sentence.

- Capitalize the first word after a colon if the word begins a complete sentence.

- Capitalize geographical and place names.

- Capitalize names of specific events and periods of time.

- Capitalize the names of organizations, government bodies, political parties, races, nationalities, languages, and religions.

Adjectives

- Capitalize most proper adjectives; for example *African* in *African American.*

- Do not capitalize certain frequently used proper adjectives; for example, *french fries, venetian blinds.*

- Capitalize a brand name used as an adjective but not the common noun it modifies; for example, *Jello pudding.*

NOTE

Concentrate on those rules that you are most likely to need for your own writing.

NOTE

Do not capitalize words that indicate direction. Do capitalize them when they name a section of a larger geographical area.

- Do not capitalize a common noun used with two proper adjectives; for example, *Iron Age tools*.

- Do not capitalize prefixes attached to proper adjectives unless the prefix refers to a nationality; for example, *pre-Columbian art* but *Franco-American music*.

Capitals in Titles

- Capitalize titles of people when used with a person's name or when used in direct address.

- Capitalize titles showing family relationships when they refer to a specific person, unless they are preceded by a possessive noun or pronoun.

- Capitalize the first word and all other key words in the titles of books, periodicals, plays, poems, stories, paintings, and other works of art.

ABBREVIATIONS

Usually, you should not use abbreviations when you are writing formal English. However, sometimes abbreviations are appropriate. The following list reviews guidelines for using abbreviations.

Names and Titles of People

- Use a person's full given name in formal writing, unless the person uses initials as part of his or her name; for example, the poet *A. E. Housman*.

- Abbreviations of social titles before a proper name begin with a capital letter and end with a period.

- Abbreviations of other titles used before proper names begin with a capital letter and end with a period.

- Abbreviations of titles after a name begin with a capital and end with a period.

- In formal writing, spell out numbers or amounts less than 100 and any other numbers that can be written in one or two words.

- Spell out all numbers found at the beginning of sentences.

- Use numerals when referring to fractions, decimals, and percentages, as well as addresses and dates.

NOTE

Abbreviations for both traditional and metric measurements should only be used in technical and informal writing and only with numerals.

END MARKS

- Use a period to end a declarative sentence, a mild imperative, or an indirect question.

- Use a question mark to end an interrogative sentence, an incomplete question, or a statement intended as a question.

- Use an exclamation mark to end an exclamatory sentence, a forceful imperative sentence, or an interjection of strong emotion.

COMMAS

- Use a comma before a conjunction that separates two independent clauses in a compound sentence.

- Use commas to separate three or more words, phrases, or clauses in a series.

- Use commas to separate adjectives of equal rank.

- Do not use commas to separate adjectives that must stay in a specific order.

- Use a comma after an introductory word, phrase, or clause.

- Use commas to set off parenthetical expressions.

- Use commas to set off nonessential expressions.

- Use commas to set off a direct quotation from the rest of the sentence.

- Use a comma to prevent a sentence from being misunderstood.

SEMICOLONS AND COLONS

- Use a semicolon to join independent clauses not already joined by a coordinating conjunction (*and, or, but, nor, so, yet*).

- Use a semicolon to join independent clauses separated by either a conjunctive adverb or a transitional expression.

- Use a colon before a list of items following an independent clause.

- Use a colon to introduce a formal or lengthy quotation or one that is missing an introductory expression.

- Use a colon to introduce a sentence that summarizes or explains the sentence before it.

NOTE

Many writers overuse commas. Make certain that you know why you are adding a comma to a sentence.

QUOTATION MARKS AND UNDERLINING

If a word, a title, or a name would be italicized in printed material, then you need to underline it when you write it by hand. If you were writing your essay on a computer, you would use the *italics* function.

TIP

Do not use quotation marks around an indirect quotation (a restatement of someone's words).

- Use quotation marks to enclose a person's exact words.

- Place a comma or a period inside the final quotation mark.

- Place a semicolon or colon outside the final quotation mark.

- Place a question mark or exclamation mark inside the final quotation if the end mark is part of the quotation.

- Place a question mark or exclamation mark outside the final quotation if the end mark is not part of the quotation.

- Use three ellipsis marks in a quotation to indicate that words have been omitted.

- Use single quotation marks for a quotation within a quotation.

- Use quotation marks around titles of short written works, episodes in a series, songs, parts of musical compositions, or collections.

- Underline (italicize) titles of long written works, shows, films, and other works of art.

- Underline (italicize) words and phrases from a foreign language when not used commonly in English.

- Underline (italicize) numbers, symbols, letters, and words used as names for themselves.

NOTE

Do not underline or place in quotation marks the titles of holy books, such as the Koran or the Bible, or their parts.

DASHES, PARENTHESES, AND BRACKETS

- Use dashes to indicate an abrupt change of thought, a dramatic interrupting idea, or a summary statement.

- Use dashes to set off a nonessential appositive, modifier, or parenthetical expression when it is long, already punctuated, or especially dramatic.

- Use parentheses to set off asides and explanations only when the material is not essential or when it consists of one or more sentences.

- Place all punctuation after the parentheses in a sentence with a set-off phrase.

- Use brackets to enclose words you insert into a quotation when you are quoting someone else.

HYPHENS

- Use a hyphen when writing out the numbers *twenty-one* through *ninety-nine.*

- Use a hyphen with fractions used as adjectives.

- Use a hyphen in words with the prefixes *all-, ex-,* and *self-* and words with the suffix *-elect.*

- Use a hyphen to connect a compound modifier before a noun, unless it includes a word ending in *-ly* or is a compound proper adjective; for example, *beautifully dressed, Native American poem.*

- If a word must be divided at the end of a line, place a hyphen between syllables.

APOSTROPHES

- Add an apostrophe and an *s* to show the possessive case of most singular nouns; for example, *cat's dish, the tomato's flavor.*

- Add an apostrophe to show the possessive case of plural nouns ending in *s* or *es;* for example, *the boys' club.*

- Add an apostrophe and an *s* to show possession with plural nouns that do not end in *s;* for example, *women's clothing, the mice's nests.*

- Add an apostrophe and an *s* or just an apostrophe (if the word is plural and ends in *s*) to the last word of a compound noun to form the possessive; for example, *the Joint Committee's decision, the mutual funds' investors.*

- To show joint ownership, make the final noun possessive. To show individual ownership, make each noun possessive; for example, *Marie and Leslie's apartment,* but *Mike's and Tom's cars.*

- Use an apostrophe and an *s* with indefinite pronouns to show possession; for example, *one's jacket, somebody's chair.*

- Use an apostrophe and an *s* to write the plurals of numbers, symbols, and letters; for example, *8's, &'s, p's.*

NOTE

Do not use an apostrophe with the possessive forms of personal pronouns; for example, hers, *not* hers'.

Diction

Word choice speaks volumes about you. (That phrase is a cliché that would be best to avoid.) The following are some suggestions to help you refine your writing and polish your choice of words.

REPLACE CLICHÉS WITH FRESHER IMAGES AND WORDS

A cliché is any stale, worn-out phrase that has been used so often it has become virtually meaningless. Clichés make your writing seem commonplace and secondhand. Some common clichés and trite expressions include the following:

CLICHÉS AND TRITE EXPRESSIONS	
Ugly as sin	Like a fish out of water
Pretty as a picture	Like finding a needle in a haystack
Happy as a lark	Like a bump on a log
Hard as a rock	Like a hot potato
Fresh as a daisy	Sky high
Skinny as a rail	Sparkling clean
Sly as a fox	Filthy rich
Stiff as a board	Dirt cheap
Old as the hills	Costing an arm and a leg
Mad as a hornet	Heart of gold
Soft as silk	One in a million
Warm as toast	Between a rock and a hard place
Dumb as a doorknob	Out of the frying pan and into the fire
Smart as a whip	When push comes to shove
Crazy as a loon	Working fingers to the bone
Honest as the day is long	Come out smelling like a rose
As much fun as a barrel of monkeys	Tooting my/your/one's own horn
Quiet as a mouse	In a New York minute
Loose as a goose	Variety is the spice of life.
Phony as a three-dollar bill	Stand up and be counted.
Pure as the driven snow	Raining cats and dogs
Crystal clear	The sixty-four-dollar question
True blue	Day in and day out
Like pulling teeth	Have a nice day.

Replace clichés and trite expressions with livelier, more concrete language; for example:

Cliché: I *was shaking in my boots* before the interview, but I was *happy as a lark* when the personnel manager offered me the job.

Improved: I was *terrified* before the interview, but I was *ecstatic* when the personnel manager offered me the job.

Cliché: Whether the author really believed what he wrote was *the sixty-four-dollar question.*

Improved: Whether the author really believed what he wrote was *difficult to determine* from the answers he gave the interviewer.

AVOID EUPHEMISMS

A euphemism is a word or phrase that is less direct but that may be considered less offensive than another word or phrase with the same meaning; for example, saying someone is *no longer with us* instead of *dead*. Euphemisms can lead to wordiness, as in the above example, because you may need several words to say what one direct word could convey. Euphemisms also lessen the impact of a thought or idea, and they can mislead your readers. Occasionally, you may choose to use a euphemism to protect someone's feelings—yours, the subject of your writing, or your audience—but eliminate euphemisms whenever possible so your writing does not seem insincere.

Euphemism: Amit could not attend the meeting Thursday because he was *indisposed*.

Improved: Amit could not attend the meeting Thursday because he was *sick*.

Euphemism: Because she was constantly late to work, Leslie was *let go*.

Improved: Because she was constantly late to work, Leslie was *fired*.

AVOID SELF-IMPORTANT LANGUAGE

A writer who tries to impress readers with unnecessarily obscure words and lengthy, complicated sentences often adopts self-important language. The result is bad tone and a confused message. When you write, avoid that type of language. Eliminate vague, general nouns and long verbs that end in *-ate* or *-ize*.

Self-important: To facilitate input by the maximum number of potential purchasers, questionnaires were designed and posted well in advance of the launch of the promotional marketing campaign.

Improved: Before we began advertising, we designed and mailed a marketing survey to find out what consumers were looking for.

AVOID FLOWERY LANGUAGE AND EMOTIONALLY LOADED WORDS

Good writing should include vivid modifiers and interesting phrases. However, your writing should never become overloaded with unnecessary adjectives and adverbs that serve only as decoration. Usually, a simpler way of expressing yourself is more effective.

Flowery: The glimmering, golden rays of the brilliant orb of the sun shimmered above the white-hot sands of the vast desert, sere and lifeless.

Improved: The rays of the sun shimmered above the hot, dry desert.

> **NOTE**
> Polysyllabic, high-sounding words can make your writing sound pretentious rather than erudite.

Similarly, overly emotional language can produce a harsh tone and make your readers reject your point of view. Avoid emotional language and substitute more rational diction.

Emotional: The idiot who wrote that essay should have his head examined.

Improved: The writer who developed that argument based it on a faulty assumption.

AVOID WORDS THAT MAY NOT BE UNDERSTOOD

You should use only vocabulary and expressions that your readers will understand. No matter what your tone, some types of language can be confusing. In general, avoid slang words and expressions because you cannot be sure that your audience is familiar with current idioms. Also, remember that slang quickly becomes dated.

Slang: Brian's mother reprimanded him for bombing his physics test.

Improved: Brian's mother reprimanded him for failing his physics test.

NOTE

Jargon is language aimed at specialists.

Similarly, jargon can confuse readers and destroy your tone. Use it only if you are writing a highly technical report and must use special terms for the topic. Your readers may easily become lost if you do not replace jargon with concrete, understandable phrases.

Jargon: Close-support, transport, and reconnaissance assistance is provided by the S-3X helicopter, which is the most cost effective in a crane configuration.

Improved: The S-3X helicopter provides support, transportation, and reconnaissance. However, the helicopter is most cost effective when it works as a crane.

ELIMINATE DEADWOOD

Check your essay for words that contribute nothing to your ideas. Discard these empty words that pad your sentences and create roundabout constructions. You will find some of the most common "empty words" in the following box.

COMMONLY USED EMPTY WORDS AND PHRASES		
a great deal of	due to	which is to say
is the one who is	it is a fact that	the area of
there is	the thing that	what I mean is
there are	of the opinion that	for the reason that
by way of	to the extent that	in a manner that

Deadwood: It is a fact that sunburn can cause skin cancer.

Improved: Sunburn can cause skin cancer.

Other deadwood you should eliminate are hedging words and phrases, or qualifiers. Writers use qualifiers to be noncommittal, but using them results in a vague and indefinite essay. However, don't eliminate all hedging words in your writing. For example, "Everyone in the stadium cheered the touchdown" needs to be qualified unless you know that the opposing team had no supporters in the stands. The following list contains words and phrases that unnecessarily qualify what you want to say:

COMMONLY USED HEDGING WORDS AND PHRASES		
almost	rather	it seems
tends to	in a way	sort of
somewhat	kind of	that may or may not

Hedging: A major earthquake that may or may not occur in this region can cause a great deal of damage.

Improved: If a major earthquake occurs in this region, it will cause a great deal of damage.

AVOID REDUNDANCY

Redundancy occurs when you repeat an idea unnecessarily. It prevents writing from being concise. Saying the same thing repeatedly not only sounds awkward but adds deadwood to your essay. To eliminate redundancy in your writing, look for words or phrases that repeat the meaning of another word.

Redundant: Tamiko prefers the written letter to the telephone.

Improved: Tamiko prefers letters to telephone calls.

Redundant: The consensus of opinion in our community is that commercial building should be restricted.

Improved: The consensus in our community is that commercial building should be restricted.

BE SUCCINCT

Less obvious than deadwood and redundant language are wordy phrases and clauses that can weaken the impact of your writing. Shorten wordy phrases and clauses if you can without changing the meaning of your sentence. Sentences can be rewritten by using appositives, prepositional phrases, adjectives, adverbs, or possessive nouns. Sometimes you can replace a phrase with a single word.

Wordy: Denee sang every Christmas carol in a loud voice.

Improved: Denee sang every Christmas carol loudly.

NOTE

To review more about combining sentences, see p. 150 in this chapter.

Wordy: Tourists from Germany and Canada love to vacation in the Caribbean.

Improved: Many German and Canadian tourists love to vacation in the Caribbean.

If your essay has a great many adjective clauses, you can simplify sentences by dropping the clause's subject, verb, and other unnecessary words. Also substitute appositives, participial phrases, and compounds for wordy clauses.

Wordy: The painting, which hangs on the museum's third floor, accurately portrays the signing of the Declaration of Independence.

Improved: The painting, on the museum's third floor, accurately portrays the signing of the Declaration of Independence.

CREATING AN IDEA BANK

NOTE

Having this list in mind will keep you from having writer's block during the test.

Before you begin practicing for the essay section of the test, brainstorm all the words and phrases you can think of to describe a literary work of nonfiction—critical essay, autobiography, biography, opinion piece, science article, and so on. Make categories under each. You might do the exercise with a friend, and then share lists to gather as many words as you can. Use this as your idea bank and your word bank, and consult it before you begin each practice essay. Here is a start to your list.

AUTOBIOGRAPHY	
Diction	**Style**
verbose	convoluted
wordy	elegant
flowery	precise

98 COMMON USAGE PROBLEMS

Many usage errors result from using colloquialisms, the language of everyday use, in formal written English. Others occur because words that are similar in meaning or spelling are confused. The following is a list of 98 common usage problems that you should avoid in your writing.

1. *a, an*
    Use the article *a* before consonant sounds and the article *an* before vowel sounds. Words beginning with *h*, *o*, and *u* can have either sound.

2. *accept, except*
    Accept is a verb meaning "to receive," and *except* is a preposition meaning "other than" or "leaving out."

3. *accuse, allege*
    Accuse means "to blame," whereas *allege* means "to state as fact something that has not been proved."

4. *adapt, adopt*
    Adapt means "to change," but *adopt* means "to take as one's own."

5. *advice, advise*
    Advice, a noun, means "an opinion." *Advise* is a verb that means "to express an opinion to."

6. *affect, effect*
    Affect is normally a verb meaning "to influence." *Effect* is usually a noun that means "result." Sometimes, *effect* is a verb that means "to cause."

7. *aggravate*
    Aggravate means "to make something worse"; it should not be used to refer to an annoyance.

8. *ain't*
    Ain't is nonstandard English.

9. *allot, a lot, alot*
    The verb *allot* means "to divide in parts" or "to give out shares." *A lot* is an informal phrase meaning "a great many," so you should not use it in formal writing. *Alot* is nonstandard spelling. It should never be used.

10. *all ready, already*
    All ready, which functions as an adjective, is an expression meaning "ready." *Already,* an adverb, means "by or before this time" or "even now."

11. *all right, alright.*
    Alright is a nonstandard spelling. Use the two-word version.

12. *all together, altogether*
    All together means "all at once." *Altogether* means "completely."

13. *A.M., P.M.*
    A.M. refers to hours before noon, *P.M.* to hours after noon. Numbers are not spelled out when you use these abbreviations, nor should you use phrases such as "in the morning" or "in the evening" with them.

14. *among, between*
    Among and *between* are prepositions. *Among* is used with three or more items. *Between* is generally used with only two items.

15. *amount, number*
    Amount is used with quantities that cannot be counted. Use *number* when items can be counted.

16. *anxious*
    Anxious means "worried" or "uneasy." It should not be used to mean "eager."

17. *anyone, any one, everyone, every one*
    Anyone and *everyone* mean "any person" and "every person." *Any one* means "any single person or thing," and *every one* means "every single person or thing."

18. *anyway, anywhere, everywhere, nowhere, somewhere*
    These adverbs should never end in *s*.

19. *as*
    As should not be used to mean "because" or "since."

20. *as to*
    As to is awkward. Substitute *about*.

21. *at*
    Eliminate *at* when used after *where*.

22. *at about*
    Eliminate *at* or *about* if you find them used together.

23. *awful, awfully*
    Awful is used informally to mean "extremely bad." *Awfully* is also informal, meaning "very."

24. *awhile, a while*
    Awhile is an adverb, meaning "for a while." *A while* is an article and a noun and is usually used after the preposition *for*.

25. *beat, win*
    Beat means "to overcome." *Win* means "to achieve victory in." Replace *win* if the sentence sense is *beat*.

26. *because*
    Eliminate *because* if it follows "the reason," or rephrase the sentence.

27. *being as, being that*
    Replace either phrase with *since* or *because*.

28. *beside, besides*
    Beside means "at the side of" or "close to." *Besides* means "in addition to." They are not interchangeable.

29. *bring, take*
    Bring means "to carry from a distant place to a nearer one." *Take* means the opposite, "to carry from a near place to a more distant place."

30. *bunch*
    Bunch means "a number of things of the same kind." Do not use *bunch* to mean "group."

31. *burst, bust, busted*
    Burst is the present, past, and past participle of the verb *to burst*. *Bust* and *busted* are nonstandard English.

32. *but what*
    But what is nonstandard English. Use *that*.

33. *can, may*
    Use *can* to mean "to have the ability to." Use *may* to mean "to have permission to."

34. *can't help but*
    Use *can't help* plus a gerund instead of *can't help but;* for example, *can't help crying*.

NOTE

In formal writing, awful *should be used to mean only "inspiring fear or awe."*

35. *condemn, condone*
These words have nearly opposite meanings. *Condemn* means "to express disapproval of." *Condone* means "to pardon" or "excuse."

36. *continual, continuous*
Continual means "occurring over and over in succession," but *continuous* means "occurring without stopping."

37. *different from, different than*
The expression *different from* is more accepted.

38. *doesn't, don't*
Use *doesn't* with third-person singular subjects.

39. *done*
Done, the past participle of the verb *to do*, follows a helping verb.

40. *dove*
Use *dived* instead of *dove* for the past tense of the verb *dive*.

41. *due to*
Use *due to* only when the words *caused by* can be substituted.

42. *due to the fact that*
Use *since* or *because* instead.

43. *each other, one another*
Most of the time these expressions are interchangeable. Sometimes *each other* is used when only two people or things are involved, and *one another* is used when more than two are involved.

44. *emigrate, immigrate*
These are opposites. *Emigrate* means "to leave a country," and *immigrate* means "to enter a country." In both cases, it is a reference to establishing a residency.

45. *enthused, enthusiastic*
Enthused is nonstandard English; therefore, use *enthusiastic*.

46. *farther, further*
Farther is a reference to distance, but *further* means "to a greater degree."

47. *fewer, less*
Fewer is properly used with things that are counted, and *less* is used with qualities or quantities that are not counted.

48. *former, latter*
In referring to two items, *former* designates the first and *latter*, the second.

49. *get, got, gotten*
Although these verbs are acceptable, it is better to select different verbs if possible, such as *become, became, have become*.

50. *gone, went*
Gone, the past participle of the verb *to go*, requires a helping verb. *Went* is the past tense of *go*, and no helping verb is required.

51. *good, lovely, nice*
Try to use more specific adjectives in their place.

52. *hanged, hung*
Hanged means "executed," and *hung* means "suspended."

53. *healthful, healthy*
Healthful is used with things (*healthful diet*), and *healthy* refers to people.

54. *if, whether*
These conjunctions are interchangeable, except when the intention is to give equal stress to alternatives, in which case *if* won't work, and *whether* must be used with *or not*. "I'll go whether you come with me or not" is not the same as "I'll go if you come with me."

55. *in, into*
In is a position reference (*the kitten drank the milk in the bowl*), but *into* implies movement (*the kitten stepped into the bowl of milk*).

56. *irregardless*
This is nonstandard English. Use *regardless* instead.

57. *judicial, judicious*
Judicial refers to a legal system. *Judicious* means "to show wisdom."

58. *just*
Place *just*, when it is used as an adverb meaning "no more than," immediately before the word it modifies.

59. *kind of, sort of*
Do not use these words to mean "rather" or "somewhat."

60. *kind of a, sort of a*
Do not use *a* following *kind of* or *sort of*.

61. *lay, lie*
Lay means "to set or put something down," and it is usually followed by a direct object. *Lie* means "to recline," and it is never followed by a direct object.

62. *learn, teach*
Learn refers to "gaining knowledge," whereas *teach* means "to give knowledge."

63. *leave, let*
Leave means "to allow to remain," and *let* means "to permit."

64. *like*
Like is a preposition and should not be used in place of *as*.

65. *loose, lose*
Loose is commonly an adjective. *Lose* is always a verb meaning "to miss from one's possession."

66. *mad*
When used in formal language, *mad* means "insane." When it is used in informal language, it means "angry."

67. *maybe, may be*
Maybe is an adverb that means "perhaps." *May be* is a verb.

68. *number, numeral*
Use *number* to mean quantity and *numeral* to mean the figure representing the number, that is, *the numeral that comes after 3 is 4.*

69. *of*
Do not use *of* after the verbs *should, would, could,* or *must*. Use *have* instead. Also eliminate *of* after the words *outside, inside, off,* and *atop*.

70. *OK, O.K., okay*
Do not use these words in formal writing.

71. *only*
Make sure to place *only* immediately preceding the word it logically modifies. *You only say you love me,* that is, you say it but you don't mean it; *You say you love only me,* that is, I am the only one you love.

NOTE

The principal parts of *lay* are *lay, laying, laid,* and *laid.* The principal parts of *lie* are *lie, lying, lay,* and *lain.*

72. *ought*
Do not use *have* or *had* with *ought*. *Ought* is used with an infinitive; for example, *ought to wash, ought not to cry.*

73. *outside of*
Do not use *outside of* to mean "besides" or "except."

74. *parameter*
Use *parameter* only in mathematical contexts to designate a variable.

75. *persecute, prosecute*
Persecute means "to subject to ill treatment," whereas *prosecute* means "to bring a lawsuit against."

76. *plurals that do not end in "s"*
Some nouns are made plural in the same way that they were in their original language. For example, *criteria* and *phenomena* are plural. Make sure that you treat them as plural, not singular, nouns.

77. *poorly*
Do not use *poorly* to mean "ill" in formal writing.

78. *precede, proceed*
Precede means "to go before," and *proceed* means "to go forward."

79. *principal, principle*
Principal can be a noun or an adjective. As a noun, it means "a person who has controlling authority," and as an adjective, it means "most important." *Principle* is always a noun, and it means "a basic law."

80. *raise, rise*
Raise normally takes a direct object, but *rise* never takes a direct object, as in "I *raised* the flag," but "I *rise* every morning at 6."

81. *real*
Do not use *real* to mean "very" or "really" in formal language.

82. *says*
Do not use *says* in place of *said.*

83. *seen*
Seen requires a helping verb, as in "I was *seen* at the movies," not "I *seen* him at the movies."

84. *set, sit*
Set is usually followed by a direct object and means "to put something in a specific place." *Sit* means "to be seated," and it is never followed by a direct object.

85. *shape*
In formal language, do not use the word *shape* to mean "condition," as in *The boxer was in good shape.*

86. *since, because*
Use *since* when time is involved and *because* when a reason is involved. *Since I last saw them, I read a book*, but *Because they came last Saturday, I did not finish the book I was reading.*

87. *slow, slowly*
It is preferable to use *slow* as the adjective and *slowly* as the adverb.

88. *than, then*
Than is a comparative and is not to be confused with *then*, which refers to time.

89. *that, which, who*
These pronouns refer to the following: *that*—people and things, *which*—only things, and *who*—only people.

ALERT!
If a word ends in *a* or *i*, be careful. It may be plural.

NOTE
You can remember the difference by thinking of "your princiPAL as your PAL."

TIP
Careful writers still use slow *only as an adjective.*

NOTE

To correct a sentence containing *them there, these here, this here,* or *that there*, delete *here* or *there*.

90. *their, there, they're*
Their is a possessive pronoun. *There* is an expletive or an adverb. *They're* is a contraction of *they are*.

91. *them there, these here, this here, that there*
These are nonstandard expressions and should not be used. Replace with *these* or *those* if an adjective is required.

92. *till, until*
These words are interchangeable, but they are often misspelled.

93. *to, too, two*
To is a preposition. *Too* is an adverb used to modify adjectives and adverbs. *Two* is a number.

94. *unique*
Unique means "one of a kind"; therefore, it should not be modified by words such as *very* or *most*.

95. *want in, want out*
These are nonstandard expressions and should not be used.

96. *ways*
Ways is plural. Do not use the article *a* immediately preceding *ways*.

97. *when, where*
Do not use these words directly after a linking verb. Also, do not use *where* as a substitute for *that*.

98. *-wise*
Do not use this suffix to create new words.

Be sure to use
but that, not *but what*
because of, not *due to*
because, not *on account of*
rarely or *hardly ever*, not *rarely ever*
kind or *kind of a*, not *sort, sort of*

SUMMING IT UP

- Any grammar questions on the test are really disguised comprehension questions. They will ask you to identify one of the parts of speech or they will ask you to classify parts of a sentence.

- Remember to use the present tense when writing about the author's intention in literary works.

- Writing timed essays, evaluating them, and then working to improve the weaknesses you identify are the best ways to prepare for the test.

PART V

TWO PRACTICE TESTS

ANSWER SHEET PRACTICE TEST 2

SECTION I

1. Ⓐ Ⓑ Ⓒ Ⓓ Ⓔ
2. Ⓐ Ⓑ Ⓒ Ⓓ Ⓔ
3. Ⓐ Ⓑ Ⓒ Ⓓ Ⓔ
4. Ⓐ Ⓑ Ⓒ Ⓓ Ⓔ
5. Ⓐ Ⓑ Ⓒ Ⓓ Ⓔ
6. Ⓐ Ⓑ Ⓒ Ⓓ Ⓔ
7. Ⓐ Ⓑ Ⓒ Ⓓ Ⓔ
8. Ⓐ Ⓑ Ⓒ Ⓓ Ⓔ
9. Ⓐ Ⓑ Ⓒ Ⓓ Ⓔ
10. Ⓐ Ⓑ Ⓒ Ⓓ Ⓔ
11. Ⓐ Ⓑ Ⓒ Ⓓ Ⓔ
12. Ⓐ Ⓑ Ⓒ Ⓓ Ⓔ
13. Ⓐ Ⓑ Ⓒ Ⓓ Ⓔ
14. Ⓐ Ⓑ Ⓒ Ⓓ Ⓔ
15. Ⓐ Ⓑ Ⓒ Ⓓ Ⓔ
16. Ⓐ Ⓑ Ⓒ Ⓓ Ⓔ
17. Ⓐ Ⓑ Ⓒ Ⓓ Ⓔ
18. Ⓐ Ⓑ Ⓒ Ⓓ Ⓔ
19. Ⓐ Ⓑ Ⓒ Ⓓ Ⓔ

20. Ⓐ Ⓑ Ⓒ Ⓓ Ⓔ
21. Ⓐ Ⓑ Ⓒ Ⓓ Ⓔ
22. Ⓐ Ⓑ Ⓒ Ⓓ Ⓔ
23. Ⓐ Ⓑ Ⓒ Ⓓ Ⓔ
24. Ⓐ Ⓑ Ⓒ Ⓓ Ⓔ
25. Ⓐ Ⓑ Ⓒ Ⓓ Ⓔ
26. Ⓐ Ⓑ Ⓒ Ⓓ Ⓔ
27. Ⓐ Ⓑ Ⓒ Ⓓ Ⓔ
28. Ⓐ Ⓑ Ⓒ Ⓓ Ⓔ
29. Ⓐ Ⓑ Ⓒ Ⓓ Ⓔ
30. Ⓐ Ⓑ Ⓒ Ⓓ Ⓔ
31. Ⓐ Ⓑ Ⓒ Ⓓ Ⓔ
32. Ⓐ Ⓑ Ⓒ Ⓓ Ⓔ
33. Ⓐ Ⓑ Ⓒ Ⓓ Ⓔ
34. Ⓐ Ⓑ Ⓒ Ⓓ Ⓔ
35. Ⓐ Ⓑ Ⓒ Ⓓ Ⓔ
36. Ⓐ Ⓑ Ⓒ Ⓓ Ⓔ
37. Ⓐ Ⓑ Ⓒ Ⓓ Ⓔ

38. Ⓐ Ⓑ Ⓒ Ⓓ Ⓔ
39. Ⓐ Ⓑ Ⓒ Ⓓ Ⓔ
40. Ⓐ Ⓑ Ⓒ Ⓓ Ⓔ
41. Ⓐ Ⓑ Ⓒ Ⓓ Ⓔ
42. Ⓐ Ⓑ Ⓒ Ⓓ Ⓔ
43. Ⓐ Ⓑ Ⓒ Ⓓ Ⓔ
44. Ⓐ Ⓑ Ⓒ Ⓓ Ⓔ
45. Ⓐ Ⓑ Ⓒ Ⓓ Ⓔ
46. Ⓐ Ⓑ Ⓒ Ⓓ Ⓔ
47. Ⓐ Ⓑ Ⓒ Ⓓ Ⓔ
48. Ⓐ Ⓑ Ⓒ Ⓓ Ⓔ
49. Ⓐ Ⓑ Ⓒ Ⓓ Ⓔ
50. Ⓐ Ⓑ Ⓒ Ⓓ Ⓔ
51. Ⓐ Ⓑ Ⓒ Ⓓ Ⓔ
52. Ⓐ Ⓑ Ⓒ Ⓓ Ⓔ
53. Ⓐ Ⓑ Ⓒ Ⓓ Ⓔ
54. Ⓐ Ⓑ Ⓒ Ⓓ Ⓔ

answer sheet

SECTION II

Question 1

_____

_____

_____

_____

_____

_____

_____

_____

_____

_____

_____

_____

_____

_____

_____

_____

_____

_____

_____

_____

_____

_____

_____

_____

_____

answer sheet

Question 2

answer sheet

Question 3

answer sheet

Practice Test 2

SECTION I

54 QUESTIONS • 60 MINUTES

> **Directions:** This section consists of selections of literature and questions on their content, style, and form. After you have read each passage, select the response that best answers the question and mark the corresponding space on the answer sheet.

QUESTIONS 1–15 REFER TO THE FOLLOWING PASSAGE. READ THE PASSAGE CAREFULLY AND THEN CHOOSE THE ANSWERS TO THE QUESTIONS.

From the "Preface" of *Modern American Poetry, a Critical Anthology*

Line   It may be difficult, if not impossible, to determine the boundaries as well as the beginnings of "modernism," but only a few appraisers will deny that American literature became modern as well as American with the advent of Mark Twain, Herman Melville, and Walt Whitman.

5   In the history of poetry the line may be drawn with a measure of certainty, and it is with the Civil War and the publication of the third edition of *Leaves of Grass* that modern American poetry is defined.

Aftermath of the Civil War

    The Civil War inspired volumes of indignant, military, religious, and
10   patriotic verse without adding more than four or five memorable pieces to the anthologies; the conflict produced a vast quantity of poems but practically no important poetry. Its end marked the end of an epoch— political, social, and literary. The arts declined; the New England group began to disintegrate. The poets had overstrained and outsung them-
15   selves; it was a time of surrender and swan-songs. Unable to respond to the new forces of political nationalism and industrial reconstruction, the Brahmins (that famous group of intellectuals who had dominated literary America) withdrew into their libraries. Such poets as Longfel- low, Bryant, Taylor, turned their eyes away from the native scene, or
20   left creative writing altogether and occupied themselves with transla- tions. "They had been borne into an era in which they had no part," writes Fred Lewis Pattee (*A History of American Literature Since 1870*), "and they contented themselves with reëchoings of the old music." For them poetry ceased to be a reflection of actuality, "an
25   extension of experience." Within a period of six years, from 1867 to 1872, there appeared Longfellow's *Divina Commedia,* C. E. Norton's

183

Vita Nuova, T. W. Parson's *Inferno,* William Cullen Bryant's *Iliad* and *Odyssey,* and Bayard Taylor's *Faust.*

30   Suddenly the break came. America developed a national consciousness; the West discovered itself, and the East discovered the West. Grudgingly at first, the aristocratic leaders made way for a new expression; crude, jangling, vigorously democratic. The old order was changing with a vengeance. All the preceding writers—poets like Emerson, Lowell, Longfellow, Holmes—were not only products of the New England colleges, but typically "Boston gentlemen of the early Renaissance." To them, the new

35   men must have seemed like a regiment recruited from the ranks of vulgarity. Walt Whitman, Mark Twain, Bret Harte, John Hay, Joaquin Miller, Joel Chandler Harris, James Whitcomb Riley—these were men who had graduated from the farm, the frontier, the mine, the pilothouse, the printer's shop! For a while, the movement seemed of little consequence; the impact of Whitman and the Westerners was averted.

40   The poets of the transition, with a deliberate art, ignored the surge of a spontaneous national expression. They were even successful in holding it back. But it was a gathering force.

—Louis Untermeyer

1. What is the meaning of the expression, "overstrained and outsung themselves" (lines 14–15)?

   (A) Tired out
   (B) Lost creativity
   (C) Worked too hard
   (D) Gone beyond their knowledge
   (E) Sought new insights

2. This selection is an example of which mode of writing?

   (A) Descriptive
   (B) Narrative
   (C) Persuasive
   (D) Expository
   (E) Argument

3. What is the best explanation of the expression, "an extension of experience" (lines 24–25)?

   (A) A reference to existentialism in poetry
   (B) Poetry as a reflection of the real world
   (C) A definition of modern poetry
   (D) A reflection of the universal nature of poetry
   (E) Poetry as an art form

4. Which of the following is the thesis that the author explores?

   (A) The Civil War inspired volumes of indignant, military, religious, and patriotic verse without adding more than four or five memorable pieces to the anthologies.
   (B) It may be difficult, if not impossible, to determine the boundaries as well as the beginnings of "modernism."
   (C) Only a few appraisers will deny that American literature became modern as well as American with the advent of Mark Twain, Herman Melville, and Walt Whitman.
   (D) The conclusion of the Civil War marked the end of an epoch—political, social, and literary.
   (E) The Brahmins withdrew from the literary scene because they could not respond to the changes made by the Civil War.

5. Which of the following changed the role of the Brahmins?

   (A) The Civil War and Reconstruction
   (B) Religious freedom and politics
   (C) Political nationalism and industrial reconstruction
   (D) Industrial growth and the westward movement
   (E) Philosophical creativity and the scientific revolution

6. Longfellow's *Divina Commedia* is an example of the author's contention that

   (A) modernism began with the end of the Civil War
   (B) the New England poets no longer created vibrant, original verse, but turned to translations
   (C) modernism developed along political lines
   (D) modern literature grew slowly in most areas
   (E) the New England writers provided a more studied view of life

7. What is meant by the expression, "'reëchoings of the old music'" (lines 23–24)?

   (A) Tired old songs
   (B) Rewriting old material
   (C) Hearing influences from the past
   (D) Metaphorical sounds of the past
   (E) Redone philosophical treatises

8. The author contends that the Brahmins viewed the new poets as

   (A) vulgar
   (B) intellectual
   (C) uneducated
   (D) simple
   (E) insightful

9. What does the author mean in the first lines of the final paragraph, "Suddenly the break came. America developed a national consciousness; the West discovered itself, and the East discovered the West."?

   (A) People in the East were moving west.
   (B) There was a break in thought between the East and West.
   (C) American modern poetry found itself.
   (D) The Brahmins and modern poets were in conflict.
   (E) Poetry from the West became the dominant verse.

10. Which of the following is the best characterization of the tone of this passage?

    (A) Harsh and scathing
    (B) Scholarly and informative
    (C) Condescending and irritating
    (D) Humorous and witty
    (E) Dry and pretentious

11. Which of the following best summarizes the thoughts of the author in this piece?

    (A) The Brahmins' poetry, although superior to modern poetry, was lost after the Civil War.
    (B) The more liberated modern American poetry outshone the older styles.
    (C) The Brahmins were essentially the creators of modern American poetry.
    (D) The Civil War marked the beginning of modern American poetry.
    (E) The experiences of the Civil War formed the basis of some of the Brahmins' work.

12. The author would agree with which of the following statements about the Civil War?

   (A) It produced a great number of poems, but little poetry.
   (B) It produced many poets.
   (C) It developed the skills of the Brahmins.
   (D) It created new advocates of poetry.
   (E) It produced a number of forums for poets.

13. What is the meaning of the sentence beginning "The poets of the transition, with a deliberate art," (line 40)?

   (A) The transitional poets were deliberate in their poetry.
   (B) The Brahmins worked to prevent changes in American poetry.
   (C) The Brahmins paid little attention to the changes in poetry.
   (D) The spontaneous growth of modern American poetry overwhelmed the Brahmins.
   (E) There was little support for the Brahmins' poetry.

14. The author characterizes the new poets as

   (A) brash and arrogant
   (B) spiritual and philosophical
   (C) malleable and whimsical
   (D) forceful and inventive
   (E) crude and cutting edge

15. The author characterizes the Brahmins as

   (A) educated and mercurial
   (B) stuffy and intransigent
   (C) light-hearted and introspective
   (D) serious but easygoing
   (E) brilliant and forgiving

QUESTIONS 16–30 REFER TO THE FOLLOWING SELECTION. READ THE PASSAGE CAREFULLY AND THEN CHOOSE THE ANSWERS TO THE QUESTIONS. THIS PIECE WAS WRITTEN IN 1780 WHEN BENJAMIN FRANKLIN WAS RESTRICTED TO HIS HOUSE DURING AN ATTACK OF GOUT.

From "Dialogue Between Gout and Mr. Franklin"

Line		
	Franklin.	How can you so cruelly sport with my torments?
	Gout.	Sport! I am very serious. I have here a list of offenses against your own health distinctly written and can justify every stroke inflicted on you.
	Franklin.	Read it, then.
5	**Gout.**	It is too long a detail, but I will briefly mention some particulars.
	Franklin.	Proceed. I am all attention.
	Gout.	Do you remember how often you have promised yourself, the following morning, a walk in the grove of Boulogne, in the garden de la Muette, or in your own garden, and have violated your promise, alleging, at one time, it was too cold, at another, too warm, too wind, too moist, or what else you pleased, when in truth it was too nothing but your insuperable love of ease?
10		
	Franklin.	That I confess may have happened occasionally, probably ten times in a year.

15   **Gout.**   Your confession is very far short of the truth. The gross amount is one
              hundred and ninety-nine times.

      Franklin. Is it possible?

      Gout.   So possible, that it is fact. You may rely on the accuracy of my statement.
              You know M. Brillon's gardens and what fine walks they contain, you
20   know the handsome flight of a hundred steps which lead from the terrace
              above to the lawn below. You have been in the practice of visiting this
              amiable family twice a week, after dinner, and it is a maxim of your own
              that "a man may take as much exercise in walking a mile up and down
              stairs as in ten on level ground." What an opportunity was here for you
25   to have had exercise in both these ways! Did you embrace it, and how
              often?

      Franklin. I cannot immediately answer that question.

      Gout.   I will do it for you: not once.

      Franklin. Not once?

30   **Gout.**   Even so. During the summer you went there at six o'clock. You found the
              charming lady with her lovely children and friends eager to walk with
              you and entertain you with their agreeable conversation, and what has
              been your choice? Why to sit on the terrace, satisfying yourself with the
              fine prospect and passing your eye over the beauties of the garden below,
35   without taking one step to descend and walk about in them. On the
              contrary, you call for tea and the chessboard, and lo! You are occupied in
              your seat till nine o'clock, and that besides two hours' play after dinner;
              and then, instead of walking home, which would have bestirred you a
              little, you step into your carriage. How absurd to suppose that all this
40   carelessness can be reconcilable with health without my interposition!

      Franklin. I am convinced now of the justness of poor Richard's remark that "Our
              debts and our sins are always greater than we think for."

      Gout.   So it is. You philosophers are sages in your maxims and fools in your
              conduct.

45   **Franklin.** But do you charge among my crimes that I return in a carriage from M.
              Brillon's?

      Gout.   Certainly, for, having been seated all the while, you cannot object the
              fatigue of the day and cannot want therefore the relief of a carriage.

      Franklin. What then would you have me do with my carriage?

50   **Gout.**   Burn it if you choose, you would at least get heat out of it once in this
              way; or, if you dislike that proposal, here's another for you: observe the
              poor peasants who work in the vineyard and grounds about the villages
              of Passy, Auteuil, Chaillot, etc., you may find every day among these
              deserving creatures four or five old men and women bent and perhaps
55   crippled by weight of years and too long and too great labor. After a most
              fatiguing day these people have to trudge a mile or two to their smoky
              huts. Order your coachman to set them down. This is an act that will be
              good for your soul; and, at the same time, after your visit to the Brillons',
              if you return on foot, that will be good for your body.

60   **Franklin.** Ah! How tiresome you are!

      Gout.   Well, then, to my office, it should not be forgotten that I am your physi-
              cian. There . . .

      Franklin. Oh! Oh!—for Heaven's sake leave me! And I promise faithfully never
              more to play at chess but to take exercise daily and live temperately.

GO ON TO THE NEXT PAGE →

65   **Gout.** I know you too well. You promise fair, but, after a few months of good
health, you will return to your old habits; your fine promises will be
forgotten like the forms of last year's clouds. Let us then finish the
account, and I will go. But I leave you with an assurance of visiting you
again at a proper time and place, for my object is your good, and you are
70   sensible now that I am your *real friend*.

—Benjamin Franklin

16. Which of the following best summarizes the theme of this excerpt?

   (A) A statement on the health of wealthy individuals
   (B) A delineation of the reasons to exercise
   (C) A fanciful discussion between a man and his disease
   (D) A lamentation of a man who is hurting
   (E) A dialogue for a morality play

17. What is the literary process that gives Gout voice?

   (A) Alliteration
   (B) Metaphor
   (C) Allegory
   (D) Personification
   (E) Simile

18. What is the tone of the dialogue?

   (A) Clinical, scientific
   (B) Reasoned, yet humorous
   (C) Formal and structured
   (D) Silly and frivolous
   (E) Objective

19. When Franklin acknowledges the justness of the statement, "Our debts and our sins are always greater than we think for," (lines 41–42) which of the following is he confirming?

   (A) We believe that many of our debts are too great.
   (B) We believe that we should not have any debts.
   (C) We believe that our debts and our sins are always smaller than they turn out to be.
   (D) We believe that committing a sin should not create a debt that we must pay.
   (E) We believe that others do not have to pay as heavily for their sins.

20. What is the best definition for the word "interposition" (line 40)?

   (A) Intercession
   (B) Interdiction
   (C) Involvement
   (D) Absence
   (E) Interview

21. Which of the following is the best characterization of Gout's reaction to Franklin's statement that Gout is sporting with him (line 1)?

   (A) Indignation
   (B) Pleased
   (C) Chastised
   (D) Contrite
   (E) Oblivious

22. From this dialogue, what assumption can be made about what Franklin advocates?

   (A) Walking when in a foreign country
   (B) Helping the poor and less fortunate
   (C) Reasonable and responsible behavior on the part of the individual
   (D) Involvement in the health practices of others
   (E) Limiting time playing games

23. Gout's attitude toward Franklin is best described as

   (A) disgusted
   (B) conciliatory
   (C) superficial
   (D) stern
   (E) pedantic

24. Why does the author elect to express his ideas with a dialogue between Gout and Franklin?

    (A) It allows clarity between Gout's thoughts and Franklin's reaction.
    (B) It makes it easier for Franklin to dispute the misinterpretation of Gout.
    (C) The author's only purpose was to be light-hearted.
    (D) It challenges the reader to take the side of either Gout or Franklin.
    (E) It leaves ambiguity as to the motives of Gout and Franklin.

25. Which of the following statements most accurately characterizes the interests of Franklin?

    (A) He likes walking in the gardens.
    (B) He enjoys being with friends.
    (C) He likes to be outside in the sun.
    (D) He enjoys a sedentary lifestyle.
    (E) He puts his work second to pleasure.

26. What is the meaning of the word "object" (line 47)?

    (A) Feel
    (B) Dispute
    (C) Argue
    (D) Silence
    (E) Save

27. The sentence "You found the charming lady with her lovely children and friends eager to walk with you and entertain you with their agreeable conversation, and what has been your choice?" contains

    I.   A participial phrase
    II. A compound verb in the past tense
    III. An infinitive

    (A) I only
    (B) II only
    (C) III only
    (D) I and III only
    (E) I, II, and III

28. What does the sentence "I cannot immediately answer that question" (line 27) say about Franklin's state of mind?

    (A) He is argumentative.
    (B) He is forgetful.
    (C) He is feeling guilty.
    (D) He is not being serious.
    (E) He is tired of Gout.

29. How does the dialogue reflect the eighteenth century's interest in science?

    (A) The mention of gardens
    (B) Recognition that walking is important exercise
    (C) Use of scientific reasons for medical conditions
    (D) Use of scientific language
    (E) Inclusion of quotations from an important scientific work

30. What is Franklin the author suggesting by Gout's statement, "So it is. You philosophers are sages in your maxims and fools in your conduct." (lines 43–44)?

    (A) Philosophers are ignorant.
    (B) Wise people are infallible.
    (C) People can make wise statements and take unwise actions.
    (D) Intelligent comments aren't always used.
    (E) People can make ill-considered statements.

practice test

QUESTIONS 31–43 REFER TO THE FOLLOWING SELECTION. READ THE PASSAGE CAREFULLY AND THEN CHOOSE THE ANSWERS TO THE QUESTIONS.

From *The Wealth of Nations*

Line
    The discovery of America, and that of a passage to the East Indies by the Cape of Good Hope, are the two greatest and most important events recorded in the history of mankind. Their consequences have already been very great: but, in the short period of between two and three centuries which has elapsed since these discoveries were made,

5   it is impossible that the whole extent of their consequences can have been seen. What benefits or what misfortunes to mankind may hereafter result from those great events, no human wisdom can foresee. By uniting, in some measure, the most distant parts of the world, by enabling them to relieve one another's wants, to increase one another's enjoyments, and to encourage one another's industry, their general tendency

10 would seem to be beneficial.

    In the meantime, one of the principal effects of those discoveries has been to raise the mercantile system to a degree of splendour and glory which it could never otherwise have attained to. It is the object of that system to enrich a great nation rather by trade and manufactures than by the improvement and cultivation of land, rather by

15 the industry of the towns than by that of the country. But, in consequence of those discoveries, the commercial towns of Europe, instead of being the manufacturers and carriers for but a very small part of the world, (that part of Europe which is washed by the Atlantic ocean, and the countries which lie round the Baltic and Mediterranean seas), have now become the manufacturers for the numerous and thriving cultivators

20 of America, and the carriers, and in some respects the manufacturers too, for almost all the different nations of Asia, Africa, and America. Two new worlds have been opened to their industry, each of them much greater and more extensive than the old one, and the market of one of them growing still greater and greater every day.

    The countries which possess the colonies of America, and which trade directly to the

25 East Indies, enjoy, indeed, the whole show and splendour of this great commerce. Other countries, however, notwithstanding all the invidious restraints by which it is meant to exclude them, frequently enjoy a greater share of the real benefit of it. The colonies of Spain and Portugal, for example, give more real encouragement to the industry of other countries than to that of Spain and Portugal. In the single article of

30 linen alone the consumption of those colonies amounts, it is said, but I do not pretend to warrant the quantity, to be more than three million sterling a year. But this great consumption is almost entirely supplied by France, Flanders, Holland, and Germany. Spain and Portugal furnish but a small part of it. The capital which supplies the colonies with this great quantity of linen is annually distributed among, and furnishes

35 a revenue to, the inhabitants of those other countries.

31. The author's tone in the passage is best described as

  (A) objective
  (B) didactic
  (C) pedantic
  (D) persuasive
  (E) reasoned

32. Which of the following best describes the author's attitude toward expansionism?

  (A) Ambivalent
  (B) Sympathetic
  (C) Very positive
  (D) Conservative
  (E) Progressive

33. In the sentence beginning "Other countries, however, notwithstanding all the invidious restraints" (line 26), the best meaning for the word "invidious" is

   (A) ensnaring
   (B) deceptive
   (C) treacherous
   (D) offensive
   (E) invincible

34. This selection is an example of which of the following modes of discourse?

   (A) Narrative
   (B) Description
   (C) Exposition
   (D) Argument
   (E) Persuasion

35. The first sentence in the first paragraph, "The discovery of America, and that of a passage to the East Indies by the Cape of Good Hope, are the two greatest and most important events recorded in the history of mankind," presents the author's view of

   I.   History
   II. Expansionism
   III. Economics

   (A) I only
   (B) II only
   (C) III only
   (D) I and II only
   (E) I, II, and III

36. This passage reads most like which of the following?

   (A) A letter
   (B) A history lesson
   (C) A current events lesson
   (D) A statement of opinion
   (E) An essay supporting expansionism

37. In the first paragraph, the sentence beginning "By uniting, in some measure, the most distant parts of the world" (lines 7–8) contains which of the following elements?

   (A) A gerund phrase
   (B) An infinitive phrase
   (C) A prepositional phrase
   (D) An adverb phrase
   (E) All of the above

38. In the sentence beginning "In the meantime, one of the principal effects of those discoveries" (line 11), the writer employs which of the following rhetorical devices?

   (A) Overstatement
   (B) Hyperbole
   (C) Conceit
   (D) Oversimplification
   (E) Imagery

39. This passage is primarily concerned with the writer's views on the

   (A) benefits of global commerce
   (B) effects of colonialism on America and the East Indies
   (C) effects of global commerce on colonies
   (D) effects of laissez-faire economics
   (E) effects of revenues on imperialist nations

40. According to this passage, what does the writer believe about European expansionism?

   I.   It is impossible to evaluate fully.
   II. It represents exploitation of native populations.
   III. It creates global commerce, which is good for all.
   IV. It enriches countries other than those possessing the colonies.

   (A) I and II only
   (B) I, II, and III only
   (C) II and III only
   (D) II, III, and IV only
   (E) I, III, and IV only

41. In the last paragraph, the writer employs which of the following stylistic devices to support his arguments?

(A) Generalization
(B) Causal relation
(C) Analogy
(D) Anecdote
(E) Example

42. What is the antecedent of "their" in the following independent clause from the first paragraph?

> . . . but, in the short period of between two and three centuries which has elapsed since these discoveries were made, it is impossible that the whole extent of their consequences can have been seen.

(A) The discovery of the Americas and the passage to the East Indies
(B) The short period
(C) These discoveries
(D) Important events
(E) Whole extent

43. Which of the following is the best rephrasing of this sentence from the final paragraph?

> In the single article of linen alone the consumption of those colonies amounts, it is said, but I do not pretend to warrant the quantity, to be more than three million sterling a year.

(A) In the single article of linen alone the consumption of those colonies' amounts, it is said, but I do not pretend to warrant the quantity, to be more than three million sterling a year.
(B) The consumption of those colonies' amounts of linen alone may be more than three million sterling a year, although I cannot warrant the quantity.
(C) Regarding the consumption of linen alone, those colonies' amounts of that article, it is said, to be more than three million sterling a year, but I do not pretend to warrant the quantity.
(D) Not pretending to warrant the quantity, in the single article of linen alone the consumption of those colonies amounts, I have heard said, to be more than three million sterling a year.
(E) In the single article of linen alone the consumption of those colonies amounts being more than three million sterling a year, but I do not confirm that quantity.

QUESTIONS 44–54 REFER TO THE FOLLOWING SELECTION.

> **Directions:** Read the passage carefully and then choose the answers to the questions.

This passage is an excerpt from an article on South American Cichlids.

Line When many people think of fish tanks in the home, they think of tropical, saltwater
fish. And there is no doubt that saltwater fish are some of the most colorful, unusual
creatures on Earth. However, if aquarists simply focus on saltwater fish, they are
missing out on a wonderful world of freshwater tropical fish. In particular, an aquarist
5 looking for lots of action in a tank in addition to lots of color should consider keeping a
tank of either South American or African Cichlids, or perhaps one tank of each. These
wonderful fish are "filled with personality and provide hours of pleasure and relax-
ation to aquarists."[1] But, before one embarks on the wonderful world of cichlids, one
must fully understand the nature of these breathtaking creatures, because to love a
10 creature is to understand a creature.

As graceful as ballet dancers and at times as aggressive as sharks, South American
Cichlids are perhaps the most interesting fish a freshwater aquarist can have. South
American Cichlids are lake fish. More specifically, they are found in the lakes of South
America and Central America. With the exception of South American Cichlids that are
15 considered dwarf fish, most South American Cichlids can grow to sizes of up to a few
feet. In a home aquarium, the fish will grow as much as the tank allows, and a cichlid
may need to be moved to a larger tank in order to avoid stunting its growth. Live
feeding, using feeder goldfish, is often recommended for South American Cichlids, but
aquarists should be aware that live feeding greatly increases the growth rate of these
20 fish. According to Stanley Almira, "live feeding is perhaps the most exciting part of
owning S.A. Cichlids, however, one should be warned of the excessive growth that can
result. One must moderate live feeding to control size and also keep in mind the
aggression live feeding can cause."[2]

As well as keeping size in control, as Almira mentions, live feeding can contribute
25 to the natural aggression seen in many South American Cichlids. In fact, regardless of
feeding habits, the aquarist must be aware of the innate aggressive (or non-aggres-
sive) tendencies of these fish. Reputable dealers of S.A. Cichlids will always let a
buyer know about the level of aggressiveness of the fish they wish to buy. Certain
types of S.A. Cichlids are classified as extremely aggressive, and these types of fish
30 often have problems living in a community tank. The most aggressive of the fish are
Managuense Cichlids (*Parachromis managuensis*) and Red Devil Cichlids (*Amphilophus labiatus*). These two types of S.A. Cichlids are so highly aggressive that even one
Managuense or Red Devil dropped into a tank of less aggressive cichlids will likely
quickly set to work killing every less aggressive fish in the tank. "Could there be more
35 evil fish than these devil fish? They seek to destroy everything in their path and are
best left to the wild,"[3] is the observation made by Gregori Anessi upon completion of
his 10 year study into the aggressive habits of Red Devils and Managuense.

The Managuense, also called the Jaguar Cichlid, originated in Nicaragua—Lake
Managua, specifically. It is gold with black markings and hints of red and blue in the
40 fins of the adult male. As they mature, Managuenses develop two "canine" type teeth
protruding from their bottom jaw. These teeth are used to tear through the delicate
flesh of other fish. Since a Managuense can grow to up to 2 feet long, fish of all
smaller sizes are in danger of becoming dinner for the great fish. The Managuense is

GO ON TO THE NEXT PAGE

also known as one of the smartest freshwater fish. In fact, for a fish, the eyes display
45   a depth of understanding counter to most people's impressions of fish as unthinking
creatures.

_____

[1] Frieshman, Gene R. *The Amazing Aquatic World of the Cichlid.* (New York: Brown and Brown, Inc., 2001), p. 305.
[2] Almira, Stanley. *Feeding and Caring for Your South American Cichlids.* (Philadelphia: Creatures of the Sea Publishing Co. 1999), Chapter 11, "Live Feeding and Its Ties to Growth/Aggression," p. 311.
[3] Anessi, Gregori. *The Managuense, Brains, Brawn, and a Killer Instinct in* Parachromis managuensis *and* Amphilophus labiatus. (California: Aquarists Press, 1961), p. 111

44. What best describes this passage?

(A) A passionate plea for increased ownership of South American Cichlids
(B) A dire warning of the danger presented by Managuense and Red Devil Cichlids
(C) An informative guide to the caring and feeding of tropical saltwater fish
(D) An instructive article for choosing and raising South American Cichlids
(E) A presentation of statistics about South American Cichlids

45. Which of the following rhetorical devices is used in the following sentence?

"Could there be more evil fish than these devil fish?"

(A) Parody
(B) Rhetorical question
(C) Emotive language
(D) Hyperbole
(E) Anecdote

46. What is the meaning of the word "innate" as used in line 26?

(A) Natural
(B) Ungrateful
(C) Learned
(D) Extraordinary
(E) Strange

47. Which of the following is an accurate reading of the information in footnote 2?

(A) Stanley Almira wrote a book called "Live Feeding and Its Ties to Growth/Aggression."
(B) Stanley Almira is the editor of "Feeding and Caring for Your South American Cichlids."
(C) Creatures of the Sea Publishing published "Feeding and Caring for Your South American Cichlids" in 1999.
(D) Chapter 11 of "Feeding and Caring for Your South American Cichlids" begins on page 311.
(E) Stanley Almira wrote his book in Philadelphia in 1999.

48. What word best describes the attitude of the author toward South American Cichlids?

(A) Condescending
(B) Indifferent
(C) Fearful
(D) Reproachful
(E) Fondness

49. What is true about the footnotes as a whole?

(A) They are all provided to show how the author researched the article.
(B) They are all cited as sources of direct quotes in the article.
(C) They are used to help promote the books written by Frieshman, Almira, and Anessi.
(D) None of the above
(E) All of the above

50. Based on the information in the last paragraph, what is the most likely reason that the Managuense is called a Jaguar Cichlid?

  (A) Because it has many teeth
  (B) Because it has blue and red markings
  (C) Because it is aggressive
  (D) Because it is gold with black markings
  (E) Because it is the smallest cichlid

51. The phrase "to love a creature is to understand a creature" in lines 9–10 is an example of

  (A) Parallel construction
  (B) Onomatopoeia
  (C) Alliteration
  (D) Personification
  (E) Analogy

52. Which book was written by Gene R. Frieshman?

  (A) *The Managuense, Brains, Brawn, and a Killer Instinct in* Parachromis managuensis *and* Amphilophus labiatus
  (B) *Feeding and Caring for Your South American Cichlids*
  (C) *The Amazing Aquatic World of the Cichlid*
  (D) *Creatures of the Sea*
  (E) *Live Feeding and Its Ties to Growth/Aggression*

53. What word would Gregori Anessi most likely use to describe Red Devils and Managuenses?

  (A) Remarkable
  (B) Placid
  (C) Incorrigible
  (D) Moral
  (E) Malevolent

54. What word is closest to the meaning of the word "great" in the sentence "Since a Managuense can grow to up to 2 feet long, fish of all smaller sizes are in danger of becoming dinner for the great fish."

  (A) Wonderful
  (B) Huge
  (C) Famous
  (D) Magnificent
  (E) Heroic

S T O P If you finish before time is called, you may check your work on this section only. Do not turn to any other section in the test.

SECTION II

3 QUESTIONS • 2 HOURS 15 MINUTES

Directions: Read the passage below carefully. Write a well-developed essay analyzing how the author uses rhetoric and style to engage the reader. Pay special attention to such elements as diction, tone, style, and narrative pace.

Question 1

SUGGESTED TIME—40 MINUTES

Line   The Publishers of the Standard Novels, in selecting *Frankenstein* for one of their
series, expressed a wish that I should furnish them with some account of the origin of
the story. I am the more willing to comply, because I shall thus give a general answer
to the question, so very frequently asked me: "How I, then a young girl, came to think
5   of, and to dilate upon, so very hideous an idea?" It is true that I am very averse to
bringing myself forward in print; but as my account will only appear as an appendage
to a former production, and as it will be confined to such topics as have connection
with my authorship alone, I can scarcely accuse myself of a personal intrusion. . . .
        I busied myself *to think of a story,* a story to rival those which had excited us to this
10   task. One which would speak to the mysterious fears of our nature and awaken
thrilling horror—one to make the reader dread to look round, to curdle the blood, and
quicken the beatings of the heart. If I did not accomplish these things, my ghost story
would be unworthy of its name. I thought and pondered—vainly. I felt that blank
incapability of invention, which is the greatest misery of authorship, when dull
15   Nothing replies to our anxious invocations. *Have you thought of a story?* I was asked
each morning, and each morning I was forced to reply with a mortifying negative. . . .
        Many and long were the conversations between Lord Byron and Shelley, to which I
was a devout but nearly silent listener. During one of these, various philosophical
doctrines were discussed, and among others the nature of the principle of life and
20   whether there was any probability of its ever being discovered and communicated. . . .
Perhaps a corpse would be reanimated: galvanism had given token such things.
Perhaps the component parts of a creature might be manufactured, brought together,
and endured with vital warmth.
        Night waned upon this talk, and even the witching hour had gone by, before we
25   retired to rest. When I placed my head on my pillow, I did not sleep, nor could I be
said to think. My imagination, unbidden, possessed and guided me, gifting the succes-
sive images that arose in my mind with a vividness far beyond the usual bounds of
reverie. I saw—with shut eyes but acute mental vision—I saw the pale student of
unhallowed arts kneeling beside the thing he had put together. I saw the hideous
30   phantasm of a man stretched out, and then, on the working of some powerful engine,
show signs of life and stir with an uneasy, half vital motion. Frightful must it be, for
supremely frightful would be the effect of any human endeavor to mock the stupen-
dous mechanism of the Creator of the world. His success would terrify the artist; he
would rush away from his odious handiwork, horror-stricken he would hope that, left
35   to itself, the slight spark of life that he had communicated would fade; that this thing,
which had received such imperfect animation, would subside into dead matter; and he
might sleep in the belief that the silence of the grave would quench forever the
transient existence of the hideous corpse that he had looked upon as the cradle of life.
He sleeps; but he is awakened; he opens his eyes; behold the horrid thing stands at

40   his bedside, opening his curtains, and looking on him with yellow, watery, but
speculative eyes.

    I opened mine in terror. The idea so possessed my mind, that a thrill of fear ran
through me, and I wished to exchange the ghastly image of my fancy for the realities
around. I see them still: the very room, the dark parquet, the closed shutters, with the

45   moonlight struggling through, and the sense I had that the glassy lake and white high
Alps were beyond. I could not so easy get rid of my hideous phantom: still it haunted
me. I must try to think of something else. I recurred to my ghost story—my tiresome
unlucky ghost story! O! if I could only contrive one that would frighten my reader as I
myself had been frightened that night!

50   Swift as light and as cheering was the idea that broke in upon me. "I have found it!
What terrified me will terrify others, and I need only describe the specter that
haunted my midnight pillow." On the morrow I announced that I had *thought of a
story.* I began that day with the words, *It was on a dreary night of November,* making
only a transcript of the grim terrors of my waking dream.

—Mary Shelley

Directions: Read carefully this passage from Ralph Waldo Emerson's speech, "The American Scholar," given as the Phi Beta Kappa address at Harvard in 1837. Write a well-organized, well-reasoned essay that critically analyzes how Emerson used the English language and conventions to promote his ideas.

Question 2

SUGGESTED TIME—40 MINUTES

Line   The theory of books is noble. The scholar of the first age received into him the world around: brooded thereon; gave it a new arrangement of his own mind, and uttered it again. . . . It can stand, and it can go. It now endures, it now flies, it now inspires. Precisely in proportion to the depth of mind from which it issued, so high does it soar,
5   so long does it sing.

Or, I might say, it depends on how far the process had gone, of transmuting life into truth. In proportion to the completeness of the distillation, so will the purity and imperishableness of the product be. But none is quite perfect. . . . Each age, it is found, must write its own books; or rather, each generation for the next succeeding.
10   The books of an older period will not fit this.

Yet hence arises a grave mischief. The sacredness which attaches to the act of creation, the act of thought, is instantly transferred to the record. The poet chanting, was felt to be a divine man. Henceforth the chant is divine also. The writer was a just and wise spirit. Henceforward it is settled, the book is perfect; as love of the hero
15   corrupts into worship of his statue. Instantly, the book becomes noxious. The guide is a tyrant. . . . The sluggish and perverted mind of the multitude, always slow to open to the incursions of Reason, having once so opened, having once received this book, stands upon it, and makes an outcry, if it disparaged. Colleges are built on it. Books are written on it by thinkers, not by Man Thinking; by men of talent, that is, who
20   start wrong, who set out from accepted dogmas, not from their own sight of principles. Meek young men grow up in libraries, believing it their duty to accept the views which Cicero, which Locke, which Bacon, have given, forgetful that Cicero, Locke and Bacon were only young men in libraries when they wrote these books.

Hence, instead of man thinking, we have the book worm. . . .

Books are the best of things, well used; abused, among the worst.

—Ralph Waldo Emerson

Directions: The following prompt is based on the following six sources. The assignment requires that you synthesize a number of the sources into a coherent, well-written essay that takes a position. Use at least three of the sources to support your position. Do not simply paraphrase or summarize the sources. Your argument should be the focus of your essay and the sources should support this argument. Remember to attribute both direct and indirect citations.

Question 3

SUGGESTED TIME—15 MINUTES FOR READING AND 40 MINUTES FOR WRITING

Introduction: In recent years, government censorship of content delivered over public airwaves has become an issue. Satellite radio delivers content to listeners who are paid subscribers. Because satellite radio is a paid service, it is not regulated by government. Traditional radio (terrestrial radio) is subject to censorship. Because of its ability to deliver uncensored content, might satellite radio eventually replace terrestrial radio?

Assignment: Read the following sources (including any introductory information) carefully. **Then, write an essay that supports, qualifies, or disputes the argument that satellite radio will replace terrestrial radio because of government censorship. Synthesize at least three of the sources to support your position.**

You may refer to the sources by their titles (Source A, Source B, etc.) or by the descriptions in parentheses.

Source A (Allsworth)

Source B (Jones and Brooks)

Source C (Gates)

Source D (McDonald)

Source E (Chart)

Source F (Lopez)

SOURCE A
Allsworth, Elissa. "New Gadgets," *Pastimes Magazine Monthly,* May 22, 2001

The following passage is excerpted from an article that talks about satellite radio as a new option for radio listening.

The communications industry is buzzing about a new product that some say may revolutionize the way people listen to the radio. That product is satellite radio. Unlike traditional radio, which works by broadcasting content over local frequencies, satellite radio content is delivered via satellite. Satellite radio has an advantage over traditional radio in that you could drive across the country and never have to change your radio station! You could pick up the same station, at the same number on your dial, in Massachusetts and in Alaska! For anyone who takes long car trips, this is a wonderful product.

In addition to the technical differences between satellite and traditional radio, there are significant content differences. Because satellite radio is delivered to paid subscribers, there is a lot of freedom in the content offered. For example, music stations can devote themselves to one very specific type of music, such as a station that plays only Elvis tunes. Because satellite radio is a paid service, commercials are not needed, so listeners can also receive commercial-free radio. In addition, those who do not agree with government censorship of music can listen to uncensored music and talk radio via satellite radio. Radio hosts who have been fired in recent years due to questionable content may find new homes on satellite radio.

SOURCE B

Jones, Janna, and Dana Brooks. "DJ Extreme Takes His Show on the Road" Available at http://talkradiomagazine.com, August 2003

The following passage is excerpted from an online article about a DJ who was fired from traditional radio and began a new show on satellite radio.

Fans of DJ Extreme were extremely disappointed last year when the popular afternoon DJ was fired from his job at WWCB radio for "a questionable bit" on his show. The bit caused the station to have to pay almost a million dollars in fines to the government for airing content that is against regulations. Says a station employee who asked not to be named, "DJ Extreme was warned numerous times about his on-air behavior, and he continued to try to push it as far as he could go. Due to this, his tenure with this radio station, and possibly his radio career, is over."

And for a while, it looked like the career of DJ Extreme was, indeed, over. After an initial flurry of talk show appearances following his ouster from the station, the DJ appeared to disappear. But last month, with almost no fanfare, he was back—but this time, on satellite radio. The lack of fanfare did not last long, though, as word spread that DJ Extreme was on the airwaves once again. And in the two weeks that followed his debut, sales of his brand of satellite radio increased by 1 million subscriptions. That's right—1 million! And according to the satellite company, the subscription numbers continue to grow. Maybe firing DJ Extreme was not such a good idea after all, because at least 1 million people have made the switch to satellite radio, possibly leaving their traditional radios in the dust.

GO ON TO THE NEXT PAGE

SOURCE C

Gates, Juan. "Terrestrial Radio Is Not Dead" *Radio Weekly,* February 15, 2005.

The following passage is excerpted from an article that refutes the idea that satellite radio will replace terrestrial radio.

Satellite radio seems to be the new fad. That's right, I said fad. Sure, it's a new product and seems to offer some exciting broadcasting possibilities, but there is a catch—you have to *pay* for this great content. And some people will pay for satellite radio; many already have. It's a neat alternative to radio, as long as you want to pay for it. It seems silly to pay for radio, since it is available for free across the nation. Sure, you have to listen to commercials, and sometimes your favorite song is censored, but is that really a problem? Who would disagree with not allowing foul language on public airwaves? It seems strange that people would get so hung up on such a small amount of censorship.

Satellite radio providers would like you to believe that soon satellite will be your only option because terrestrial radio will become a thing of the past. Please! In the few years that satellite radio has been available, there have been large numbers of initial subscribers. But what the satellite companies don't want you to know is that a high percentage of subscribers do not renew their subscriptions because they do not want to pay for them. In addition, of all people who have won satellite receivers and free one-year subscriptions in nationwide contests, almost 60 percent do not renew their subscription after their free year is up. This says that although many people may enjoy the content, when it comes down to it, they don't want to pay for it. And for this reason, traditional radio will never die. And I predict that as the years go by, more and more people will come to their senses and stop paying for something you can get for free.

> **SOURCE D**
>
> McDonald, Aurora. "We Are Hiding from the Issue" *Issues Digest,* April 2006

The following passage is excerpted from a letter to the editor of Issues Digest *about the necessity of censorship in some cases.*

Satellite radio versus terrestrial radio seems to be an ongoing theme in the communications industry lately. Will satellite replace terrestrial radio? Should we let that happen? I don't think so. The battle between satellite and terrestrial radio has become a broad battle about supposedly "free speech." Proponents of uncensored free radio seem to think that regulating the airwaves is a free speech issue. And while it is true that free speech is protected, not *all* speech is protected. It is not legal to slander someone. It is not legal to yell "fire!" in a crowded theater, and everyone seems to agree with these regulations. But when it comes to bleeping out a dirty word on public air, some people get all up in arms.

We are hiding from the issue that censorship is simply necessary in some cases. The advent of satellite radio is simply clouding the issue. It should not even come up in censorship discussions. People pay for satellite radio. If they do not like the content, they can stop paying. Now, some may tell you that if you don't like the content on a public radio station, you should simply change the station. But these people perhaps have never been riding in a van full of children and been a bit to slow to change the station before a chorus of "what does that mean," or "ohhh, she said a bad word" fills the car. Yes, one can simply change the station. However, isn't it nice that the government makes it possible that we don't have to? The issue is our children being protected from unsuitable content. While parents of course share in this responsibility, it is wonderful to know that there is a government agency on our side.

SOURCE E

Adapted from *Satellite Versus Terrestrial: Who Listens to What*. Illinois: The Research Group, 2006

Satellite Radio vs. Terrestrial Radio: Numbers for all four quarters of 2005. Numbers are percentages of people who listen to terrestrial radio, satellite radio, or both. 19,000 people responded to the poll.

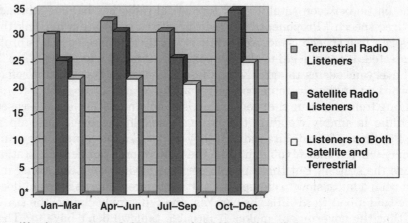

*Numbers represent 0–35 percent of 19,000 people polled.

practice test

> **SOURCE F**
>
> Lopez, Angelo. "The Radio Renaissance" *The Past Magazine,* October 1, 2004

The following passage is excerpted from an article about how satellite radio programming is bringing more people to radio.

The best thing that could happen to radio happened: the advent of satellite radio. Satellite radio has saved a dying medium. Who listens to the radio for anything but music, anymore? Sure, there are some successful talk stations, but not too many, and there is a lack of variety at that. The golden days of radio, where a family might gather around the living room to listen to a show, seemed to be over, completely replaced by television. And then, television seemed to be replaced by video games, excluding adults altogether. This is the direction family entertainment has taken, I often thought to myself.

But then, something amazing happened. My son won a satellite radio receiver and subscription a few months ago. I have to admit I was at first worried about the kind of content he would find, and the fact that the content is not regulated did give me pause. But I trusted my son, and I turned out to be right. After playing with the radio for a few weeks, he discovered a wonderful station that replays old radio shows from the 1930s. Who would think a 13-year-old would be interested in old radio shows? It turns out, my son is. And better yet, he got his little sister interested as well. Now, every Wednesday, our whole family gathers around the radio to listen to a radio show! Not the TV, the radio! It has been a wonderful experience. TV and video games have not been replaced, but, somehow, more family time has been added to our week due to the radio show. It is nice to know that my family is spending the kind of time together that my parents and grandparents did.

S T O P If you finish before time is called, you may check your work on this section only. Do not turn to any other section in the test.

ANSWER KEY AND EXPLANATIONS

Section I

1. B	12. A	23. D	34. E	45. B
2. D	13. B	24. A	35. A	46. A
3. B	14. E	25. D	36. E	47. C
4. C	15. B	26. C	37. E	48. E
5. A	16. C	27. C	38. A	49. B
6. B	17. D	28. C	39. A	50. D
7. B	18. B	29. C	40. E	51. A
8. A	19. C	30. C	41. E	52. C
9. C	20. B	31. D	42. C	53. E
10. B	21. A	32. C	43. B	54. B
11. D	22. C	33. D	44. D	

1. **The correct answer is (B).** The context is that the New England group was beginning to fall apart. As poets, this means that they were beginning to lose their creativity. Although choices (A), (C), (D), and (E) may express some of the feelings and experiences of the New England group, none addresses the core problem of these poets in the manner that choice (B) does.

2. **The correct answer is (D).** This selection is not descriptive, so the mode cannot be description, choice (A). It does not attempt to argue or persuade, so it cannot be persuasive, choice (C), or argumentative, choice (E), writing. Nor does it tell a story; therefore, it is not a narrative, choice (B). It simply presents the facts—exposition, choice (D).

3. **The correct answer is (B).** The sentence cited contains the statement, "a reflection of actuality, 'an extension of experience.'" Choice (B) closely matches that thought. There is no development of an existential subject, choice (A). Modern poetry is not defined, choice (C). Choices (D) and (E) are similarly not discussed in the excerpt.

4. **The correct answer is (C).** All of these statements are true. The trick here is to figure out which gives the author's main idea. The writer is discussing the beginning of modern American writing. That is what choice (C) is presenting. The other choices, (A), (B), (D), and (E), are facts that support and illuminate the writer's thesis.

5. **The correct answer is (A).** The correct answer is developed in the first paragraph with the observation that the Civil War marked the start of modern poetry. In the second paragraph, a link is shown between the close of the Civil War and the decline of the New England group, also known as the Brahmins. Religious freedom and politics, choice (B), were never shown to be an issue. Political nationalism, industrial growth, and philosophical creativity were also never developed as an influence on the Brahmins, choices (C), (D), and (E).

6. **The correct answer is (B).** In the second paragraph, Louis Untermeyer states that some of the Brahmins "occupied themselves with translations." *Divina Commedia* is such a translation. This makes choice (B) the correct answer. Choice (A) is true, but incorrect because it is not relevant to the question. Choices (C), (D), and (E) are not related to the question, and the author does not explore them.

7. **The correct answer is (B).** The context of this expression is another way that Untermeyer shows that the creativity of the Brahmins had been lost. In this case, he is saying that the Brahmins were satisfied with the sounds of old music, an allusion to their focus on translations of old writings. The author is not speaking of sounds per se—that eliminates choices (A), (C), and (D). The author is not speaking of philosophical concepts, choice (E).

8. **The correct answer is (A).** This question is from the point of view of the Brahmins, not the author. It probably does not reflect the thoughts of the author. In the third paragraph, Untermeyer writes, "To them [the Brahmins], the new men must have seemed like a regiment recruited from the ranks of vulgarity." This passage is a direct response to the question and is represented by choice (A). Choices (B), (C), (D), and (E) do not express the point of view of the New England poets.

9. **The correct answer is (C).** The passage from the final paragraph is the identification by the author of the change from the Brahmin-influenced era to modern American poetry. This can be most readily seen by Untermeyer's comment that "America developed a national consciousness." Choices (A) and (D) are true but do not reflect the writer's thoughts in this passage. Choices (B) and (E) are neither true nor relevant.

10. **The correct answer is (B).** Although the Brahmins might have been harsh and scathing in their commentary about modern American poets, the passage itself does not have that tone; therefore, choice (A) is incorrect. There is no wit or humor contained in the excerpt, making choice (D) incorrect. The remaining three answers have some elements that may seem to be true. A reader may see the article as dry or even irritating, but not condescending, choice (C), or pretentious, choice (E). Only one of these three answer choices has both elements that are true. Choice (B), scholarly and informative, correctly answers the question.

11. **The correct answer is (D).** The author never made a judgment about which type of poetry was superior, so choice (A) is incorrect. The same can be said of choice (B). The Brahmins were not identified as the creators of modern American poetry, choice (C). The author specifically said that the Civil War produced little quality poetry, eliminating choice (E). The author develops the Civil War as the starting point of modern American poetry in the first two paragraphs, choice (D).

12. **The correct answer is (A).** The author says in the first sentence of the second paragraph "the conflict . . . produced a vast quantity of poems but practically no important poetry." Choice (A) mirrors Untermeyer's commentary. If Untermeyer says that no poetry was produced, that implies that no poets were produced, so choice (B) cannot be correct. Choices (C), (D), and (E) do not accurately reflect this passage.

13. **The correct answer is (B).** The sentence taken from the end of the concluding paragraph is a reference to the Brahmins' attempt to keep their style of poetry the dominant form. Untermeyer does not suggest that the poets of transition were deliberate in the execution of their art as indicated in choice (A). The author proposes that the poets of transition resisted the change; therefore, they were aware of it, making choice (C) incorrect. The author states neither of the meanings described in choices (D) and (E).

14. **The correct answer is (E).** In the third sentence of the final paragraph, Untermeyer identifies the new poetic expression as "crude, jangling, vigorously democratic." Choice (E) repeats the description as crude, and it relies on the reader to recognize that a democratic form of poetry is cutting edge. The descriptions of the poets in choices (A), (B), (C), and (D) are not consistent with the description or even mentioned by the author.

15. **The correct answer is (B).** Untermeyer describes the Brahmins as educated, but he does not contend that they are mercurial, choice (A). The author leaves the reader with the impression that the Brahmins are anything but lighthearted or easygoing, choices (C) and (D). They are portrayed as brilliant but not forgiving; thus, choice (E) is incorrect. This leaves (B) as the correct answer. Untermeyer does give the impression that the Brahmins were stuffy and intransigent.

16. **The correct answer is (C).** Each of the choices has a small element of correctness. The characters do make comments about health, choice (A), and some discussion about exercise takes place, choice (B). Franklin does mention the pain of the gout attack, choice (D). Dialogue occurs, although not suited for a morality play, choice (E). However, because the question asks for the theme of the passage, only choice (C) is correct.

17. **The correct answer is (D).** An alliteration is the repetition of initial consonant sound, choice (A). A metaphor is a figure of speech in which one thing is spoken of as though it were something else, choice (B). An allegory is a literary work with two or more levels of meaning; one of which is literal and others symbolic, choice (C). A simile is a figure of speech that compares two unlike things by using words such as *like* or *as,* choice (E). None of these applies to the selection. Allowing the disease to speak is personification, the giving of human characteristics to nonhuman things, choice (D).

18. **The correct answer is (B).** Choices (A), (C), and (E), but not choice (D), seem reasonable. However, only choice (B) includes both elements of the tone—the humor and the reasoned presentation of the medical information given.

19. **The correct answer is (C).** Franklin is lamenting the thought that people's debts and sins are always greater than people imagine them to be. Choice (A) restates part of the maxim, while choices (B), (D), and (E) are not accurate restatements.

20. **The correct answer is (B).** If you did not know what *interposition* means, you could try your knowledge of prefixes to determine that it means to be placed between; it's the noun form of the verb *interpose.* Choice (A) means an intervention between parties with a view to reconciling differences; this does not fit Gout's role in the piece. Choice (B) means the act of prohibiting or restraining someone from doing something; it is much stronger than choice (C), involvement. Gout is very much in evidence, so choice (D), absence, is illogical. Based on the context—Gout has just recited a list of Franklin's transgressions—choice (E), interview, seems too mild a meaning. Choice (B) is the strongest word and seems to best match Gout's tone.

21. **The correct answer is (A).** (The character of Gout is female in the dialogue.) Gout states that she is very serious and she can justify every action (lines 2–3). She is indignant, or righteously angry, choice (A), and is not pleased, choice (B), or feeling chastised, choice (C), or contrite, choice (D). Gout certainly is not oblivious, choice (E), but very concerned about Franklin's health.

22. **The correct answer is (C).** On the surface, all these choices seem correct because each is mentioned in the selection. However, choices (A), (B), (D), and (E) are specific details of Franklin's point that reasonable and responsible behavior cures the gout, choice (C).

23. **The correct answer is (D).** The challenge of determining the correct answer is between choices (D) and (E) because the other choices do not express the tone of Gout's comments. If Gout were disgusted, choice (A), she would not bother trying to reason with Franklin. There is no conciliation in her tone, choice (B), nor are her arguments superficial, choice (C). Gout is not dealing with trivial ideas in a narrow bookish manner, so choice (D) is the correct description.

24. **The correct answer is (A).** Choice (B) is incorrect because Gout is not misinterpreting Franklin the character's actions; Franklin agrees with Gout. The topic is serious—Franklin the character agrees with Gout—so Franklin the author's purpose is more than to write some lighthearted prose, choice (C). The theme is developed in such a way as to make Gout's argument more persuasive, thus eliminating choice (D) as untrue. Choice (E) is inaccurate because the motives are clearly developed. Choice (A) is the best answer in that the use of dialogue permits Franklin the writer to focus on Gout's comments and easily refute Franklin the character's defense.

25. **The correct answer is (D).** The key here is to notice that the word *interests* is plural. Franklin does enjoy being with friends, choice (B), but that is only one interest. He says he likes walking in the gardens, choice (A), but does not act as if he does. There is no information in the selection to support choice (C). Knowing Franklin as a historical figure would help you see that choice (E) is incorrect. Therefore, the statement that best characterizes what we do know about Franklin from the selection is that he enjoys those interests that do not require him to do anything more than sit, choice (D).

26. **The correct answer is (C).** First, read the sentence. While *object* may be a noun or a verb, it is used as a verb in this sentence. The answer choices are either verbs or may be used as verbs (*dispute* and *silence*), so you can't eliminate any choices immediately. Next, substitute each answer choice in the sentence to see which best fits the context. If you realize the sentence means that Franklin cannot use the fatigue of the day as an excuse (argument) for needing a carriage, choice (C) is clearly the answer. While *object* can mean *dispute,* choice (B), it does not have that meaning in this passage. Choices (A), (D), and (E) make little or no sense in context.

27. **The correct answer is (C).** First, you need to determine which points are true about the sentence. The sentence has neither a participial phrase (I) nor a compound verb in the past tense, so points I and II are incorrect. There is an infinitive (III). Then determine which answer choice has only III—choice (C).

28. **The correct answer is (C).** Franklin will not answer because he knows he did not follow his own advice. At this point in the dialogue, he is not arguing with Gout nor is there any sign that he has tired of the conversation, so choices (A) and (E) are incorrect. Franklin has not shown himself to be forgetful, thus eliminating choice (B). While the tone of the passage is amusing, the Franklin of the dialogue is serious, thus eliminating choice (D).

29. **The correct answer is (C).** Use of scientific reasoning, rather than superstitions or religious beliefs, for medical conditions was a discovery of the eighteenth century. Neither choice (D) nor choice (E) is true of the selection. Choice (A) is irrelevant, and although choice (B) is true, choice (C) is a better overall statement.

30. **The correct answer is (C).** The statement in question contrasts two sets of circumstances. The correct answer must then have two sets of answers as well. Only choice (C) fulfills the requirement (sages/fools; wise statements/unwise actions). Choices (A), (B), (D), and (E) all deal with single concepts.

31. **The correct answer is (D).** The passage is not objective, but strongly one-sided, so choice (A) is incorrect. The author is not attempting to teach you about his position; therefore, choices (B) and (C) are incorrect. The passage is reasoned, but the writer presents his arguments to convince the reader of his position. This makes the better choice (D) rather than choice (E).

32. **The correct answer is (C).** A review of the first sentence of the last paragraph of the passage contains the phrase "the whole show and splendour of this great commerce." The wording clearly indicates that the author is "very positive," choice (C), about commerce and expansionism. The essay's purpose is to persuade you of the greatness of expansionism. Choice (B) has the right sentiment but is not strong enough. Choice (A) is contrary to the tone of the selection, as is choice (D). Choice (E) is a distracter.

33. **The correct answer is (D).** The word *invidious* means "to create ill will or envy" or "to give offense." If you did not know that, you could use the context to realize that choice (E) makes no sense. While the author is obviously expressing the opinion that the restraints are negative, he does not imply that they are entrapping, deceitful, or untrustworthy, choices (A), (B) and (C), respectively.

34. **The correct answer is (E).** This question is similar to, but not the same as, question 31. The author is not relating a story, so choice (A) is incorrect. He is not merely describing an event or place, so choice (B) is incorrect. Choice (C) is incorrect because the author is not simply explaining a topic. Argument, choice (D), is writing that attempts to prove a point with a well-reasoned discussion. The writer of this passage is doing more than that; he is attempting to persuade the reader to accept his position, choice (E).

35. **The correct answer is (A).** The opening sentence of the first paragraph identifies what the writer believes to be the most important events in history (I). The sentence does not mention expansionism (II) or economics (III), so choices (B), (C), (D), and (E) are incorrect. The only answer that identifies only the element of history is choice (A).

36. **The correct answer is (E).** With no salutation, direct address, or closing, the selection gives no evidence of correspondence, eliminating choice (A). Since the selection discusses history, choice (C) is unlikely. Choices (B), (D), and (E) all apply to the passage, but the correct answer is the most precise, choice (E).

37. **The correct answer is (E).** You could determine the answer to this question even if you could not remember what all the grammatical terms mean. Once you recognized two of the grammatical elements, perhaps an infinitive, choice (B), and a prepositional phrase, choice (C), you know that the answer must be choice (E), since only choice (E) allows for multiple answers.

38. **The correct answer is (A).** Although you may not recognize overstatement, choice (A), as a rhetorical device, you could establish that it is the correct answer through the process of elimination. Choice (B) may seem to apply, but hyperbole is not intended to be taken literally, so choice (B) cannot be correct. Likewise, a conceit may seem to be correct, but it is an analogy and there is none in the sentence, thus making choice (C) incorrect. The sentence certainly is not an oversimplification nor is there any imagery, so choices (D) and (E) do not apply.

39. **The correct answer is (A).** At first glance, all the choices may seem to pertain to the passage, so you must decide which most accurately applies to the entire essay. The passage deals more with the effects of the colonial production than the effects of colonialism on the colonies, so choices (B) and (C) are not the best alternatives. Choices (D) and (E) are distracters.

40. **The correct answer is (E).** The passage does not recognize the exploitation involved in colonization (II), so any answer that includes II should be eliminated—choices (A), (B), (C), and (D).

41. **The correct answer is (E).** The writer uses the example of linen production to support his point, making choice (E) correct. The use of examples to support his argument makes the piece specific, so choice (A) is incorrect. There is no comparison or story, eliminating choices (C) and (D). You might have thought that the writer employs causal relation by arguing that expansionism results in economic wealth for noncolonial nations, choice (B), but that is an organizational technique, not a method of support.

42. **The correct answer is (C).** An antecedent is the noun or noun phrase to which a pronoun refers. Only choices (A) and (C) make sense in the context of the clause. You need to pick the alternative that exactly reflects the words of the sentence, which would eliminate choice (A). The other possibilities, choices (B), (D), and (E), are distracters.

43. **The correct answer is (B).** Choice (A) corrects the possessive, *colonies',* but otherwise is identical to the convoluted original. Choice (C) moves one clause but does little else to clarify the sentence's meaning. Choice (D) is grammatically incorrect. Choice (E) is a lengthy but incomplete sentence.

44. **The correct answer is (D).** To answer this question correctly, you must select the answer choice that provides the best summary or description of the contents of the passage. Choice (A) is incorrect; the author states that people should consider owning South American Cichlids, but does not make a passionate plea to increase ownership. The author does include warnings about the aggressive nature of Managuenses and Red Devils, choice (B), but this is not the central focus of the passage. Choice (C) is incorrect because the article is about South American Cichlids, not saltwater fish. Choice (E) is incorrect because the article presents almost no statistical information. This leaves choice (D), which is the best answer among the choices given.

45. **The correct answer is (B).** This sentence is an example of rhetorical question, that is, a question that does not require an answer but is asked to make a point. Choice (A) is incorrect, because a parody is a humorous imitation. Choice (C) is also incorrect. The sentence does not contain emotive language. The sentence does not use exaggeration to make a point, so choice (D) is incorrect. An anecdote is a story told to illustrate a point, so you can eliminate choice (E).

46. **The correct answer is (A).** The word "innate" is found in the sentence "In fact, regardless of feeding habits, the aquarist must be aware of the innate aggressive (or nonaggressive) tendencies of these fish." Use context clues to help you determine the answer. Choice (A), natural, is correct. The sentence speaks about the aggressive tendencies of fish *regardless* of feeding habits. This should tip you off that the aggressive tendencies may not be affected by outside stimuli and also rules out choice (C). Choice (B) simply does not make sense. There is no indication from the context that the aggressive tendencies are extraordinary, choice (D). Tendencies are by definition ordinary.

47. **The correct answer is (C).** To answer this question, carefully read footnote 2. The footnote references a book titled "Feeding and Caring for Your South American Cichlids," written by Stanley Almira. You can immediately eliminate choice (A), because it substitutes the chapter title that appears in the reference with the title of the book. Choice (B) is incorrect, because Stanley Almira is the *author,* not the editor. If he were the editor, it would be indicated with "ed." Choice (C) is correct; the title is correct and Creatures of the Sea Publishing is the publisher of the book. Choice (D) is incorrect because the footnote indicates that the quote can be found on page 311 in Chapter 11, but there is no indication that page 311 is the first page of Chapter 11. Choice (E) is incorrect because the footnote indicates that the publisher, Creatures of the Sea, is located in Philadelphia and that the book was published, not written, in 1999.

48.   The correct answer is (E). The author recommends owning South American Cichlids, which he refers to in the first paragraph as "breathtaking creatures." Condescending implies that the author looks down on the fish, and this is untrue, so choice (A) is not correct. The author clearly has strong feelings about South American Cichlids, so you can eliminate choice (B). The author does not express fear, so choice (C) is incorrect. Finally, choice (D) is incorrect, because the author does not disapprove of the fish.

49.   The correct answer is (B). To answer this question, locate the footnote references in the passage. The footnotes that are included in the article all relate directly to quotes used in the article, so choice (B) is correct. It is reasonable to assume that the author used the books for research because the author quotes the books. However, the footnotes are not included to show research but as sources for quotes.

50.   The correct answer is (D). To answer this question correctly, it is helpful to know what a jaguar looks like, but not necessary. A jaguar is gold with black spots, so choice (D) is correct. The paragraph states that the fish is "gold with black markings." Remember that you are looking for the *most likely* answer. Choice (A) is incorrect, because the passage states that Managuense have two teeth, not many teeth. Even if you are not sure of the markings of a jaguar, it is reasonable to assume that a big cat is not blue and red, so eliminate choice (B). The fish is aggressive, choice (C), and jaguars may be aggressive, but this is a general description and would not be the *best* answer among the choices. Choice (E) is simply untrue. There is nothing in the passage to suggest that the Managuense is the smallest cichlid.

51.   The correct answer is (A). Parallel construction is when similar words or phrases are kept in the same form, in order to show a similar relationship between two or more things. In this case, parallel construction is the repetition of verb phrases using "to:" "*to* love . . . is *to* understand . . ." Onomatopoeia, choice (B), occurs when a word is used to represent a sound, so eliminate choice (B). Alliteration is a literary device in which words in a phrase all begin with the same letter, such as All Around An Alligator. That is not evident, so eliminate choice (C). Personification, choice (D), is the attribution of human characteristics to animals or inanimate objects, so discard that answer. An analogy, choice (E), draws a comparison, and does not make sense as an answer to this question.

52.   The correct answer is (C). Choice (A) is the title of the book written by Gregori Anessi. Choice (B) is the book written by Stanley Almira. Choice (D) is the name of one of the publishing companies mentioned in the footnotes. Choice (E) is a chapter title, not a book title.

53.   The correct answer is (E). Anessi describes Managuenses and Red Devils as evil, so look for a synonym for evil among the answer choices. Choice (E), malevolent, fits and is the correct answer. Remarkable, choice (A), has a positive connotation and is incorrect. The fish are aggressive, not placid, so choice (B) is incorrect. Incorrigible, choice (C), is incorrect. There is no evidence the fish are unmanageable. Morality is not a characteristic that is applied to fish, so choice (D) is incorrect.

54.   The correct answer is (B). In this sentence, "great" is used to mean huge or large. You can determine this from the context of the sentence, which mentions that the fish can grow to be up to two feet long and smaller fish are in danger of being "dinner" for the Managuense. The words in the other answer choices are all synonyms for "great," but none fits in the context of the sentence.

Section II

SUGGESTIONS FOR QUESTION 1

You might have chosen the following points to include in your essay on Mary Shelley's *Introduction to Frankenstein*. Consider them as you complete your self-evaluation. Revise your essay using points from the list to strengthen it.

Form or Mode

- Prose; an introduction to the third edition of *Frankenstein*

- Narrative

Theme

- Origins of the horror novel

- Aspects of writing a horror novel

Characters/Individuals

- Mary Shelley, the speaker

- Percy Bysshe Shelley

- Lord Byron

- Audience, readers of the novel

Conflict/Issue/Challenge

- Challenge from without: to write a horror story equal to those previously written

- Challenge from within: to think of a story

Content/Important Points

- Challenge among friends

- Inspired by conversations with Byron and Shelley

- Vivid dreams

- Gothic tradition

- Dangers of technology/science in the wrong hands

Development

- Chronological

- Slowly builds pace

Literary Conventions

- Point of view: first person

- Setting: Switzerland during a rainy summer; confined to the house

- Tone: emotional, personal, somewhat dark

Diction/Syntax/Style

- Use of both internal and external dialogue

- Vivid language

- Specific details

- Figurative language

- Complex sentence structure

- Chronological development; musical

- Word choice: sophisticated but comprehensible

SUGGESTIONS FOR QUESTION 2

You might have chosen the following points to include in your essay analyzing Emerson's speech on books. Consider them as you complete your self-evaluation. Revise your essay using points from the list to strengthen it.

Form or Mode

- Speech

- Persuasive/argument

Theme

- Books can be the best of things or the worst of things

Conflict/Issue/Challenge

- To overcome rigid reverence of great books

- To prevent transferring of respect for acts of creation (thought) to an imperfect outcome of that thought

Content/Important Points

- Indictment of bookworms

- Greatest thinkers were once students

- Should not worship profound works to the extent that their creators are forgotten

- Respect books in moderation

- Individual thought paramount (an argument misused to deny the importance of the past)

- Write books of own truths

- Undertake own acts of creation

- Implies ideas are not great in and of themselves

Literary Conventions

- Point of view: first person

- Audience: students

- Setting: university campus

- Tone: strident, argumentative

Diction/Syntax/Style

- Sentences fairly short and not extremely complex; straightforward

- Language overstated; "tyrant," "sluggish," "perverted," "Meek men grow up in libraries"

- Use of active and passive voice

- Sentence variety

- Some parallel structure: "Colleges are built on it. Books are written on it . . ."

SUGGESTIONS FOR QUESTION 3

This question asks for a synthesis essay that supports, qualifies, or disputes the argument that satellite radio will replace terrestrial radio because of government censorship. It does not matter which position you take as long as you provide adequate support for your argument using your own opinions along with information from the sources. Consider the following as you complete your self-evaluation. Revise your essay using points from the list to strengthen it if necessary. Remember to proofread your response and make sure your grammar, syntax, and spelling are correct.

Thesis statement/introduction

- Clear definition of the issue—in this case, terrestrial radio being made obsolete by satellite radio

- Clear statement of your position on the issue: statement of the reason you agree or disagree with the statement that satellite radio will replace terrestrial radio because satellite radio does not have to conform to government regulations

Supporting details

- Support is based on your own opinions about the position you take but information in the sources should also be used

- Show a clear connection among the sources you choose to cite

- Sources are seamlessly integrated with appropriate transitions

- At least three of the six sources are used

- Explain the logic of how you arrived at the conclusion you did based on the information provided in the sources

- Acknowledge opposing arguments and refute them

- Attribute both direct and indirect citations

Conclusion

- Includes a restatement of your thesis tied into the supporting evidence you used. (ex: In sum, there can be no other conclusion drawn from the evidence except to say that people will always accept a bit of censorship in exchange for free entertainment.)

- Conclusion neatly sums up your argument.

SELF-EVALUATION RUBRIC FOR THE FREE RESPONSE ESSAYS

	8–9	6–7	5	3–4	1–2	0
Overall Impression	Demonstrates excellent control of the literature and outstanding writing competence; thorough and effective; incisive	Demonstrates good control of the literature and good writing competence; less thorough and incisive than the highest papers	Reveals simplistic thinking and/or immature writing; adequate skills	Incomplete thinking; fails to respond adequately to part or parts of the question; may paraphrase rather than analyze	Unacceptably brief; fails to respond to the question; little clarity	Lacking skill and competence
Understanding of the Text	Excellent understanding of the text; exhibits perception and clarity; original or unique approach; includes apt and specific references	Good understanding of the text; exhibits perception and clarity; includes specific references	Superficial understanding of the text; elements of literature vague, mechanical, overgeneralized	Misreadings and lack of persuasive evidence from the text; meager and unconvincing treatment of literary elements	Serious misreadings and little supporting evidence from the text; erroneous treatment of literary elements	A response with no more than a reference to the literature; blank response, or one completely off the topic
Organization and Development	Meticulously organized and thoroughly developed; coherent and unified	Well organized and developed; coherent and unified	Reasonably organized and developed; mostly coherent and unified	Somewhat organized and developed; some incoherence and lack of unity	Little or no organization and development; incoherent and void of unity	No apparent organization or development; incoherent
Use of Sentences	Effectively varied and engaging; virtually error free	Varied and interesting; a few errors	Adequately varied; some errors	Somewhat varied and marginally interesting; one or more major errors	Little or no variation; dull and uninteresting; some major errors	Numerous major errors
Word Choice	Interesting and effective; virtually error free	Generally interesting and effective; a few errors	Occasionally interesting and effective; several errors	Somewhat dull and ordinary; some errors in diction	Mostly dull and conventional; numerous errors	Numerous major errors; extremely immature
Grammar and Usage	Virtually error free	Occasional minor errors	Several minor errors	Some major errors	Severely flawed; frequent major errors	Extremely flawed

SELF-EVALUATION RUBRIC FOR THE SYNTHESIS ESSAYS

	8–9	6–7	5	3–4	1–2	0
Overall Impression	Demonstrates excellent control of effective writing techniques, sophisticated argumentation, and well integrated synthesis of source information; uses citations convincingly	Demonstrates good control of effective writing techniques; somewhat thorough and incisive; uses citations appropriately	Demonstrates general competence in stating and defending a position; some inconsistencies and weaknesses in argumentation	Demonstrates some skill but lacks understanding of question and sources	Demonstrates little skill in taking a coherent position and defending it or in using sources	Lacks skill and competence
Understanding of the Text	Takes a clear position that defends, challenges, or qualifies the question accurately	Demonstrates a somewhat superficial understanding of the sources	Displays some misreading of the sources or some stretching of information to support the chosen position	Takes a position that may misread or simplify the sources; may present overly simple argument	Misreads sources, or lacks an argument, or summarizes the sources rather than using them to support a position	Position does not accurately reflect the sources; no more than a listing of the sources
Organization and Development	Clearly states a position; uses at least three sources to support that position convincingly and effectively; coherent and unified	Clearly states a position; uses at least three sources to support that position; adequate development of ideas but less convincing; coherent and unified	Generally clearly stated position and links between position and cited sources; some weaknesses in logic; cites three sources	Creates weak connections between argument and cited sources; cites only two sources	Lacks coherent development or organization; cites one or no sources	No apparent organization or development; incoherent; cites no sources
Use of Sentences	Effectively varied and engaging; close to error free	Varied and interesting; a few errors	Adequately varied; some errors	Somewhat varied and marginally interesting; one or more major errors	Little or no variation; dull and uninteresting; some major errors	Numerous major errors
Word Choice	Uses the vocabulary of the topic as evident in the sources; interesting and effective; virtually error free	Demonstrates ease in using vocabulary from the sources	Occasional use of vocabulary from the sources; occasionally interesting and effective	Somewhat dull and ordinary; some errors in diction; no attempt to integrate vocabulary from the sources	Mostly dull and conventional; no attempt to integrate vocabulary from the sources	Numerous major errors; extremely immature
Grammar and Usage	Virtually error free	Occasional minor errors	Several minor errors	Some major errors	Severely flawed; frequent major errors	Extremely flawed

Using the rubrics on the previous pages, rate yourself in each of the categories below for each essay on the test. Enter on the lines below the number from the rubric that most accurately reflects your performance in each category. Then calculate the average of the six numbers to determine your final score. It is difficult to score yourself objectively, so you may wish to ask a respected friend or teacher to assess your writing for a more accurate reflection of its strengths and weaknesses. On the AP test itself, a reader will rate your essay on a scale of 0 to 9, with 9 being the highest.

Rate each category from 9 (high) to 0 (low).

Question 1

SELF-EVALUATION

Overall Impression   _____
Understanding of the Text   _____
Organization and Development   _____
Use of Sentences   _____
Word Choice (Diction)   _____
Grammar and Usage   _____

TOTAL   _____
   Divide by 6 for final score   _____

OBJECTIVE EVALUATION

Overall Impression   _____
Understanding of the Text   _____
Organization and Development   _____
Use of Sentences   _____
Word Choice (Diction)   _____
Grammar and Usage   _____

TOTAL   _____
   Divide by 6 for final score   _____

Question 2

SELF-EVALUATION

Overall Impression   _____
Understanding of the Text   _____
Organization and Development   _____
Use of Sentences   _____
Word Choice (Diction)   _____
Grammar and Usage   _____

TOTAL   _____
   Divide by 6 for final score   _____

OBJECTIVE EVALUATION

Overall Impression   _____
Understanding of the Text   _____
Organization and Development   _____
Use of Sentences   _____
Word Choice (Diction)   _____
Grammar and Usage   _____

TOTAL   _____
   Divide by 6 for final score   _____

Question 3

SELF-EVALUATION

Overall Impression   _____
Understanding of the Text   _____
Organization and Development   _____
Use of Sentences   _____
Word Choice (Diction)   _____
Grammar and Usage   _____

TOTAL   _____
   Divide by 6 for final score   _____

OBJECTIVE EVALUATION

Overall Impression   _____
Understanding of the Text   _____
Organization and Development   _____
Use of Sentences   _____
Word Choice (Diction)   _____
Grammar and Usage   _____

TOTAL   _____
   Divide by 6 for final score   _____

ANSWER SHEET PRACTICE TEST 3

SECTION I

1. (A) (B) (C) (D) (E)   19. (A) (B) (C) (D) (E)   35. (A) (B) (C) (D) (E)
2. (A) (B) (C) (D) (E)   20. (A) (B) (C) (D) (E)   36. (A) (B) (C) (D) (E)
3. (A) (B) (C) (D) (E)   21. (A) (B) (C) (D) (E)   37. (A) (B) (C) (D) (E)
4. (A) (B) (C) (D) (E)   22. (A) (B) (C) (D) (E)   38. (A) (B) (C) (D) (E)
5. (A) (B) (C) (D) (E)   23. (A) (B) (C) (D) (E)   39. (A) (B) (C) (D) (E)
6. (A) (B) (C) (D) (E)   24. (A) (B) (C) (D) (E)   40. (A) (B) (C) (D) (E)
7. (A) (B) (C) (D) (E)   25. (A) (B) (C) (D) (E)   41. (A) (B) (C) (D) (E)
8. (A) (B) (C) (D) (E)   26. (A) (B) (C) (D) (E)   42. (A) (B) (C) (D) (E)
9. (A) (B) (C) (D) (E)   27. (A) (B) (C) (D) (E)   43. (A) (B) (C) (D) (E)
10. (A) (B) (C) (D) (E)   28. (A) (B) (C) (D) (E)   44. (A) (B) (C) (D) (E)
11. (A) (B) (C) (D) (E)   29. (A) (B) (C) (D) (E)   45. (A) (B) (C) (D) (E)
12. (A) (B) (C) (D) (E)   30. (A) (B) (C) (D) (E)   46. (A) (B) (C) (D) (E)
13. (A) (B) (C) (D) (E)   31. (A) (B) (C) (D) (E)   47. (A) (B) (C) (D) (E)
14. (A) (B) (C) (D) (E)   32. (A) (B) (C) (D) (E)   48. (A) (B) (C) (D) (E)
15. (A) (B) (C) (D) (E)   33. (A) (B) (C) (D) (E)   49. (A) (B) (C) (D) (E)
16. (A) (B) (C) (D) (E)   34. (A) (B) (C) (D) (E)   50. (A) (B) (C) (D) (E)
17. (A) (B) (C) (D) (E)
18. (A) (B) (C) (D) (E)

SECTION II

Question 1

_____

_____

_____

_____

_____

_____

_____

_____

_____

_____

_____

_____

_____

_____

_____

_____

_____

_____

_____

_____

_____

_____

_____

_____

_____

_____

answer sheet

Question 2

_____

_____

_____

_____

_____

_____

_____

_____

_____

_____

_____

_____

_____

_____

_____

_____

_____

_____

_____

_____

_____

_____

_____

_____

answer sheet

Question 3

_____

_____

_____

_____

_____

_____

_____

_____

_____

_____

_____

_____

_____

_____

_____

_____

_____

_____

_____

_____

_____

_____

_____

_____

_____

_____

_____

answer sheet

Practice Test 3

SECTION I

50 QUESTIONS • 60 MINUTES

> **Directions:** This section consists of selections of literature and questions on their content, style, and form. After you have read each passage, select the response that best answers the question and mark the corresponding space on the answer sheet.

QUESTIONS 1–13 REFER TO THE FOLLOWING SELECTION—A SPEECH BY QUEEN ELIZABETH I TO PARLIAMENT. READ THE PASSAGE CAREFULLY AND THEN CHOOSE THE ANSWERS TO THE QUESTIONS.

Line   To be a King, and wear a Crown, is a thing more glorious to them that
see it, than it is pleasant to them that bear it: for my self, I never was
so much inticed with the glorious name of a King, or the royal authority of a Queen, as delighted that God hath made me His Instrument to
5   maintain His Truth and Glory, and to defend this kingdom from
dishonor, damage, tyranny, and oppression. But should I ascribe any of
these things unto my self, or my sexly weakness, I were not worthy to
live, and of all most unworthy of the mercies I have received at God's
hands, but to God only and wholly all is given and ascribed.
10   The cares and troubles of a Crown I cannot more fitly resemble than
to the drugs of a learned physician, perfumed with some aromatical
savour, or to bitter pills gilded over, by which they are made more
acceptable or less offensive, which indeed are bitter and unpleasant to
take, and for my own part, were it not for conscience sake to discharge
15   the duty that God hath laid upon me, and to maintain His glory and
keep you in safety, in mine own disposition I should be willing to
resign the place I hold to any other, and glad to be freed of the glory
with the labors, for it is not my desire to live nor to reign longer than
my life and reign shall be for your good. And though you have had and
20   may have many mightier and wiser Princes sitting in this Seat, yet
you never had nor shall have any that will love you better.
      Thus Mr. Speaker, I commend me to your loyal loves, and yours to
my best care and your further councels, and I pray you Mr. Controller,
and Mr. Secretary, and you of my Councell, that before these Gentlemen depart unto their countries, you bring them all to kiss my hand.

1. It can be inferred from her use of the words "my sexly weakness" (line 7) that Elizabeth believes

   (A) she herself is weak
   (B) she is unworthy of God's mercies
   (C) she is too emotional
   (D) women are the weaker sex
   (E) kings make better monarchs

2. The passage as a whole can best be described as which of the following modes of discourse?

   (A) Narrative
   (B) Argument
   (C) Exposition
   (D) Description
   (E) Persuasion

3. Elizabeth's use of the phrase "pills . . . which indeed are bitter and unpleasant to take" (lines 12–14) is an example of which of the following figures of speech?

   (A) Simile
   (B) Metaphor
   (C) Imagery
   (D) Personification
   (E) Hyperbole

4. Which of the following best describes the tone of this passage?

   (A) Religious
   (B) Regal
   (C) Persuasive
   (D) Powerful
   (E) Benevolent

5. In the second paragraph, Elizabeth says ". . . in mine own disposition I should be willing to resign the place I hold to any other" (lines 16–17) in order to

   I. give credence to the idea that she rules because of Divine Will
   II. confide that she is tired of the responsibilities of the monarchy
   III. suggest that she is willing to resign and let another ruler take over

   (A) I only
   (B) II only
   (C) III only
   (D) I and II only
   (E) II and III only

6. What does Elizabeth imply when she says "To be a King, and wear a Crown, is a thing more glorious to them that see it, than it is pleasant to them that bear it" (lines 1–2)?

   (A) The monarchy is a glorious thing to behold.
   (B) The responsibilities of a ruler are a heavy burden.
   (C) It is sometimes pleasant to be queen.
   (D) Do not challenge my royal authority.
   (E) The Crown brings with it both good things and bad.

7. Which of the following definitions best suits the words "fitly resemble" (line 10) in the context?

   (A) Closely approximate
   (B) Aptly describe
   (C) Accurately compare
   (D) Perfectly mirror
   (E) Closely relate to

8. In the first paragraph, by choosing the word "Instrument" Elizabeth wishes to emphasize specifically

   (A) the nature of her political power
   (B) an almost musical delight with being the Queen
   (C) her promise to God that she will rule fairly
   (D) her obedience to God's will
   (E) that her authority comes from the line of succession

9. In this address, what does Elizabeth say are her duties as monarch?

   (A) To reign with truth and glory
   (B) To overcome her sexly weakness
   (C) To love her subjects better than her predecessors did
   (D) To take her medicine dutifully
   (E) To defend England from tyranny and oppression

10. Rhetorically, the last sentence in the second paragraph (lines 19–21) is best described as

   (A) an extended metaphor supporting the antecedent metaphor
   (B) reductio ad absurdem
   (C) a promise to care for her subjects
   (D) argumentum ad hominem
   (E) an attempt to balance possible weakness with a greater virtue

11. In the context of her speech, what does Elizabeth mean when she says "Thus . . . I commend me to your loyal loves" (line 22)?

   (A) I want you to remember me to your families.
   (B) I continue to be devoted to you.
   (C) I demand your continued allegiance.
   (D) I ask for your continued affection.
   (E) I will love those of you who are loyal to me.

12. Given the speaker's rhetoric, what can one infer is the primary purpose of Elizabeth's address?

   (A) To curry favor with her subjects by expressing her affection
   (B) To elicit compassion for herself as a woman
   (C) To explain that she rules by divine will
   (D) To convince parliament that her motives are purely altruistic
   (E) To dispel any ill will that may exist

13. The metaphor that Elizabeth develops in the second paragraph is an attempt to inform Parliament that

   (A) the burdens of being queen have made her ill
   (B) she is no longer willing to accept the yoke of power
   (C) monarchs who rule irresponsibly are an offense to God
   (D) the privileges of power do not compensate for its burdens
   (E) she rules only from her conscience and her duty to God

GO ON TO THE NEXT PAGE

practice test

QUESTIONS 14–26 REFER TO THE FOLLOWING SELECTION. READ THE PASSAGE CAREFULLY AND THEN CHOOSE THE ANSWERS TO THE QUESTIONS.

White's Chocolate House, June 6

Line   A letter from a young lady, written in the most passionate terms, wherein she laments the misfortune of a gentleman, her lover, who was lately wounded in a duel, has turned my thoughts to that subject and inclined me to examine into the causes which precipitate men into so fatal a folly. And as it has been proposed to treat of subjects of
5   gallantry in the article from hence, and no one point in nature is more proper to be considered by the company who frequent this place than that of duels, it is worth our consideration to examine into this chimerical groundless humor, and to lay every other thought aside, until we have stripped it of all its false pretenses to credit and reputation amongst men.
10   But I must confess, when I consider what I am going about and run over in my imagination all the endless crowd of men of honor who will be offended at such a discourse, I am undertaking, methinks, a work worthy an invulnerable hero in romance, rather than a private gentleman with a single rapier; but as I am pretty well acquainted by great opportunities with the nature of man, and know of a truth that
15   all men fight against their will, the danger vanishes, and resolution rises upon this subject. For this reason, I shall talk very freely on a custom which all men wish exploded, though no man has courage enough to resist it.
        But there is one unintelligible word, which I fear will extremely perplex my dissertation, and I confess to you I find very hard to explain, which is the term "satisfaction." An honest country gentleman had the misfortune to fall into company with two
20   or three modern men of honor, where he happened to be very ill treated, and one of the company, being conscious of his offense, sends a note to him in the morning, and tells him he was ready to give him satisfaction. "This is fine doing," says the plain fellow; "last night he sent me away cursedly out of humor, and this morning he fancies
25   it would be a satisfaction to be run through the body."
        As the matter at present stands, it is not to do handsome actions that denominates a man of honor; it is enough if he dares to defend ill ones. Thus you often see a common sharper in competition with a gentleman of the first rank; though all mankind is convinced that a fighting gamester is only a pickpocket with the courage of an
30   highwayman. One cannot with any patience reflect on the unaccountable jumble of persons and things in this town and nation, which occasions very frequently that a brave man falls by a hand below that of a common hangman, and yet his executioner escapes the clutches of the hangman for doing it. I shall therefore hereafter consider how the bravest men in other ages and nations have behaved themselves upon such
35   incidents as we decide by combat; and show, from their practice, that this resentment neither has its foundation from true reason nor solid fame: but is an imposture, made of cowardice, falsehood, and want of understanding. For this work, a good history of quarrels would be very edifying to the public, and I apply myself to the town for particulars and circumstances within their knowledge, which may serve to embellish
40   the dissertation with proper cuts. Most of the quarrels I have ever known have proceeded from some valiant coxcomb's persisting in the wrong, to defend some prevailing folly, and preserve himself from the ingenuity of owning a mistake.
        By this means it is called "giving a man satisfaction" to urge your offense against him with your sword; which puts me in mind of Peter's order to the keeper, in *The*
45   *Tale of a Tub*. "If you neglect to do all this, damn you and your generation forever: and so we bid you heartily farewell." If the contradiction in the very terms of one of our challenges were as well explained and turned into downright English, would it not run after this manner?

Sir,

50   Your extraordinary behavior last night and the liberty you were pleased to take
with me makes me this morning give you this, to tell you, because you are an
ill-bred puppy, I will meet you in Hyde Park an hour hence; and because you
want both breeding and humanity, I desire you would come with a pistol in your
hand, on horseback, and endeavor to shoot me through the head to teach you
55   more manners. If you fail of doing me this pleasure, I shall say you are a rascal,
on every post in town: and so, sir, if you will not injure me more, I shall never
forgive what you have done already. Pray, sir, do not fail of getting everything
ready; and you will infinitely oblige, sir, your most obedient humble servant,
etc. . . .

14. In the second sentence of the first paragraph, what is the best meaning for the word "chimerical"?

(A) Meritless
(B) Imaginary
(C) Monstrous
(D) Unjustified
(E) Musical

15. The passage as a whole is an example of which of the following modes of discourse?

(A) Description
(B) Exposition
(C) Narration
(D) Argument
(E) Persuasion

16. What does the writer say is the purpose of his essay?

(A) To educate his readers about dueling
(B) To offer alternatives to dueling
(C) To write amusing essays for his readers
(D) To discredit the practice of dueling
(E) To change a barbaric custom

17. What is meant by the phrase "giving a man satisfaction" (line 43)?

(A) To kill or wound another man
(B) To repay a debt
(C) To offer the opportunity to restore one's honor
(D) To challenge a man with swords
(E) To discredit an enemy

18. In the fourth paragraph, what does the author mean when he says "a brave man falls by a hand below that of a common hangman" (lines 31–32)?

  I. Dueling is a crime punishable by hanging.
 II. Gentlemen and commoners alike die by dueling.
III. A gentleman could be killed by a person of a lower class.

(A) I only
(B) II only
(C) III only
(D) I and II only
(E) II and III only

19. What literary device does the writer employ in the third paragraph to attack the practice of dueling?

(A) Anecdote
(B) Satire
(C) Imagery
(D) Allegory
(E) Parable

20. According to this passage, what does the writer believe about the practice of dueling?

(A) It is a time-honored custom.
(B) It is against the nature of man.
(C) Men of honor have no alternative.
(D) Men of honor must defend their reputation.
(E) It is understandable in certain circumstances.

GO ON TO THE NEXT PAGE

21. Which of the following best describes the writer's style?

(A) Formal diction, compound-complex sentences

(B) Idiomatic vocabulary, sentence fragments

(C) Colloquial diction, simple declarative sentences

(D) Colloquial diction, rambling sentences

(E) Idiomatic vocabulary, idiomatic punctuation

22. Which of the following best characterizes the tone of this selection?

(A) Persuasive, reasonable

(B) Serious, introspective

(C) Satirical, witty

(D) Impassioned, ardent

(E) Educated, scholarly

23. What is the rhetorical function of the first paragraph?

I. To present the main purpose of the article

II. To tell readers the genesis of the article

III. To explain why the author has chosen this subject

(A) I only

(B) II only

(C) III only

(D) I and II only

(E) I, II, and III

24. The first sentence of the first paragraph beginning "A letter from a young lady, written in the most passionate terms" (line 1) contains all of the following elements EXCEPT a(n)

(A) adjectival phrase

(B) gerund phrase

(C) adverbial phrase

(D) prepositional phrase

(E) participial phrase

25. In the first sentence of the last paragraph, the phrase "you are an ill-bred puppy" (lines 51–52) is an example of a(n)

(A) simile

(B) metaphor

(C) personification

(D) analogy

(E) overstatement

26. What is the rhetorical function of the last paragraph?

I. It illustrates the contradictory nature of giving "satisfaction."

II. It paraphrases a challenge to a duel.

III. It pokes fun at the custom of dueling.

(A) I only

(B) II only

(C) III only

(D) I and II only

(E) I, II, and III

QUESTIONS 27–37. READ THE FOLLOWING PASSAGE CAREFULLY BEFORE YOU CHOOSE YOUR ANSWERS.

This passage is an excerpt about the history of the American judiciary by Simeon E. Baldwin, L.L.D.

Line   The colonial charters, whether of the proprietary, provincial or republican type, were all equally charters for Englishmen, based on the common law of the English people. So far as they granted legislative power, it was generally declared that it should be exercised in conformity, so far as might be practicable, with the laws of England. The

5 proviso to this effect in the roving patent given by Queen Elizabeth to Sir Walter Raleigh may be taken as a type: "so always as the said statutes, lawes, and ordinances may be, as neere as conveniently may be, agreeable to the forme of the lawes, statutes, government, or pollicie of England."[1]

In the Southern New England colonies, when first settled, the common law of

10 England was disowned. They made the little law which they needed for themselves, and as cases which this might not provide for arose, they were to be decided by such rules as the magistrates might think right and warranted by the precepts found in the Bible. Connecticut continued to insist on this view, with general consistency, until the days of the Stamp Act, when it became the interest of her people to claim the benefit

15 of the principles of the English constitution and of the common law, on which it was built up.[2]

In early Massachusetts the written pleadings often referred to the Bible, quoting a text from it as an authority, just as citations now might be made in a lawyer's brief from a legal treatise or reported case.[3]

20 As was anticipated in the Raleigh patent, it was found from the first and everywhere that if the common law was to be applied to the rough conditions of colonial life some modifications were necessary. These, the colonists were, in the main, left free to make at their pleasure. Much of this work came to be done by their legislative assemblies; more by their courts. The assemblies sat but for a few days in the year: the

25 courts were always open to suitors, and sessions of the inferior ones were frequent.

The assemblies, however, were themselves courts. At first they kept in their own hands a large share of judicial power. They acted as the early parliaments of England had acted, both as a legislature and a judicial tribunal. In several colonies they long kept to themselves the right of deciding private controversies on equitable principles.

30 They sat as a court of review, to grant new trials or review judgments. They passed acts of attainder. They settled insolvent estates.[4]

This mingling of judicial with legislative functions is a thing to be tolerated only while the foundations of a government are being laid. As the Roman plebeian, in the days before the Twelve Tables, clamored for a known and certain law, so the common

35 people of the early colonies insisted that from a similar want they held their rights too much at the will of their rulers. In the colony of New Haven a code was early framed; but there they built on a written law—the Bible.[5] In Massachusetts, where they were more anxious to avoid conflict with the common law, the problem was a serious one.

---

[1] Poore, "Charters and Constitutions," II,1381.

[2] Colonial Records of Conn., 1689–1706, 261; Conn. Stat., ed. of 1769, 1. Cf. citations by D. Davenport, arguendo, in Flynn v. Morgan, 55 Connecticut Reports, 132–134, from MSS. in the State archives.

[3] Publications of the Colonial Society of Mass., III, 324.

[4] Wheeler's Appeal, 45 Connecticut Reports, 306, 314.

[5] New Haven Colony Records, I, 12, 115, 116; II, 569, 570.

27. The second paragraph can best be summarized by which of the following statements?

- **(A)** The Southern New England colonies always based their law on English common law.
- **(B)** The Southern New England colonies originally based their laws on the Bible but saw the benefit of using English common law around the time of the Stamp Act.
- **(C)** The Southern New England colonies always based their law on the Bible.
- **(D)** The Southern New England colonies originally based their law on an equal combination of English common law and the Bible.
- **(E)** The Stamp Act caused the Southern New England colonies to become disillusioned with law based on English common law.

28. The number 1381 in footnote 1 most likely represents

- **(A)** the year "Charters and Constitutions" was published
- **(B)** the total number of pages in "Charters and Constitutions"
- **(C)** the page number in "Charters and Constitutions" where the citation can be found
- **(D)** the number of charters mentioned in the book
- **(E)** the year that the first charter was published

29. In the following sentence from the fourth paragraph, what word does "these" refer to?

"These, the colonists were, in the main, left free to make at their pleasure."

- **(A)** Modifications
- **(B)** Conditions
- **(C)** Laws
- **(D)** Colonists
- **(E)** Patents

30. Which of the following is closest in meaning to the word "disowned" as used in the first sentence of the second paragraph?

- **(A)** Ignored
- **(B)** Sold
- **(C)** Adhered to
- **(D)** Presented
- **(E)** Revised

31. What is the purpose of footnote 3?

- **(A)** To credit a direct quotation
- **(B)** To show the reader the basis for the information in the third paragraph
- **(C)** To provide the reader with sources for further reading
- **(D)** None of the above
- **(E)** All of the above

32. This excerpt is most likely taken from

- **(A)** a historical novel
- **(B)** a scientific journal
- **(C)** a biography
- **(D)** an encyclopedia
- **(E)** a history book

33. It is reasonable to conclude from the footnotes as a whole that

- **(A)** the author gives little credence to original documents
- **(B)** the author used as many primary sources as possible to research the information in the passage
- **(C)** the passage is based on little fact
- **(D)** the passage is simply a compilation of facts from the cited sources
- **(E)** the author was an important government official

34. The language used in lines 30–31 is an example of

- **(A)** Simile
- **(B)** Foreshadowing
- **(C)** Sarcasm
- **(D)** Parallel construction
- **(E)** Imagery

35. With which statement would the author of the passage most likely agree?

   (A) The judiciary and legislature should always be mingled.
   (B) The judiciary is more important than the legislature as a part of government.
   (C) Government works best when the judiciary and legislature are kept separate.
   (D) English common law is the best way to govern all societies.
   (E) The colonies should not have protested the Stamp Act.

36. The word "type" as used in line 6 of the first paragraph most likely means

   (A) kind
   (B) font
   (C) category
   (D) example
   (E) manner

37. The author's tone can best be described as

   (A) strident
   (B) pleading
   (C) emotional
   (D) cold
   (E) scholarly

QUESTIONS 38–50 REFER TO THE FOLLOWING SELECTION. IN THIS EXCERPT FROM *MY BONDAGE AND MY FREEDOM* BY FREDERICK DOUGLASS, THE AUTHOR SPEAKS ABOUT HIS YOUTH AS A SLAVE. READ THE PASSAGE CAREFULLY AND THEN CHOOSE THE ANSWERS TO THE QUESTIONS.

Line When I was about thirteen years old and had succeeded in learning to read, every
increase of knowledge, especially respecting the free states, added something to the
almost intolerable burden of the thought—"I am a slave for life." To my bondage I saw
no end, it was a terrible reality, and I shall never be able to tell how sadly that
5   thought chafed my young spirit. Fortunately, or unfortunately, about this time in my
life, I had made enough money to buy what was then a very popular schoolbook, the
Columbian Orator. I bought this addition to my library, of Mr. Knight, on Thames
street Fell's Point, Baltimore, and paid him fifty cents for it. I was first led to buy this
book, by hearing some little boys say they were going to learn some little pieces out of
10   it for the Exhibition. This volume was, indeed, a rich treasure, and every opportunity
afforded me, for a time, was spent in diligently perusing it. . . . The dialogue and the
speeches were all redolent of the principles of liberty and poured floods of light on the
nature and character of slavery. As I read, behold! The very discontent so graphically
predicted by Master Hugh had already come upon me. I was no longer the light-
15   hearted, gleesome boy, full of mirth and play, as when I landed first at Baltimore.
Knowledge had come. . . . This knowledge opened my eyes to the horrible pit and
revealed the teeth of the frightful dragon that was ready to pounce upon me, but it
opened no way for my escape. I have often wished myself a beast, or a bird—anything,
rather than a slave. I was wretched and gloomy. Beyond my ability to describe. I was
20   too thoughtful to be happy. It was this everlasting thinking which distressed and
tormented me; and yet there was no getting rid of the subject of my thoughts. All

GO ON TO THE NEXT PAGE

nature was redolent of it. Once awakened by the silver trump* of knowledge, my spirit was roused to eternal wakefulness. Liberty! The inestimable birthright of every man, had, for me, converted every object into an asserter of this great right. It was heard in
25   every sound, and beheld in every object. It was ever present, to torment me with a sense of my wretched condition. The more beautiful and charming were the smiles of nature, the more horrible and desolate was my condition. I saw nothing without seeing it. I do not exaggerate, when I say, that it looked from every star, smiled in every calm, breathed in every wind, and moved in every storm.

—Frederick Douglass

---

* trumpet

38. This passage is primarily concerned with

    (A) the importance of reading for Frederick Douglass
    (B) Douglass's conclusion that slavery is intolerable
    (C) the author's experiences at the hands of white boys
    (D) the writer's knowledge of the constitution of the United States
    (E) reasons why he was no longer a happy youngster

39. Which of the following describes the tone of the passage?

    (A) Light and humorous
    (B) Ironic
    (C) Academic
    (D) Sincere and powerful
    (E) Angry and violent

40. This passage is an example of a

    (A) slave narrative
    (B) picaresque novel
    (C) biography
    (D) historical text
    (E) secondary source

41. The style of this excerpt can best be described as

    (A) elaborate, complex, and circumspect
    (B) poetic
    (C) plain, forceful, and direct
    (D) obscure and difficult
    (E) Elizabethan

42. According to the author, why is education incompatible with slavery?

    (A) The system keeps slaves from living in harmony with their souls.
    (B) Education makes slaves dissatisfied with their position.
    (C) Slaves learn about the Constitution and the Bill of Rights.
    (D) Education makes slaves dangerous to their masters.
    (E) Owners do not want slaves wasting work time by reading and learning.

43. What effect does reading the *Columbian Orator* have upon young Douglass?

    (A) He decides to buy the book for fifty cents.
    (B) Douglass decides to enter the Exhibition and compete against white boys.
    (C) The book increases his longing for freedom.
    (D) He discovers that he is a victim of an oppressive system.
    (E) He develops a plan to escape north.

44. Which of the following is not an accurate analysis of this passage?

    (A) Douglass's descriptions are straightforward.

    (B) The author offers little interpretation of the significance of events.

    (C) The passage is factual.

    (D) The author employs many literary allusions.

    (E) Douglass allows readers to draw their own conclusions.

45. When Douglass writes "This knowledge opened my eyes to the horrible pit and revealed the teeth of the frightful dragon that was ready to pounce upon me," (lines 16–17) he was referring to

    (A) Mr. Hugh, his owner

    (B) the effects of education

    (C) the *Columbian Orator*

    (D) the institution of slavery

    (E) events that had happened to him

46. What structure does Douglass employ in the sentence "The more beautiful and charming were the smiles of nature, the more horrible and desolate was my condition." (lines 26–27)?

    (A) Metaphors

    (B) Parallelism

    (C) Exaggeration

    (D) Eloquence

    (E) Cacophony

47. In the sentence "It was this everlasting thinking which distressed and tormented me; and yet there was no getting rid of the subject of my thoughts" (lines 20–21), the word "thinking" is which of the following?

    (A) Participle

    (B) Verb

    (C) Infinitive

    (D) Adverbial phrase

    (E) Gerund

48. What significant change does Douglass describe in the lines "As I read, behold! The very discontent so graphically predicted by Master Hugh had already come upon me" (lines 13–14)?

    (A) The young Douglass came to the conclusion that slavery was wrong.

    (B) Douglass decided he would pursue a higher education.

    (C) The writer decided he would act light-hearted and mirthful while planning his escape.

    (D) His spirit awakened.

    (E) Douglass found his soul.

49. Douglass uses the word "redolent" twice (line 12 and line 22). What does the word mean?

    (A) Filled with

    (B) Sweet-smelling

    (C) Evocative

    (D) Excessive

    (E) Exuding

50. Which of the following best describes the mode of discourse of this article?

    (A) Exposition

    (B) Narrative

    (C) Argument

    (D) Description

    (E) Persuasion

S T O P If you finish before time is called, you may check your work on this section only. Do not turn to any other section in the test.

SECTION II

3 QUESTIONS • 2 HOURS 15 MINUTES

Directions: Read the following passage carefully. Write a well-organized essay in which you explain how Thoreau developed and supported his core theme, or argument. Be sure to consider rhetorical and stylistic devices such as diction, imagery, tone, theme, and mode of discourse.

Question 1

SUGGESTED TIME—40 MINUTES

From *Civil Disobedience*

Line I heartily accept the motto, "That government is best which governs least"; and I should like to see it acted up to more rapidly and systematically. Carried out, it finally amounts to this, which also I believe: "That government is best which governs not at all"; and when men are prepared for it, that will be the kind of government which they will have.
5   Government is at best but an expedient; but most governments are usually, and all governments are sometimes, inexpedient. The objections which have been brought against a standing army, and they are many and weighty, and deserve to prevail, may also at last be brought against a standing government. The standing army is only an arm of the standing government. The government itself, which is only the mode which
10   the people have chosen to execute their will, is equally liable to be abused and perverted before the people can act through it. Witness the present Mexican war, the work of comparatively a few individuals using the standing government as their tool; for in the outset, the people would not have consented to this measure.
      This American government—what is it but a tradition, though a recent one, endeav-
15   oring to transmit itself unimpaired to posterity, but each instant losing some of its integrity? It has not the vitality and force of a single living man; for a single man can bend it to his will. It is a sort of wooden gun to the people themselves; and, if ever they should use it in earnest as a real one against each other, it will surely split. But it is not the less necessary for this; for the people must have some complicated machinery or
20   other, and hear its din, to satisfy that idea of government which they have. Govern-
      ments show thus how successfully men can be imposed on, even impose on themselves, for their own advantage. It is excellent, we must all allow; yet this government never of itself furthered any enterprise, but by the alacrity with which it got out of its way. It does not keep the country free. It does not settle the West. It does not educate. The
25   character inherent in the American people has done all that has been accomplished; and it would have done somewhat more, if the government had not sometimes got in its way. For government is an expedient by which men would fain succeed in letting one another alone; and, as has been said, when it is most expedient, the governed are most let alone by it. Trade and commerce, if they were not made of India rubber, would never manage
30   to bounce over the obstacles which legislators are continually putting in their way; and, if one were to judge these men wholly by the effects of their actions, and not partly by their intentions, they would deserve to be classed and punished with those mischievous persons who put obstructions on the railroads.
      But, to speak practically and as a citizen, unlike those who call themselves no-
35   government men, I ask for, not at once no government, but *at once* a better government. Let every man make known what kind of government would command his respect, and that will be one step toward obtaining it. . . .

Directions: Read the passage below carefully. Write a well-organized essay presenting a logical argument for or against Woodrow Wilson's Appeal for Neutrality. Address your personal position regarding U.S. involvement in foreign conflict. Include evidence from your own observation, experience, or reading to support your position.

Question 2

SUGGESTED TIME—40 MINUTES

Line The people of the United States are drawn from many nations, and chiefly from the
nations now at war. It is natural and inevitable that there should be the utmost
variety of sympathy and desire among them with regard to the issues and circumstances of the conflict. Some will wish one nation, others another, to succeed in the
5 momentous struggle. It will be easy to excite passion and difficult to allay it. Those
responsible for exciting it will assume a heavy responsibility, responsibility for no less
a thing than that the people of the United States, whose love of their country and
whose loyalty to its Government should unite them as Americans all, bound in honor
and affection to think first of her and her interests, may be divided in camps of hostile
10 opinion, hot against each other, involved in the war itself in impulse and opinion if not
in action.

Such divisions amongst us would be fatal to our peace of mind and might seriously
stand in the way of the proper performance of our duty as the one great nation at
peace, the one people holding itself ready to play a part of impartial mediation and
15 speak the counsels of peace and accommodation, not as a partisan, but as a friend.

Directions: The following prompt is based on the following six sources. The assignment requires that you synthesize a number of the sources into a coherent, well-written essay that takes a position. Use at least three of the sources to support your position. Do not simply paraphrase or summarize the sources. Your argument should be the focus of your essay and the sources should support this argument. Remember to attribute both direct and indirect citations.

Question 3

SUGGESTED TIME—15 MINUTES FOR READING AND 40 MINUTES FOR WRITING

Introduction: Advertising on television used to consist of commercials only. That changed with the advent of product placement, in which advertisers pay television shows to prominently display their products. Some feel that this form of advertising is sneaky. Some feel that it is the most effective form of advertising. Is one form of advertising on television more effective than another?

Assignment: Read the following sources (including any introductory information) carefully. **Then, write an essay that supports, qualifies, or disputes the argument that product placement is the most effective form of television advertising. Synthesize at least three of the sources to support your position.**

You may refer to the sources by their titles (Source A, Source B, etc.) or by the descriptions in parentheses.

Source A (Jennworth)

Source B (Allison)

Source C (chart)

Source D (Wilson and Marino)

Source E (Ad Advertising)

Source F (Zuckerman)

SOURCE A

Jennworth, David. "The New Generation of Advertising" *Advertising Yearly,* 2006.

The following passage is excerpted from an article about product placement as an effective form of advertising.

Product placement has created a revolution in television advertising. By no means has it replaced traditional television commercials, but recent studies show it has as much effect as commercials, if not more. The problem with commercials has always been the ability of a viewer to change the channel during commercials and watch something else. Many people do not like to watch commercials, and this presented a problem for advertisers. Aside from producing compelling commercials that people want to watch, how else could advertisers reach viewers? After all, even if a commercial is compelling, if it is not the first commercial of the break, the viewer may have already changed the channel. Enter product placement.

The concept is simple: display products prominently on popular television shows. This display of products is effective in two ways. First, simply showing the product exposes viewers to it. Second, and even more effective (and expensive), having a popular character on a show *use* a product even more overtly exposes viewers to it. Advertisers reason that if a popular character uses a product, viewers will, too. This effect is intensified if the product is used by a character on a reality television show. People may be more likely to buy a product if a "real" character is using it.

SOURCE B

Allison, James. "You Can't Fool Me—Or My Friends" *Advertising Watch,* April 2004.

The following passage is excerpted from an article that discusses the effects of product placement on the viewing public.

You can't fool me with product placement advertising. You can't fool my friends, either. We've been watching TV for too long. We know all about advertising and, frankly, we are tired of being sold to. Regular commercials were bad enough, but product placement is downright insulting! Do advertisers think that by simply having a character drink a certain drink, or eat a certain food, or wear a certain outfit that viewers will be compelled to use those products? Please! A note to advertisers: we know what you are up to, and we won't let it work.

Product placement may be beginning to have the an effect opposite what was originally intended. Instead of a successful "soft sell," advertisers have actually created animosity among viewers. It seems that advertisers think that viewers are too stupid to realize they are being sold to. Surely, tricking viewers into subconsciously wanting products was the original motivation behind product placement. It is as if advertisers are saying "you can't avoid us by changing the channel anymore; we are always selling to you." Well, who watches TV to be sold to? People just want to be entertained. That's it. If I want to watch commercials, I will. But don't force me to.

SOURCE C

Adapted from the Advertising on TV Council Annual Effectiveness Survey.

Traditional Advertising Versus Product Placement.

Yummy Soft Drink Advertising Effectiveness for 2005

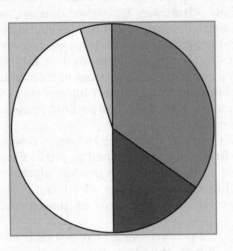

- Commercials
- Print advertising
- Product placement on TV
- Other

GoFast Auto Company Advertising Effectiveness for 2005

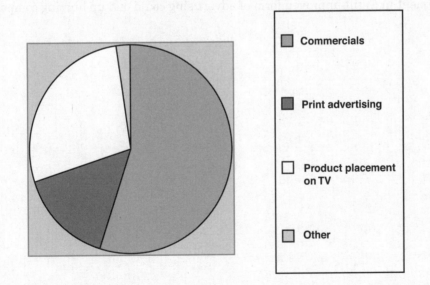

- Commercials
- Print advertising
- Product placement on TV
- Other

SOURCE D

Wilson, Amy, and Joanne Marino. "Product Placement in Advertising" *Discussion Magazine,* 2005.

The following passage is excerpted from an article that discusses product placement as an effective form of advertising.

How effective is product placement? How fair is product placement? How cost-effective is product placement? These are all questions advertisers and agencies must ask themselves when formulating an advertising campaign. Product placement is an intriguing way to advertise, but there is a fear in the industry that its effectiveness is overblown. These numbers can be hard to determine, as most companies do not share their internal advertising effectiveness numbers. It is much easier to gauge the effectiveness of traditional commercial advertising. The numbers that are available show that commercials are very effective means of advertising, especially to targeted audiences. Why then, has product placement become so popular with so little proof of its effectiveness?

The answer is that product placement is popular right now. In fact, it seems that the idea that product placement is the wave of the future has been created by product placement itself. Companies reason that if other companies are using so much product placement, it must be working. In addition, even if a company has doubts as to the effectiveness, they feel that if their competitors use it, they must, too. In this way, product placement seems to be selling itself!

More research is needed into the effect of product placement before it can be officially crowned the "best way to advertise." In addition, the phenomenon is so new that it would behoove companies to wait and see how it develops. There is a trend in many companies to forego a large amount of traditional commercial advertising in favor of product placement. This investment in a still-unproven form of advertising could end up hurting companies in the long run.

SOURCE E
The Ad Advertising Agency memo to Tasty Potato Chips, Inc., 2006.

The following passage is excerpted from a memo from an advertising agency to try to convince the client, Tasty Potato Chips, to use product placement on a popular TV show.

To: The Board of Tasty Potato Chips
From: Ad Advertising

Re: Product Placement on *The Stress House*

The Stress House is one of the most popular reality series on television today. It consistently ranks tops in ratings for its time slot on both days that it airs: Mondays and Fridays. In addition, it is most popular with our targeted age group of 18 to 25. Informal discussions with other advertisers have revealed that product placement on *The Stress House* has increased their profits in the target age group by 25 percent. If we place Tasty Potato Chips on *The Stress House,* we believe that we can increase your revenue by at least that percentage, as well.

Ad Advertising has secured a commitment from the producers of *The Stress House* to feature only Tasty Potato Chips on their show. For an additional fee, the producers promise to feature Tasty Potato Chips in one of the show's challenges.

We strongly urge you to take advantage of this deal. We are sure that placing Tasty Potato Chips on *The Stress House* will increase your sales from television advertising. In addition, by using product placement rather than purchasing your traditional 30-second advertising spot from the network, you can save almost 30 percent of your television advertising dollars.

GO ON TO THE NEXT PAGE

SOURCE F

Zuckerman, Deena. "The Product Placement Revolution" *College Magazine,* 2004.

The following passage is excerpted from an article about the prominence of product placement.

Not since the "invention" of television commercials has a form of advertising taken the world by storm the way product placement has. And no topic in advertising has been more polarizing. It seems that for every person who supports product placement, there is one who is vehemently opposed. Why does this issue contribute to such intense feelings in people?

Those who support product placement tend to be the advertisers themselves. For less money and less time than they would spend on traditional 30-second commercials, companies can often see the same results from product placement advertising. Not everyone who supports product placement is an advertiser, though. There are a surprising number of viewers who prefer product placement to regular commercials. In fact, one person I spoke to expressed the hope that product placement would completely replace commercials. "Wouldn't it be great if there weren't any commercial breaks?" asked one student, Chris Rose. He continued, "That way, there would be more time for the actual show. You could get to see a whole 30 minutes of your favorite sit-com instead of the 20 minutes of show and 10 minutes of breaks that you seem to see now."

Opponents of product placement take a dim view of the motives of advertisers. The 18-to-24 generation has been sold to by television since their childhood, and some seem to resent additional intrusion by advertisers. "It's bad enough I have to suffer through commercials," says Beck Borenstein, "now I have to see commercials inside my favorite shows. It's just not fair. It makes me not want to buy a product."

Beck's comments notwithstanding, the product placement revolution continues. It seems advertisers are willing to bet (or are simply holding out hope) that more people out there agree with Chris than Beck.

STOP If you finish before time is called, you may check your work on this section only. Do not turn to any other section in the test.

ANSWER KEY AND EXPLANATIONS

Section I

1. D	11. A	21. A	31. B	41. C
2. E	12. D	22. A	32. E	42. B
3. B	13. D	23. E	33. B	43. C
4. C	14. B	24. B	34. D	44. D
5. A	15. E	25. B	35. C	45. D
6. B	16. D	26. E	36. D	46. B
7. C	17. C	27. B	37. E	47. E
8. D	18. C	28. C	38. B	48. A
9. E	19. A	29. A	39. D	49. C
10. E	20. B	30. A	40. A	50. B

1. **The correct answer is (D).** Whenever a series of answer choices includes broad statements or generalizations, check to see if the generalization may be the best response. In this case, choices (D) and (E) refer to concepts rather than to specific instances. Choice (D) relates directly to the phrase Elizabeth uses in her speech, whereas choice (E) does not relate to the content of the paragraph. Eliminate choice (E). A careful rereading of the sentence, in the context of the paragraph, will tell you that choices (A), (B), and (C) can be eliminated. Elizabeth does not say she is weak, choice (A), nor too emotional, choice (C). She would consider herself unworthy of God's mercies only if she believed that she ruled based on her own right rather than through God's will. Because she does not believe this, choice (B) is incorrect. Choice (D), the notion of women as the weaker sex, a belief widely held at the time, is the best answer.

2. **The correct answer is (E).** If you did not know immediately that this is a persuasive speech, using the process of elimination would tell you. You could rule out choice (A), because Elizabeth is not telling a story. Elizabeth is not presenting a well-reasoned argument, so cross off choice (B). Choice (C) is not correct because Elizabeth is not explaining something, and choice (D) can be eliminated because Elizabeth is not describing something to her audience. Choice (E) is the best answer because judging from her tone, diction, and content, Elizabeth is attempting to persuade her audience of something, to convince them of her position or point of view.

3. **The correct answer is (B).** This question asks you to identify a figure of speech. Elizabeth is comparing "pills" to the "cares and troubles of a Crown," so that rules out choices (C), (D), and (E), that have nothing to do with comparison. A simile must use *like* or *as*, which eliminates choice (A). That leaves choice (B), a metaphor.

4. **The correct answer is (C).** Although the passage has a bit of each of the choices, overall, given the speaker's rhetoric and purpose, the best answer is choice (C), persuasive.

5. **The correct answer is (A).** Elizabeth's purpose in this paragraph is to reinforce the premise that she rules by virtue of divine will (I), not by her own will. Elizabeth may indeed be tired of the burden of ruling (II), but that is not stated or implied here. She is saying that she *cannot* resign because God has given this burden to her, so item III is incorrect. Only item I is correct, and only choice (A) has item I.

6. **The correct answer is (B).** This is an inference question. If you don't know the answer right away, then try educated guessing. It is easy to rule out choices (D) and (E), because they are obviously wrong. Do not be distracted by choices (A) and (C) simply because they contain words that you see in the sentence. Choice (B) is the best inference from the sentence.

7. **The correct answer is (C).** Remember that you are dealing with definition and context. Remember also that Elizabeth is making a comparison. Always substitute the answer choices in the sentence to see which one makes the most sense. Choices (B), (C), and (E) seem likely possibilities, but choices (A) and (D) don't make sense. Elizabeth can neither approximate nor mirror "the cares and burdens of a Crown . . . than to the drugs of a learned physician." Because of the words *than to*, choice (C), *accurately compare*, fits within the construction and makes sense.

8. **The correct answer is (D).** Go back to the passage and read the entire sentence. The clue is in the clause "that God hath made me His Instrument to maintain His Truth and Glory." Choice (D) states the general idea that being God's instrument is synonymous with being obedient to God. Choice (B) has nothing to do with the passage. Choices (A) and (C) relate to Elizabeth's actions, whereas choice (D) restates God's action and is a truer statement of the clause. Choice (E) is the direct opposite of the clause.

9. **The correct answer is (E).** This is a recall question, that is, the answer is stated directly in the first paragraph of the passage. Of the answer choices, only choice (E) is contained there. The other choices are not.

10. **The correct answer is (E).** If you don't know the Latin terms, skip them and try to find the answer in another way. If you do know the Latin terms, you know that they are incorrect and do not apply here. Reductio ad absurdem, choice (B), is a proposition that proves to be absurd when carried to its logical conclusion. Argumentum ad hominem, choice (D), is an argument that appeals to the emotions rather than the intellect (a secondary meaning of ad hominem is the manner in which one attacks an opponent's character rather than addresses the person's contentions). Don't be fooled by choice (C). Love is mentioned, but it's not the point. That leaves choices (A) and (E). There is no comparison in the sentence, so there can be no metaphor, thus eliminating choice (A). Choice (E) is the best answer.

11. **The correct answer is (A).** Once in a while you may get a seemingly easy question. This is one such question, and don't read too much into it. It is just what you think it is at first glance. Elizabeth wants to be remembered to her hearers' loved ones. A clue is in the next phrase when she commends "yours to my best care." The *yours* refers to the loved ones again.

12. **The correct answer is (D).** Remember that tone and style are clues to purpose. If you answered question number 4 correctly, you know that the tone of the passage is persuasive. Choice (D) contains the word *convince*, which is part of the purpose of persuasion. Don't be distracted by the other choices. Choice (A) does not reflect the tone accurately; Elizabeth's expression of affection is secondary to her main point. Choice (B) is a misreading of Elizabeth's character, based on her speech. Choice (C) is one piece of support for her thesis. Choice (E) asks you to make an assumption without any basis in the passage and can be eliminated.

13. **The correct answer is (D).** Choices (A), (B), and (C) are not stated or implied in this paragraph. In fact, choice (B) is the opposite of what Elizabeth is saying. Choice (E) does not represent a comparison, leaving choice (D) as the answer.

14. **The correct answer is (B).** This is a straightforward vocabulary question. Choices (A), (D), and (E) are distracters. You may remember that the chimera was a mythical

monster, but in the context of the selection, the connotation is on the word *mythical*. Imaginary then, choice (B), is a better answer than choice (C). A bit later on, the author reinforces this idea by talking about the "false pretenses" that go with dueling.

15. **The correct answer is (E).** Choices (A), (B), and (C) are easily ruled out, because the writer is not simply describing, explaining, or telling a story. Choice (D) can be eliminated because an argument implies a premise/conclusion relationship, which is not the case here. The writer seeks to persuade the reader to think as he does; therefore, choice (E) is the correct answer.

16. **The correct answer is (D).** The writer states in the first paragraph that "it is worth our consideration to examine into this chimerical groundless humor [dueling], and to lay every other thought aside, until we have stripped it of all its false pretenses . . . ." This statement indicates that choices (B), (C), and (E) are incorrect. The author says nothing about alternatives or changes in dueling, and the tone of the piece is not amusing. The process of elimination then leaves choices (A) and (D). While the article may indeed educate the reader, choice (A), the stated purpose is to discredit the practice of dueling, choice (D).

17. **The correct answer is (C).** This is one of those questions in which each of the answer choices seems a little bit true. Go back to the passage. The writer makes repeated use of the word *honor*, which should give you a clue. In addition, choice (B) would be correct only if the writer were speaking metaphorically about a debt of honor, which he isn't. Choice (E) is incorrect because the last sentence in paragraph 4 indicates that the real purpose of the duel is to allow some foolhardy coxcomb to avoid having to admit he was wrong. That leaves choices (A), (C), and (D). While both choices (A) and (D) are true statements about duels, they do not answer the question, leaving choice (C) as the correct answer.

18. **The correct answer is (C).** A "brave man" is a gentleman, and a "hand below that of a common hangman" means a person of a lower social class than a hangman. Item I is not stated or implied in the passage, which rules out choices (A) and (D). Item II is true, but it does not relate to the statement from the passage, eliminating choices (B), (D), and (E). Only point III relates to the statement, so choice (C), item III only, is correct.

19. **The correct answer is (A).** In the third paragraph, the writer gives us an anecdote of "a country gentleman" to strengthen his position. Choice (B), satire, is a literary work that uses sarcasm and ridicule to expose vices and follies; this work is too serious in tone to be satire. There is little imagery, choice (C), in the third paragraph. In an allegory, characters and events represent abstract qualities, which is not true of the country gentleman. A parable, choice (E), is a short tale that teaches a moral. The purpose of the tale of the country gentleman is not to teach a moral but to illustrate the author's point.

20. **The correct answer is (B).** This is a recall question, meaning that the answer is stated directly in the text. In the second paragraph, the writer states "that all men fight against their will." Choice (A) can be eliminated because the question asks only about what the writer believes. Choice (C) is incorrect because the author is offering an alternative—not to duel. The author skewers choice (D) in his essay, and choice (E) is not stated in the text.

21. **The correct answer is (A).** In line 5, the author implies that he is writing an article, so he must be writing for a newspaper or magazine. (This piece is by Richard Steele of *Tatler* and *Spectator* fame.) Therefore, this is a professional piece with formal diction, quickly and easily eliminating choices (B), (C), (D), and (E).

22. **The correct answer is (A).** Looking for consistency among answers will help you rule out choice (C), because we already eliminated satire in question 19, and although the writer uses humor, the piece is not particularly witty. The piece is serious but not introspective, that is, told from the deep feelings of the author, choice (B). Neither is the piece impassioned or ardent, choice (D). While the author is obviously educated, the piece is not filled with allusions or factual references, thus eliminating choice (E). The piece is written to be persuasive using a reasonable tone, choice (A).

23. **The correct answer is (E).** In checking points I, II, and III against the first paragraph, you can see that all three are true about the rhetorical function of the first paragraph. Only answer choice (E) has all three items.

24. **The correct answer is (B).** This *not/except* question tests your knowledge of English grammar. The phrase "from a young lady" is an adjectival phrase, so choice (A) is true about the sentence and an incorrect answer to the question. "Into so fatal a folly" is an adverbial phrase, making choice (C) true and incorrect. Both are examples of prepositional phrases, so choice (D) is true and incorrect. "Written in the most passionate terms" is a participial phrase, so choice (E) is incorrect. A gerund is a word ending in -*ing*, and there is none in the sentence, so choice (B) is not true and the right answer.

25. **The correct answer is (B).** Recalling the figures of speech, you might remember that a simile, choice (A), requires the words *like* or *as*. Choice (C), personification, is the giving of human qualities to a nonhuman thing. An analogy, choice (D), is a comparison to a directly parallel case. Choice (E), an overstatement, is an exaggeration. Choice (B), a metaphor, is the only one that fits. A metaphor is a comparison of two things, often related, and does not employ *like* or *as*.

26. **The correct answer is (E).** Each item, I, II, and III, is true. None of them can be eliminated; therefore, choice (E), which contains all three items, is the correct answer.

27. **The correct answer is (B).** When you are asked to find the best summary of a paragraph, it is a good idea to read over that paragraph with the answer choices in mind. Choice (B) is correct, based on the information in the second paragraph. Choice (A) is incorrect; the paragraph states that the original laws ignored English common law in favor of the Bible or the judgment of magistrates. Based on this, choice (D) is also incorrect. Choice (C) is incorrect; at the time of the Stamp Act, the colonies saw the benefit of English common law.

28. **The correct answer is (C).** Because this is an older work, the citations look different from those you may be used to seeing. Choice (A) is incorrect. Queen Elizabeth and Sir Walter Raleigh were not born until the sixteenth century, so they could not be referenced in a book published in the 1300s. Choice (B) is incorrect because it would make no sense to include the total number of pages in a book in a citation. Choice (C) makes the most sense. The number 1381 follows the Roman numeral II. It is reasonable to assume that the II is a part number, and 1381 is a page number. Remember, the purpose of a footnote of this type is to refer the reader to the original source of the information cited. There is no support in the paragraph for choices (D) and (E).

29. **The correct answer is (A).** The sentence that precedes the one in the question reads "As was anticipated in the Raleigh patent, it was found from the first and everywhere that if the common law was to be applied to the rough conditions of colonial life some modifications were necessary." It is the modifications that the colonists were free to make at their pleasure. Therefore, choice (A) is correct.

30. **The correct answer is (A).** In the context of the paragraph, "ignored" makes the most sense. The paragraph explains that at first, the colonist made up their own laws as

needed. Choice (B) does not make sense; people do not sell laws. Choice (C) is incorrect; the colonists ignored English common law, they did not adhere to (stick to) it. Choice (D) also does not make sense. Choice (E) is incorrect; the colonists created their own laws. They did not revise common law.

31. **The correct answer is (B).** There is no direct quotation in the third paragraph, so you can eliminate choice (A). However, you can infer from the footnote that the third paragraph shows the source the author used to come to the conclusion expressed in the third paragraph. The footnote is not included to provide suggestions for further reading.

32. **The correct answer is (E).** To correctly answer this question, think about your general impressions of the passage. The passage presents facts and does not include any characters, so you can eliminate choice (A). Choice (B) does not work; although it is scholarly, the passage does not involve science. There is no indication the passage is about the history of a specific person, so choice (C) is incorrect. The passage is too long and detailed to be an encyclopedia entry. This leaves you with choice (E). The passage discusses the history of law in the colonies, and presents historical facts, so you can conclude that choice (E) is correct.

33. **The correct answer is (B).** With the exception of footnote 1, which cites a book written by another author, all of the other footnotes cite original publications and reports for the states of Connecticut and Massachusetts. As the footnotes cite original documents, choice (A) is incorrect. Choice (C) is incorrect; the footnotes provide the sources of the facts in the passage. The author used the sources for support and draws conclusions, so choice (D) cannot be true. There is no evidence to support the claim made in choice (E).

34. **The correct answer is (D).** The repetition of the word "They" followed by a past-tense verb is an example of parallel construction; that is, for emphasis, the sentences are put together in a similar manner. There is no comparison made, so simile is incorrect. Foreshadowing is when an author hints at later events in story and is incorrect. There is no evidence of sarcasm in the sentences, so choice (C) is not correct. The sentences do not provide visual or other sensory descriptions, so rule out choice (E).

35. **The correct answer is (C).** Support for the assertion made in choice (C) can be found in the last paragraph, "This mingling of judicial with legislative functions is a thing to be tolerated only while the foundations of a government are being laid." Therefore, choice (C) is correct and you can eliminate choice (A), as well. There is no support in the passage for choice (B). Choice (D) is also not supported in the passage—the author makes references to the use (or disuse) of English common law in colonial government but makes no statement to support the idea that it is the best way to govern all societies. There is no support for choice (E).

36. **The correct answer is (D).** Here, the word type is used to mean example. In this case, it may be helpful to substitute the word "type" with each of the answer choices. The proviso of Queen Elizabeth is an example used to illustrate why colonial laws should conform as much as possible to English common law. The other choices are all synonyms of type but do not fit in the context of the paragraph.

37. **The correct answer is (E).** The passage talks about the history of colonial government. Choice (A), strident, does not fit—there is no sense of urgency in the author's tone. The author is not pleading, so choice (B) is incorrect. The tone is academic, not emotional, so choice (C) is incorrect. The tone is not emotional, but neither is it cold, so you can eliminate choice (D). This leaves choice (E), scholarly, which is the best description of the tone of the article.

38. **The correct answer is (B).** While choices (A) and (E) are mentioned in the selection, they only support the main idea—that slavery is intolerable—they do not restate it. While white children are mentioned in the passage, Douglass does not describe experiences with them, so choice (C) is incorrect. Choice (D) is wrong because there is no mention of the Constitution.

39. **The correct answer is (D).** The question is easily answered by working through the choices and eliminating the wrong ones. There is nothing amusing, ironic, or academic in this passage; thus, choices (A), (B), and (C) are eliminated. While the writer has every right to be angry, he does not express that emotion in this passage, eliminating choice (E). Certainly, the passage is both powerful and sincere, choice (D).

40. **The correct answer is (A).** If you know who Frederick Douglass was, you will know that his autobiographies are considered classic examples of the slave narrative genre. If you do not know who he is, then you will have to work your way through the choices. A picaresque novel, choice (B), is a fictional account of the adventures of a vagabond or rogue, which does not fit the life described here. Thus choice (B) is incorrect. Since Douglass wrote this, evidenced by the use of the first-person pronouns, it cannot be a biography, choice (C), nor can it be a textbook. The same logic eliminates choice (E), since a secondary source is a work written about another person or another time.

41. **The correct answer is (C).** If you correctly answered the question about tone, this one should have been easy. The style is plain, easy to understand, and eloquent in its simplicity. There are no tortured sentences, choices (A) and (D), or Shakespearean phrases, choice (E). While the writer does use some figurative language, the effect is not poetic, choice (B).

42. **The correct answer is (B).** This is another good question on which to use the process of elimination. At first glance, choice (A) seems as if it might have some validity; however, there is little mention of spiritual aspects in the passage. Likewise, choice (D) has possibilities, but the writer does not talk about dangers to owners, only the debilitating effects on those enslaved. Choice (C) is wrong because Douglass does not discuss the Constitution or the Bill of Rights. The issues in choice (E) do not appear in the selection.

43. **The correct answer is (C).** This is a comprehension question. Douglass states that the book created in him a discontent with his status as a slave. You might feel that choice (D) is correct, but be aware that the writer already knew that he was a slave. The question asks about something that happened after Douglass bought the book, so choice (A) is incorrect since it states how much he paid for the book. Neither choice (B) nor choice (E) is mentioned in the selection.

44. **The correct answer is (D).** There are no literary allusions in the passage. An allusion is a passing reference to people, places, or events that readers will recognize. The writer does refer obliquely to the Declaration of Independence once, but that hardly qualifies as many allusions, and it is not a literary but a political allusion in any case. If you got question 41 right, you will know that Douglass's descriptions are straightforward, choice (A). Because choice (B) is an accurate description of the selection, so then is choice (E). The passage is also factual in nature, recounting what Douglass did and felt, choice (C).

45. **The correct answer is (D).** Here, the writer is using figurative language to emphasize the horror of slavery. He likens slavery to a dragon's lair. To answer this question, you need to figure out to what the "this knowledge" refers. It would be unlikely that Douglass was referring to a person with this phrase, eliminating choice (A). The closest reference is to the contents of the volume he was reading, but not the volume itself,

Columbian Orator, choice (C). The contents relate to the value of liberty to illustrate the ills of slavery, choice (D). Choice (E) is too broad, and choice (B) is not relevant to the context.

46. **The correct answer is (B).** Structure refers to the design or arrangement of parts in a work of literature. Metaphors are figures of speech that compare two unlike things, so choice (A) does not apply. Choice (C), exaggeration, is overstatement, usually for the purpose of creating humor or horror, neither of which is the case in this passage. While the selection is eloquent, choice (D), eloquence is not a recognized structure. Cacophony, choice (E), is a sound device, not a structure.

47. **The correct answer is (E).** A gerund is a verb form ending in *-ing* that functions as a noun. *Thinking*, in this sentence, functions as a predicate nominative, or *noun*. A participle, choice (A), may also end in *-ing* (or *-ed*) but functions as an adjective, not a noun. A verb, choice (B), is the predicate in a sentence, the action word. An infinitive, choice (C), is almost always made up of *to* plus a verb. An adverbial phrase, choice (D), modifies a verb or adjective. None of these applies to the word *thinking*.

48. **The correct answer is (A).** This question tests your comprehension. The lines you are asked about record Douglass's recognition that slavery is intolerable. The writer can no longer be happy in his state of bondage. Choice (B) does not relate to anything in the selection. The words *gleesome* and *mirth* are used in the selection, but there is no mention of escape, choice (C). Choices (D) and (E) would require a metaphysical interpretation that you are not asked to make.

49. **The correct answer is (C).** *Redolent* does mean sweet-smelling, choice (B), as well as evocative, choice (C), but in context, choice (C) is the correct answer. Choice (A) might seem to fit with the speeches, but nature is not filled with liberty. Choices (D) and (E) are distracters.

50. **The correct answer is (B).** If you got question 40 right, this answer was easy. As a slave narrative, the mode of discourse is choice (B), narrative. Because slavery is described from the point of view of a personal story, the selection is more than exposition, choice (A), and description, choice (D). Although Douglass may wish to persuade the reader of the dehumanizing effects of slavery, his tone is neither argumentative nor persuasive.

Section II

SUGGESTIONS FOR QUESTION 1

The following are points that you might have chosen to include in your essay on *Civil Disobedience*. Consider them as you complete your self-evaluation. Revise your essay using points from the list to strengthen it.

Form

- Excerpt from an essay

Mode

- Persuasion

Subject

- Government

- The type of government Thoreau considers the best

- What's wrong with the government of his day

Author

- Henry David Thoreau, Transcendentalist

Theme

- Government should do as little as possible

Tone

- Sincere

- Persuasive

- Light and humorous

Diction/Syntax/Style

- Sophisticated diction

- Complex sentence structure

- Use of first-person plural pronoun: "us against them" relationship

- Humor through use of images such as wooden gun, punishment of obstructive legislators

- Order of importance organization

Literary Devices

- Metaphor of wooden gun for the government

- Comparison of commerce and trade to rubber, able to bounce over obstructions that the government puts in their path

- Simile for government legislators

SUGGESTIONS FOR QUESTION 2

The following are points that you might have chosen to include in your essay on Woodrow Wilson's *Appeal for Neutrality*. Consider them as you complete your self-evaluation. Revise your essay using points from the list to strengthen it.

Form

- Speech

- A formal proclamation of neutrality

Mode

- Argument

Tone

- Persuasive

- Paternal

Speaker

- President Woodrow Wilson

Subject

- Maintain U.S. neutrality in World War I

Theme

- Neutrality

- Unity

- America first

- Division fatal to peace

Diction/Structure/Style

- Formal diction

- Educated vocabulary

- Varied sentence structure

- Easily understood by all citizens

Purpose

- Formal declaration of U.S. neutrality

- Appeal to citizens for impartiality in spirit as well as in actions

- Appeal for unity

Note: The discussion of your own attitude toward U.S. involvement in world conflicts should reflect a thoughtful review of the pros and cons of Wilson's argument in light of current world politics and the role of the United States.

SUGGESTIONS FOR QUESTION 3

This question asks for a synthesis essay that supports, qualifies, or disputes the argument that product placement is the most effective form of television advertising. It does not matter which position you take as long as you provide adequate support for your argument using your own opinions along with information from the sources. Consider the following as you complete your self-evaluation. Revise your essay using points from the list to strengthen it if necessary. Remember to proofread your response and make sure your grammar, syntax, and spelling are correct.

Thesis statement/introduction

- Clear definition of the issue—in this case, the effectiveness of product placement as a form of advertising

- Clear statement of your position on the issue: statement of the reason you agree or disagree with the statement that product placement is the most effective form of advertising

Supporting details

- Support is based on your own opinions about the position you take but the information in the sources is also used

- Show a clear connection between the sources you choose to cite

- Sources are seamlessly integrated with appropriate transitions

- At least three of the six sources are used

- Explain the logic of how you arrived at the conclusion you did, based on the information provided in the sources

- Acknowledge opposing arguments and refute them

- Attribute both direct and indirect citations

Conclusion

- Include a restatement of your thesis tied into the supporting evidence you used. (ex: In sum, there can be no other conclusion drawn from the evidence except that there is no more effective form of advertising than product placement.) Conclusion neatly sums up your argument.

SELF-EVALUATION RUBRIC FOR THE FREE RESPONSE ESSAYS

	8–9	6–7	5	3–4	1–2	0
Overall Impression	Demonstrates excellent control of the literature and outstanding writing competence; thorough and effective; incisive	Demonstrates good control of the literature and good writing competence; less thorough and incisive than the highest papers	Reveals simplistic thinking and/or immature writing; adequate skills	Incomplete thinking; fails to respond adequately to part or parts of the question; may paraphrase rather than analyze	Unacceptably brief; fails to respond to the question; little clarity	Lacking skill and competence
Understanding of the Text	Excellent understanding of the text; exhibits perception and clarity; original or unique approach; includes apt and specific references	Good understanding of the text; exhibits perception and clarity; includes specific references	Superficial understanding of the text; elements of literature vague, mechanical, overgeneralized	Misreadings and lack of persuasive evidence from the text; meager and unconvincing treatment of literary elements	Serious misreadings and little supporting evidence from the text; erroneous treatment of literary elements	A response with no more than a reference to the literature; blank response, or one completely off the topic
Organization and Development	Meticulously organized and thoroughly developed; coherent and unified	Well organized and developed; coherent and unified	Reasonably organized and developed; mostly coherent and unified	Somewhat organized and developed; some incoherence and lack of unity	Little or no organization and development; incoherent and void of unity	No apparent organization or development; incoherent
Use of Sentences	Effectively varied and engaging; virtually error free	Varied and interesting; a few errors	Adequately varied; some errors	Somewhat varied and marginally interesting; one or more major errors	Little or no variation; dull and uninteresting; some major errors	Numerous major errors
Word Choice	Interesting and effective; virtually error free	Generally interesting and effective; a few errors	Occasionally interesting and effective; several errors	Somewhat dull and ordinary; some errors in diction	Mostly dull and conventional; numerous errors	Numerous major errors; extremely immature
Grammar and Usage	Virtually error free	Occasional minor errors	Several minor errors	Some major errors	Severely flawed; frequent major errors	Extremely flawed

SELF-EVALUATION RUBRIC FOR THE SYNTHESIS ESSAYS

	8–9	6–7	5	3–4	1–2	0
Overall Impression	Demonstrates excellent control of effective writing techniques; sophisticated argumentation, and well integrated synthesis of source information; uses citations convincingly	Demonstrates good control of effective writing techniques; somewhat thorough and incisive; uses citations appropriately	Demonstrates general competence in stating and defending a position; some inconsistencies and weaknesses in argumentation	Demonstrates some skill but lacks understanding of question and sources	Demonstrates little skill in taking a coherent position and defending it or in using sources	Lacks skill and competence
Understanding of the Text	Takes a clear position that defends, challenges, or qualifies the question accurately	Demonstrates a somewhat superficial understanding of the sources	Displays some misreading of the sources or some stretching of information to support the chosen position	Takes a position that may misread or simplify the sources; may present overly simple argument	Misreads sources, or lacks an argument, or summarizes the sources rather than using them to support a position	Position does not accurately reflect the sources; no more than a listing of the sources
Organization and Development	Clearly states a position; uses at least three sources to support that position convincingly and effectively; coherent and unified	Clearly states a position; uses at least three sources to support that position; adequate development of ideas but less convincing; coherent and unified	Generally clearly stated position and links between position and cited sources; some weaknesses in logic; cites three sources	Creates weak connections between argument and cited sources; cites only two sources	Lacks coherent development or organization; cites one or no sources	No apparent organization or development; incoherent; cites no sources
Use of Sentences	Effectively varied and engaging; close to error free	Varied and interesting; a few errors	Adequately varied; some errors	Somewhat varied and marginally interesting; one or more major errors	Little or no variation; dull and uninteresting; some major errors	Numerous major errors
Word Choice	Uses the vocabulary of the topic as evident in the sources; interesting and effective; virtually error free	Demonstrates ease in using vocabulary from the sources	Occasional use of vocabulary from the sources; occasionally interesting and effective	Somewhat dull and ordinary; some errors in diction; no attempt to integrate vocabulary from the sources	Mostly dull and conventional; no attempt to integrate vocabulary from the sources	Numerous major errors; extremely immature
Grammar and Usage	Virtually error free	Occasional minor errors	Several minor errors	Some major errors	Severely flawed; frequent major errors	Extremely flawed

Using the rubrics on the previous pages, rate yourself in each of the categories below for each essay on the test. Enter on the lines below the number from the rubric that most accurately reflects your performance in each category. Then calculate the average of the six numbers to determine your final score. It is difficult to score yourself objectively, so you may wish to ask a respected friend or teacher to assess your writing for a more accurate reflection of its strengths and weaknesses. On the AP test itself, a reader will rate your essay on a scale of 0 to 9, with 9 being the highest.

Rate each category from 9 (high) to 0 (low).

Question 1

SELF-EVALUATION

Overall Impression _____
Understanding of the Text _____
Organization and Development _____
Use of Sentences _____
Word Choice (Diction) _____
Grammar and Usage _____

TOTAL _____
    Divide by 6 for final score _____

OBJECTIVE EVALUATION

Overall Impression _____
Understanding of the Text _____
Organization and Development _____
Use of Sentences _____
Word Choice (Diction) _____
Grammar and Usage _____

TOTAL _____
    Divide by 6 for final score _____

Question 2

SELF-EVALUATION

Overall Impression _____
Understanding of the Text _____
Organization and Development _____
Use of Sentences _____
Word Choice (Diction) _____
Grammar and Usage _____

TOTAL _____
    Divide by 6 for final score _____

OBJECTIVE EVALUATION

Overall Impression _____
Understanding of the Text _____
Organization and Development _____
Use of Sentences _____
Word Choice (Diction) _____
Grammar and Usage _____

TOTAL _____
    Divide by 6 for final score _____

Question 3

SELF-EVALUATION

Overall Impression _____
Understanding of the Text _____
Organization and Development _____
Use of Sentences _____
Word Choice (Diction) _____
Grammar and Usage _____

TOTAL _____
    Divide by 6 for final score _____

OBJECTIVE EVALUATION

Overall Impression _____
Understanding of the Text _____
Organization and Development _____
Use of Sentences _____
Word Choice (Diction) _____
Grammar and Usage _____

TOTAL _____
    Divide by 6 for final score _____

APPENDIXES

College-by-College Guide to AP Credit and Placement

For the past two decades, national and international participation in the AP Program has grown steadily. Colleges and universities routinely award credit for AP test scores of 3, 4, or 5, depending on the test taken. The following chart indicates the score required for AP credit, how many credits are granted, what courses are waived based on those credits, and other policy stipulations at more than 400 selective colleges and universities.

Use this chart to discover just how valuable a good score on the AP English Language & Composition Test can be!

appendix a

School Name	Required Score	Credits Granted	Course Waived	Stipulations
Agnes Scott College (GA)	4–5	4	ENG 110	Students who score 4–5 on both English exams get 8 hours and fulfill the literature distribution in addition to the Specific 1 standard.
Albany College of Pharmacy of Union University (NY)	4–5			
Albertson College of Idaho (ID)	3–5			
Albion College (MI)	4		ENGL 101 & WCE	
Albright College (PA)	4–5			
Allegheny College (PA)	4–5			
Alma College (MI)	3		ENG 100(4)	
Asbury College (KY)	3	3	ENG 110	
	4	3	ENG 251	School only listed this category as English. It was not divided into sub categories.
Auburn University (AL)	4–5	3	ENGL 1100	
Augustana College (IL)	4	3	None	
Augustana College (SD)	4–5			
Austin College (TX)	4–5		English Elective	English Elective and 1/2 Writing Credit.
Azusa Pacific University (CA)	3–4	3	Freshman Writing Seminar	
	5	6	Freshman Writing Seminar/3 units non-GS elective	If score is a 5 in both English Language and English Literature, student receives 9 units of credit - ENGL110, ENGL111, 3 units non-GS elective.
Babson College (MA)	4–5			
Baldwin-Wallace College (OH)	3–5	3	ENG 111	
Bard College (NY)	5			
Barnard College (NY)	4–5	3		English was only AP Test they had. There was no split between Lang & Comp, Lit & Comp.
Bates College (ME)	4–5		1 Unspecified	
Baylor University (TX)	4		ENGL 1302	For the minimum score: 4, plus ACT English 29+, or SAT Verbal/Critical Reading 670+.
Belmont University (TN)	4–5		ENG 1010	
Beloit College (WI)	4–5	4		Credit will be granted once a student matriculates to Beloit College and provides official score reports to the Registrar's Office.
Benedictine University (IL)	3	3	RHET 101	

School Name	Required Score	Credits Granted	Course Waived	Stipulations
Bentley College (MA)	4–5			High school graduates who have taken the AP exams may be awarded credit for scores of 4 or 5, on any subject test.
Berea College (KY)	3–5			
Bernard M. Baruch College of the City University of New York (NY)	4–5			
Birmingham-Southern College (AL)	5		EH 102	
Boston College (MA)	4–5			
Boston University (MA)	4–5		WR 099	
Bradley University (IL)	3–5	3	ENG 101	
Brandeis University (MA)	4–5			
Brigham Young University (UT)	3–5	6	ENGL 115	
Bryan College (TN)	3–5			
Bryn Mawr College (PA)	5			
Bucknell University (PA)	4–5			Credit is awarded for only 1 English AP exam.
Butler University (IN)	4–5	3	EN 102	
Calvin College (MI)	4	3	ENGL 101	
	5	6	ENGL 101 & ENGL 201	
Canisius College (NY)	3	3	Free elective	
	4–5	6	ENG 101 and 1 Free elective	If Honors student, 2 Free electives.
Carleton College (MN)	4–5	6		Score of 5: Part I of Writing Requirement fulfilled.
Carnegie Mellon University (PA)	4–5			
Carroll College (MT)	3–5			
Carson-Newman College (TN)	4–5			
Case Western Reserve University (OH)	4–5	3	ENGL 150	
Cedarville University (OH)	3–5	0	None	
Central College (IA)	3–5			
Centre College (KY)	4–5			
Chapman University (CA)	4	3	ENG 103	
Christian Brothers University (TN)	4–5			
Clarkson University (NY)	4–5		COMM 210	
Clark University (MA)	4–5			
Clemson University (SC)	3–4	3	ENGL 101	

School Name	Required Score	Credits Granted	Course Waived	Stipulations
Clemson University—*continued*	5	6	ENGL 101 & ENGL 103	
Coe College (IA)	4–5			
Colby College (ME)	4–5			
Colgate University (NY)	4–5			
College of Charleston (SC)	3	3 or 6	ENGl 101 & ENGL 102	3 = ENGL 101, 4 or 5 = ENGL 101 & 102
The College of New Jersey (NJ)	4–5		Elective	Student with a minimum score of 4 in any AP History or English receives waiver of WRI 102 Academic Writing.
College of Saint Benedict (MN)	5	4	ENGL 211	
The College of St. Scholastica (MN)	4–5	4	ENG 1110	
College of the Atlantic (ME)	4–5			
College of the Holy Cross (MA)	4–5			
The College of William and Mary (VA)	4–5		Writing 101	
The College of Wooster (OH)	4–5			
Colorado Christian University (CO)	3–5			
The Colorado College (CO)	5			
Colorado School of Mines (CO)	4–5	3	Free elective	
Colorado State University (CO)	4–5	3	COCC 150	
Columbia College (NY)	5	3	No exemption	
Columbia University, The Fu Foundation School of Engineering and Applied Science (NY)	5	3	No exemption	
Concordia College (MN)	3		Disc 101	
	4		Disc 101 & 102	
Connecticut College (CT)	4–5			
Converse College (SC)	3	3		Students who score 3 in English will be placed in English 290 (Advanced Composition) and will receive the AP credit only upon successful completion of English 290.
	4–5	6		
Cornell College (IA)	4–5			
Cornerstone University (MI)	4–5	4	ENG 113	Credit will not be granted for both English Lang & Comp and English Lit & Comp.
Covenant College (GA)	4	3	ENG 111	
Creighton University (NE)	5	3	ENG 150	

School Name	Required Score	Credits Granted	Course Waived	Stipulations
Dartmouth College (NH)	5			
Davidson College (NC)	4–5		ENG 199	AP credit does not satisfy the composition requirement, which must be met by a W-course at Davidson. ENG 110 satisfies the literature requirement.
Denison University (OH)	4–5		FYS 101	
DePauw University (IN)	4–5	4	ENG 130	
Dickinson College (PA)	4–5		ENG 211	Although students receive credit for ENGL 211, this credit does NOT fulfill the Writing Intensive requirement.
Dominican University (IL)	3–5	6	ENGL 101	
Drew University (NJ)	4–5	4	ENGL 1	English Comp only.
Drexel University (PA)	4–5			
Drury University (MO)	3–5	3	ENGL 150	
Duke University (NC)	4–5		ENGL 29	
Earlham College (IN)	5	6		
Elizabethtown College (PA)	3–5	3	EN 100	
Elmira College (NY)	3	3	3 elective credits	
	4	6	6 elective credits	
	5	9		Registrar and Writing Faculty will determine placement.
Elon University (NC)	4–5	4	ENG 110	
Embry-Riddle Aeronautical University (AZ)	3–5			
Emerson College (MA)	4–5		WP 101	
Emory University (GA)	4–5	4		In the case of two AP results for individual language examinations (i.e., English Literature and English Language), credit may be awarded for either examination but not for both.
Erskine College (SC)	4–5			
Eugene Lang College The New School for Liberal Arts (NY)	4–5			
Fairfield University (CT)	4–5	3	EN 11	
Florida Institute of Technology (FL)	4–5	3	Composition and Rhetoric	
Florida International University (FL)	3	3	ENC 1101	
	4–5	6	ENC 1101 & ENC 1102	
Florida State University (FL)	3	3	ENC 1101	

School Name	Required Score	Credits Granted	Course Waived	Stipulations
Florida State University—*continued*	4–5	6	ENC 1101 & ENC 1102	
Fordham University (NY)	3–5			Currently, a grade of 3 will be accepted as elective credit. However, grades of 4 or 5 may be applied towards the core curriculum.
Franciscan University of Steubenville (OH)	4–5			
Franklin and Marshall College (PA)	4–5		General elective	
Furman University (SC)	4–5		ENGL 12	
George Fox University (OR)	3–5	3	WRIT 110	
Georgetown College (KY)	3–5	3–6		
Georgetown University (DC)	4–5	3		If a student takes both tests, then the higher score is used because credit is awarded only once for both tests. No credit for a score of 3.
The George Washington University (DC)	4	3	ENGL 99	
	5	6	ENGL 99	
Georgia Institute of Technology (GA)	4–5	3	ENGL 1101	
Georgia State University (GA)	3–5			
Gettysburg College (PA)	4–5	4		
Gonzaga University (WA)	4	3	Elective	Credits will be awarded which may be used to fulfill the overall credit requirements for graduation, but may not be used to fulfill core curriculum or major requirements.
	5	3	ENGL 101	
Gordon College (MA)	4–5			
Goshen College (IN)	3	3	elective; must take Engl 110 or 204 for Gen Ed	
	4–5	3	Engl 110/Gen Ed	
Goucher College (MD)	4–5			
Grinnell College (IA)	4–5	4		
Grove City College (PA)	4–5			
Gustavus Adolphus College (MN)	4–5			

School Name	Required Score	Credits Granted	Course Waived	Stipulations
Hamilton College (NY)	4–5			Recipients of scores of 4 or 5 on either or both of the AP examinations in English may place directly into one of several 200-level courses.
Hamline University (MN)	4–5		Elective Credit	
Hampshire College (MA)	3–5			
Hanover College (IN)	3–5			
Harding University (AR)	3	3	ENG 111	
Harvard University (MA)	5		No equivalent	Placement in Expository Writing (required of all freshmen)
Haverford College (PA)	4–5			The registrar will award one course credit for an AP score of 5 and one-half course credit for a score of 4. No credit is awarded for scores under 4.
Hendrix College (AR)	4–5		ENGL 110	
Hillsdale College (MI)	3	3		
	4–5	6		
Hiram College (OH)	4–5			
Hobart and William Smith Colleges (NY)	4–5			
Hope College (MI)	4–5			
Houghton College (NY)	4–5	3	Principles of Writing	Should a student take both AP English exams, he/she would receive credit for both POW and Lit of West World.
Illinois College (IL)	4–5			
Illinois Institute of Technology (IL)	4–5	3	COM 101	
Illinois Wesleyan University (IL)	4–5			a student can earn a Writing Intensive Flag if his or her score is a 4 or 5 on the English Language and Composition Exam and a grade of B or higher was received in the Gateway Colloquium course.
Iowa State University of Science and Technology (IA)	3–5			
Ithaca College (NY)	4–5	6	ENG 377–1 & ENG 307–1	Adv. Placement is granted for only one English exam.
James Madison University (VA)	4–5	3	GWRIT 103	
John Brown University (AR)	3–5		EGL 1013	
John Carroll University (OH)	4–5	6	EN 111 & EN 112	
Juniata College (PA)				
Kalamazoo College (MI)	4–5			

School Name	Required Score	Credits Granted	Course Waived	Stipulations
Kenyon College (OH)	4–5		ENGL 111Y-112Y or ENGL 103 & 104	Placement in any 200-level course.
Knox College (IL)	3		ENG 101	
	4–5		ENG 101 & ENG 102	
Lafayette College (PA)	4–5		ENG 110	Can only receive credit for English 110 once.
Lake Forest College (IL)	4–5			
Lawrence Technological University (MI)	4	3		Enroll in LLT 1213. If the student earns a "C" or better in the first attempt, he/she should contact the Student Service Center to request credit for COM 1103.
	5	3	COM 1103	
Lawrence University (WI)	4–5			
Lebanon Valley College (PA)	4–5	6	ENG 111 & ENG 112	
Lehigh University (PA)	4	3	Freshman English	These students will complete the six-hour requirement by taking an English course suggested by the department, typically ENGL 11.
	5	6	Freshman English	
LeTourneau University (TX)	4–5	3	ENGL 1013	A student with scores of 4–5 on both the English Language and the English Literature tests will receive 3 hours in ENGL 1013 and 3 hours in a Literature Elective for a total of 6 hours of credit.
Lewis & Clark College (OR)	4–5			Placement into English 205 or 206.
Linfield College (OR)	4–5			
Lipscomb University (TN)	3	6	EN 1113	
	4–5	6	EN 1113 & EN 1123	
Louisiana State University and Agricultural and Mechanical College (LA)	3	3	ENG 1001	
	4	6	ENG 1001 & ENG 1002	
	5	9	ENG 1001, 1002 & 2025 or ENG 2027, 2029 or 2123	

School Name	Required Score	Credits Granted	Course Waived	Stipulations
Loyola College in Maryland (MD)	4–5			
Loyola Marymount University (CA)	4–5	3	ENG 110	
Loyola University Chicago (IL)	4–5	3	ENGL 105	
Luther College (IA)	4–5	4		
Lycoming College (PA)	4–5	8	ENGL 106 & ENGL 215	
Lyon College (AR)	4–5			
Macalester College (MN)	4–5		ENGL 101	AP Credit in English may not be included in the minimum number of courses for a major or minor in English.
Marist College (NY)	3–4	3	ENG 116L	
	5	6	ENG 116L & ENG 117L	
Marlboro College (VT)	4–5	8		
Marquette University (WI)	4	3	ENGL 1	
	5	6	ENGL 1 & ENGL 2	
Maryville College (TN)	3–5			
Maryville University of Saint Louis (MO)	3–5			
The Master's College and Seminary (CA)	3–5			
McDaniel College (MD)	4–5			Students may receive advanced placement plus up to 8 hours credit.
McGill University (QC)	4–5	6		May not take Effective Communication or English for Academic Purposes.
McKendree College (IL)	3–5	3	None	
Mercer University (GA)	3–5			
Messiah College (PA)	3–5	3	English elective	
Miami University (OH)	4	3	ENG 111	Then enroll in English 113.
	5	6	ENG 111 & ENG 112	
Michigan State University (MI)	3	0	WRA 150	
	4–5	4	WRA 150	
Michigan Technological University (MI)	4–5	3	UN 1001	Or 3 credits for UN 2001 if student is already receiving credit UN 1001.
Middlebury College (VT)	4–5			Only one English exam will receive credit; this cannot be used toward the English major.

School Name	Required Score	Credits Granted	Course Waived	Stipulations
Milligan College (TN)	4–5	6	HUMN 101W & General elective	
Millsaps College (MS)	4–5	6	General elective credit only	
Mills College (CA)	4–5			
Mississippi College (MS)	4–5	3	ENG 101	
Missouri State University (MO)	4–5	3	ENG electives	
Moravian College (PA)	4–5			
Morehouse College (GA)	4–5			
Mount Holyoke College (MA)	4–5	4		
Mount Saint Vincent University (NS)	4–5			
Muhlenberg College (PA)	3–5			
Murray State University (KY)	3–4	3	ENG 101	If you get a score of 3 take ENG 102, if you get a score of 4 take ENG 104.
	5	6	ENG 101 & ENG 102	
New College of Florida (FL)	4–5			
New Jersey Institute of Technology (NJ)	4–5	3	HSS 101	
New Mexico Institute of Mining and Technology (NM)	4–5	3	ENGL 111	Proceed directly into ENGL 112.
New York University (NY)	0	0	No course equivalent	
North Carolina State University (NC)	4			Eligible to submit portfolio to apply for ENG 101 credit.
	5	4	ENG 101	
North Central College (IL)	4–5		ENG 115	
Northwestern College (IA)	4–5	4	Elective	
Northwestern College (MN)	3–5	4	ENG 1105	
Northwestern University (IL)	5		2 English electives	
Occidental College (CA)	4–5			
Oglethorpe University (GA)	3	4		Essay will be evaluated by English faculty
	4–5	4	Elective credit	
Ohio Northern University (OH)	3	4	ENGL 110	
	4	8	ENGL 110 & ENGL 111	

School Name	Required Score	Credits Granted	Course Waived	Stipulations
Ohio Northern University—*continued*	5	12	ENGL 110, 111, & 204	
The Ohio State University (OH)	4	5	ENG 110.01	
	5	5	ENG H110.01	
Ohio Wesleyan University (OH)	4–5		ENG 105	
Oklahoma City University (OK)	4–5	3	ENGL 1113	
Oklahoma State University (OK)	3	3	ENGL 1113	
	4–5	6	ENGL 1113 & ENGL 1213	
Pacific Lutheran University (WA)	4–5	4	Elective	
Pacific University (OR)	4–5	3		
Peabody Conservatory of Music of The Johns Hopkins University (MD)	4–5			
The Pennsylvania State University University Park Campus (PA)	0	0	None	For a grade of three, four, or five, no credit is awarded. With a grade of four or five, a student is invited by the English Department to schedule English 030—Honors Freshman Composition.
Pepperdine University (CA)	4–5	3	ENG 101.01	
Pitzer College (CA)	4–5			
Point Loma Nazarene University (CA)	3	3		
	4–5	6		
Polytechnic University, Brooklyn Campus (NY)	4–5		EN 1014	
Pomona College (CA)	4–5			When both have been taken, credit will be given for the Literature exam.
Presbyterian College (SC)	0	0	No credit	
Princeton University (NJ)	5		No course equivalent	AP credit is not awarded for the International English Language AP exam.
Providence College (RI)	4–5			
Purdue University (IN)	4–5	4	ENGL 106	
Queen's University at Kingston (ON)	4–5			TBA
Quincy University (IL)	4–5			
Quinnipiac University (CT)	4–5	3	EN 101	
Randolph-Macon Woman's College (VA)	4–5			
Reed College (OR)	4–5			

School Name	Required Score	Credits Granted	Course Waived	Stipulations
Rensselaer Polytechnic Institute (NY)	4–5	4		
Rhodes College (TN)	4–5	8	ENG 151 & one unspecified course	
Rice University (TX)	4–5	3	ENGL 121	
Rochester Institute of Technology (NY)	3–5			
Rollins College (FL)	4–5	4	Writing Gen Ed	
Rose-Hulman Institute of Technology (IN)	4–5	4	RH 131	
Rutgers, The State University of New Jersey, Newark (NJ)	4–5			
Rutgers, The State University of New Jersey, New Brunswick/ Piscataway (NJ)	4–5			
Saint Francis University (PA)	3		ENG 104	
	4–5		English writing elective & ENG 104	
Saint John's University (MN)	5	4	ENGL 211	
Saint Joseph's University (PA)	4–5	3	ENG 1011 or ENG 1021	
St. Lawrence University (NY)	4–5	0	None	
St. Louis College of Pharmacy (MO)	3–5			
Saint Louis University (MO)	4–5	3	ENGA 190	
Saint Mary's College (IN)	4–5	6	ENWR 100 level	
Saint Mary's College of California (CA)	3		ENGL 00E	
	4–5		ENGL 4	
St. Mary's College of Maryland (MD)	4–5			
St. Norbert College (WI)	3–5			
St. Olaf College (MN)	5			Credit awarded for only one English AP exam not both Lang/Comp and Lit/Comp
Salem College (NC)	4–5		English course credit	1 English course credit plus placement in English 103.
Samford University (AL)	4–5	4	UCCA 101	

School Name	Required Score	Credits Granted	Course Waived	Stipulations
San Diego State University (CA)	3–4	6		San Diego State University course equivalent is Rhetoric and Writing Studies 100 and 3 units of Rhetoric and Writing Studies 299.
	5	6	Rhetoric and Writing Studies 100 and 200	Exempts from CSU English Placement Test and satisfies Writing Competency.
Santa Clara University (CA)	4–5	4	ENG 1	
Sarah Lawrence College (NY)	4–5			
Scripps College (CA)	4–5			
Seattle Pacific University (WA)	3–5	5	Elective course	
Seattle University (WA)	4–5	5	ENGL 110	A maximum of 10 credits will be granted for English even if two exams are completed.
Sewanee: The University of the South (TN)	4–5	4		
Siena College (NY)	4–5			
Simpson College (IA)	3–5			
Skidmore College (NY)	4–5			
Smith College (MA)	4–5			
Southern Methodist University (TX)	4	3	ENGL 1301	
	5	6	ENGL 1301 & ENGL 1302	
Southwest Baptist University (MO)	3–5	3	ENG 1113	
Southwestern University (TX)	4–5	3–4	ENG 10-013	If both, extra hours are given.
State University of New York at Binghamton (NY)	3–5	4	Elective credit	
State University of New York at Buffalo (NY)	3–5			
State University of New York College at Geneseo (NY)	3–4	6	ENGL 1TR	Not for Major credit. Maximum of 9 credits awarded if both exams taken.
	5	6	ENGL 142(for major), ENGL 1TR(Not for Major credit	Maximum of 9 credits awarded if both exams taken.
State University of New York College of Environmental Science and Forestry (NY)	3–5			
Stetson University (FL)	4–5	3	EH 121	

School Name	Required Score	Credits Granted	Course Waived	Stipulations
Stevens Institute of Technology (NJ)	4–5	3	Humanities course	You may receive credit for a spring semester freshman- or sophomore-level humanities course in Group A: Literature/ Philosophy as a result of a successful AP exam in English.
Stonehill College (MA)	4–5	6	Two General electives	
Stony Brook University, State University of New York (NY)	3–5	3	None	
Susquehanna University (PA)	4–5			In exceptional cases, the department may also recommend credit for scores of 3.
Swarthmore College (PA)	4–5			Does not count toward English major.
Sweet Briar College (VA)	4–5			
Syracuse University (NY)	3–5	6	WRT 105 & WRT 205	Management credit accepted as Humanities elective Education (inclusive) will accept a score of 3 only after a grade of B+ or higher is earned in an SU writing course.
Tabor College (KS)	3–5	6	EN 101 3 hrs. electives	
Taylor University (IN)	4–5	3	ENG 110	There must be an essay included with a score of 4.
Tennessee Technological University (TN)	4	3	ENGL 1010	
	5	6	ENGL 1010 & ENGL 1020	
Texas A&M University (TX)	3	3	ENGL 104	
	4–5	6	ENGL 104 & ENGL 241	
Texas Christian University (TX)	3	3	10803	
	4–5	6	10803, 20803	
Texas Tech University (TX)	3	3	ENGL 1301	
	4–5	6	ENGL 1301 & ENGL 1302	
Transylvania University (KY)	4–5			
Trinity College (CT)	4–5			Neither can be counted toward the English major.
Trinity University (TX)	5	3	ENGL 1302	
Truman State University (MO)	3–5	3	ENG 190	

School Name	Required Score	Credits Granted	Course Waived	Stipulations
Tufts University (MA)	4			If both tests are taken, only one acceleration credit is awarded to the student. Exemption from the first semester of the College Writing Requirement (placement in English 2 or an equivalent course); one acceleration credit.
	5			If both tests are taken, only one acceleration credit is awarded to the student. Exemption from the College Writing Requirement; one acceleration credit.
Tulane University (LA)	4–5	4	ENGL 101	
Union College (NE)	3–5			
Union College (NY)	4–5			
Union University (TN)	3–5	3	ENG 111	
The University of Alabama in Huntsville (AL)	3	3	EH 101	
	4–5	6	EH 101 & EH 102	
The University of Arizona (AZ)	4–5	0-3		If student completes ENGL 109H with a grade of C or better, student will have 3 units from 109H, plus 3 ENGL department elective credits from AP. Without a grade of C in 109H, student will not receive AP credit.
University of Arkansas (AR)	3–4		ENGL 1013	
	5		ENGL 1013 & ENGL 1023	
University of California, Berkeley (CA)	3–5			A score of 3 satisfies Entry Level Writing. A score of 4 or 5 satisfies Entry Level Writing and the first half of R&C.
University of California, Davis (CA)	3	8		Maximum credit allowed: 8 units for all English exams. A score of 3, 4 or 5 on the English AP examination satisfies the University of California Entry Level Writing Requirement (formerly known as the Subject A requirement).
	4–5	8	English 1, 3	Maximum credit allowed: 8 units for all English exams. A score of 3, 4 or 5 on the English AP examination satisfies the University of California Entry Level Writing Requirement (formerly known as the Subject A requirement).

School Name	Required Score	Credits Granted	Course Waived	Stipulations
University of California, Irvine (CA)	3	8	Elective credit only	Fulfills UC Entry Level Writing requirement.
	4–5	8		One course toward category IV of the UCI breadth requirement from the English 28 series plus 4 units of elective credit; may not replace English major, minor, or School of Humanities requirements.
University of California, Los Angeles (CA)	3–5			
University of California, Riverside (CA)	3	8	ENGL 001A & elective	Or 8 elective units if the student enrolls in ENGL 001A.
	4–5	8	ENGL 001A & ENGL 001B	
University of California, Santa Barbara (CA)	3	8	Writing 1, 1E, 1LK	
	4	8	Writing 1, 1E, 1LK, 2, 2E, 2LK	
	5	8	Writing 1, 1E, 1LK, 2, 2E, 2LK, 50, 50E, 50LK	
University of California, Santa Cruz (CA)	3–5	8		Satisfies one IH and Entry Level Writing Requirement. AP score of 4 or 5 satisfies "C-1". Maximum of 8 credits granted.
University of Central Arkansas (AR)	3		WRTG 1310	
	4–5		WRTG 1310 & WRTG 1320	
University of Central Florida (FL)	3		ENC 1101	
	4–5		ENC 1101 & ENC 1102	
University of Colorado at Boulder (CO)	4	3	WRTG 1150	
	5	6	WRTG 1150 & WRTG 1250	
University of Connecticut (CT)	4–5	4	ENGL 104	The AP Examination in English Language or English Literature does not fulfill the University of Connecticut Writing Competency requirement.
University of Dallas (TX)	3–5	6	ENG credit	Only 6 total credits of English awarded for either or both exams.
University of Dayton (OH)	4	3		One English Exam only.

School Name	Required Score	Credits Granted	Course Waived	Stipulations
University of Dayton—*continued*	5	6		One English Exam only.
University of Delaware (DE)	3	3	ENGL 166	
	4	3	ENGL 266	
	5	6	ENGL 166 & ENGL 266	
University of Denver (CO)	3	4	4 First Year Writing	
	4	8	8 First Year Writing	
	5	12	8 First Year Writing/ 4 elective	
University of Evansville (IN)	4–5			
University of Florida (FL)	3	3	ENC 1101	Writing Requirement (6000 words).
	4–5	6	ENC 1101 & ENC 1102	
University of Georgia (GA)	3–4	3	ENGL 1101	
	5	6	ENGL 1101 & ENGL 1102	
University of Illinois at Chicago (IL)	4–5	3	ENGL 160	
University of Illinois at Urbana–Champaign (IL)	4–5	4	Rhetoric 105 & Composition I requirement	
The University of Iowa (IA)	4–5	4	010:003	
University of Kansas (KS)	3	0	ENGL 101	Placement in ENGL 105
	4–5	3	ENGL 105	Placement in ENGL 205
University of Kentucky (KY)	3	3	ENG 101	3 credit hours for ENG 101 with a grade of CR. Choose either ENG 102 or ENG 104 (recommended).
	4–5	4	ENG 104	
University of Maryland, Baltimore County (MD)	4–5	3	ENGL 100	
University of Maryland, College Park (MD)	3	3	LL elective	
	4–5	3	ENGL 101	Students with score of 4 or 5 on Lang and Comp exam satisfy CORE-Fundamental Studies Freshman Writing requirement (*ENGL 101).
University of Mary Washington (VA)	3–5	3	ENGL 0101	

School Name	Required Score	Credits Granted	Course Waived	Stipulations
University of Miami (FL)	5	6	ENG 105 & ENG 106	
University of Michigan (MI)	4–5	3		Does not satisfy the English Composition or distribution requirements in English.
University of Michigan–Dearborn (MI)	3–4		COMP 105	
	5		COMP 105 & ENGL 231	
University of Minnesota, Morris (MN)	3–5	4	ENGL 1011	
University of Minnesota, Twin Cities Campus (MN)	3–5	4	COMP 1011	Fulfills freshman writing requirement.
University of Missouri–Columbia (MO)	4–5	3	ENG 1000	
University of Missouri–Kansas City (MO)	4–5	3	ENGL 110	
University of Missouri–Rolla (MO)	3–5	3	ENGL 20	
University of Nebraska–Lincoln (NE)	4–5	3	English Composition 150	
The University of North Carolina at Asheville (NC)	5	4	LANG 120	
The University of North Carolina at Chapel Hill (NC)	4–5	3	ENGL 101	
The University of North Carolina Wilmington (NC)	3	3	ENG 101	
	4–5	3	ENG 103	
University of North Florida (FL)	3	3	ENC 1101	
	4–5	6	ENC 1101 & ENC 1102	
University of Notre Dame (IN)	4–5	3	First Year Composition 13100	
University of Oklahoma (OK)	3–4		ENGL 1113	
	5		ENGL 1113 & ENGL 1123	
University of Pennsylvania (PA)	5		English Freshman Free	
University of Pittsburgh (PA)	4–5	3	ENGLIT 0000	
	5	6	ENGCMP 0200 & ENGLIT 0000	with 500 on verbal SAT

School Name	Required Score	Credits Granted	Course Waived	Stipulations
University of Puget Sound (WA)	4–5		Elective	Credit is not allowed for both exams.
University of Redlands (CA)	3–5			
University of Rhode Island (RI)	3–5	3	Writing 104	
University of Richmond (VA)	4–5	3	ENGL 103	
University of Rochester (NY)	4–5		No credit	
University of St. Thomas (MN)	3–5		ENG 100	Does not fulfill the Literature and Writing requirement.
University of San Diego (CA)	3–5			
The University of Scranton (PA)	3–5	3–6		
University of South Carolina (SC)	3–4		ENGL 101	
	5		ENGL 101 & ENGL 102	
University of Southern California (CA)	3–5	4		
The University of Tennessee at Chattanooga (TN)	3	3	ENGL 121	
	4–5	6	ENGL 121 & ENGL 122	
The University of Texas at Austin (TX)	3		RHE 306, CR	
	4		RHE 306, B	
	5		RHE 306, A	
The University of Texas at Dallas (TX)	3		3 SCH free electives	
	4–5		RHET 1300	
University of the Sciences in Philadelphia (PA)	4–5			
University of Tulsa (OK)	4–5	3	ENGL 1033	
University of Utah (UT)	3–5	8	Writing 2010	
University of Virginia (VA)	5	3	ENWR 110	
University of Washington (WA)	4–5	5	ENGL 109	AP English. Counts toward Visual, Literary, and Performing Arts general education requirement for graduation.
University of Wisconsin–La Crosse (WI)	3	3	ENGL 110	
	4–5	3	ENGL 110 & 300 level writing course	
University of Wisconsin–Madison (WI)	3	3	English Composition Electives	

School Name	Required Score	Credits Granted	Course Waived	Stipulations
University of Wisconsin–Madison—*continued*	4–5	3	English Composition Electives	Exempt from GER Communication A.
University of Wisconsin–River Falls (WI)	3	3	English Elective	Possibly receive credit for ENGL 100.
	4–5	3	ENGL 100	
Ursinus College (PA)	4–5			
Valparaiso University (IN)	4–5	3	ENGL 100	
Vanderbilt University (TN)	4–5	6	ENGL 104W & ENGL 105W	
Vassar College (NY)	4–5			
Villanova University (PA)	4–5			
Virginia Military Institute (VA)	3–5	6	EN 101 & EN 102	
Virginia Polytechnic Institute and State University (VA)	3	3	ENGL 1105	
	4–5	6	ENGL 1105 & ENGL 1106	
Wabash College (IN)	4–5			
Wagner College (NY)	4–5			
Wake Forest University (NC)	4–5	4	ENG 111	Only 4 total hours of ENG 111 credit will be awarded.
Wartburg College (IA)	3		EN 111	
	4–5		EN 112	
Washington & Jefferson College (PA)	4–5			
Washington and Lee University (VA)	5	3	ENG 11N	
Washington College (MD)	4–5	8	ENG 201 & ENG 202	
Washington University in St. Louis (MO)	5	3		3 credits of elective credit (L13–0001) contingent upon completing L13–100 with a grade of B or better. Please note, no credit is given for wiriting or literature courses.
Wellesley College (MA)	4–5		No exact equivalent	
Wells College (NY)	4–5			
Wesleyan College (GA)	4–5			
Wesleyan University (CT)	4–5			No more than one credit will be awarded even if students take both exams.
Western Washington University (WA)	3	4	Humanities GUR	Student may receive credits for either English exam, but not both

School Name	Required Score	Credits Granted	Course Waived	Stipulations
Western Washington University—*continued*	4–5	8	ENGL 101 & Humanities GUR	Student may receive credits for either English exam, but not both
Westminster College (UT)	4–5	8	ENGL 110 & ELEC 100T	
Westmont College (CA)	4–5			
Wheaton College (IL)	3	2		
	4–5	4		
Wheaton College (MA)	4–5			
Whitman College (WA)	5	4	ENGL 110	
Whitworth College (WA)	3–4	3	ENGL 110	
	5	6	ENGL 110	
Willamette University (OR)	4–5		ENGL 100	Non-major credit in these departments. Contact Art, Environmental Science, French, Music, or Spanish departments regarding possible assignment of specific course equivalencies in these areas.
William Jewell College (MO)	4–5	4	GEN 102	
Winona State University (MN)	3–5			
Wittenberg University (OH)	4–5			
Wofford College (SC)	4–5	3	ENG 101	
Xavier University (OH)	4–5	3	ENGL 101	
Yale University (CT)	5			

A Quick Review of Literary and Rhetorical Terms

You will not find any questions on the test that ask you to define a literary or rhetorical term, but you may find questions that give you an example and ask you to identify what it *is* an example of. As you study for your AP test, review the terms in the following list. As you read your assignments in English class, find examples of the concepts that underlie these literary and rhetorical terms. When you write your critical essays for class, incorporate terms and concepts from the list, where appropriate, to make your essays more precise.

A

allegory: an extended narrative in prose or verse in which characters, events, and settings represent abstract qualities and in which the writer intends a second meaning to be read beneath the surface story; the underlying meaning may be moral, religious, political, social, or satiric

alliteration: the repetition of consonant sounds at the beginning of words that are close to one another; for example, "beautiful blossoms blooming between the bushes"

allusion: a reference to another work or famous figure that is assumed to be well-known enough to be recognized by the reader

anachronism: an event, object, custom, person, or thing that is out of order in time; some anachronisms are unintentional, such as when an actor performing Shakespeare forgets to take off his watch; others are deliberately used to achieve a humorous or satiric effect, such as the sustained anachronism of Mark Twain's *A Connecticut Yankee in King Arthur's Court*

analogy: a comparison of two similar but different things, usually to clarify an action or a relationship, such as comparing the work of a heart to that of a pump

anaphora: specific type of repetition; word, phrase, or clause repeated at the beginning of two or more sentences in a row

anecdote: a short, simple narrative of an incident; often used for humorous effect or to make a point

aphorism: a short, often witty statement of a principle or a truth about life

apostrophe: usually in poetry but sometimes in prose; the device of calling out to an imaginary, dead, or absent person or to a place, thing, or personified abstraction

argumentation: writing that attempts to prove the validity of a point of view or an idea by presenting reasoned arguments; *persuasive writing* is a form of argumentation

assonance: the repetition of vowel sounds between different consonants, such as in *neigh/fade*

authority: support for an argument that is based on recognized experts in the field

B

burlesque: broad parody; whereas a parody will imitate and exaggerate a specific work, such as *Romeo and Juliet*, a burlesque will take an entire style or form, such as myths, and exaggerate it into ridiculousness

C

cacophony: harsh, awkward, or dissonant sounds used deliberately in poetry or prose; the opposite of **euphony**

caricature: descriptive writing that greatly exaggerates a specific feature of a person's appearance or a facet of personality

classicism: the principles and styles admired in the classics of Greek and Roman literature, such as objectivity, sensibility, restraint, and formality

coherence: quality of a piece of writing in which all the parts contribute to the development of the central idea, theme, or organizing principle

colloquialism: a word or phrase used in everyday conversation and informal writing but that is often inappropriate in formal writing

conceit: an elaborate **figure of speech** in which two seemingly dissimilar things or situations are compared

connotation: implied or suggested meaning of a word because of its association in the reader's mind

consonance: the repetition of identical consonant sounds before and after different vowel sounds, as in *boost/best*; it can also be seen within several compound words, such as *fulfill* and *Ping-Pong*

conundrum: a riddle whose answer is or involves a pun; it may also be a paradox or difficult problem

D

denotation: literal meaning of a word as defined

description: the picturing in words of something or someone through detailed observation of color, motion, sound, taste, smell, and touch; one of the four **modes of discourse**

diction: word choice, an element of style; also called **syntax**

discourse: spoken or written language, including literary works; the four traditionally classified **modes of discourse** are **description, exposition, narration,** and **persuasion**

dissonance: harsh or grating sounds that do not go together

E

epigram: a concise, witty saying in poetry or prose that either stands alone or is part of a larger work; it may also refer to a short poem of this type

euphony: a succession of harmonious sounds used in poetry or prose; the opposite of **cacophony**

exemplum: a brief tale used in medieval times to illustrate a sermon or to teach a lesson

exposition: the immediate revelation to the audience of the setting and other background information necessary for understanding the plot; also, explanation; one of the **four modes of discourse**

F

figurative language: language that contains **figures of speech,** such as similes and metaphors, in order to create associations that are imaginative rather than literal

figures of speech: expressions, such as similes, metaphors, and personifications, that make imaginative, rather than literal, comparisons or associations

folklore: traditional stories, songs, dances, and customs that are preserved among a people; folklore usually precedes literature, being passed down orally from generation to generation until recorded by scholars

foreshadowing: the use of a hint or clue to suggest a larger event that occurs later in the work

G

genre: a type of literary work, such as a novel or poem; there are also subgenres, such as science fiction or sonnet, within the larger genres

H

hubris: the excessive pride or ambition that leads a tragic hero to disregard warnings of impending doom, eventually causing his or her downfall

humor: anything that causes laughter or amusement; up until the end of the Renaissance, humor meant a person's temperament

hyperbole: deliberate exaggeration in order to create **humor** or emphasis

I

idyll: a short descriptive narrative, usually a poem, about an idealized country life; also called a **pastoral**

imagery: words or phrases that use a collection of images to appeal to one or more of the five senses in order to create a mental picture

interior monologue: writing that records the conversation that occurs inside a character's head

inversion: reversing the customary order of elements in a sentence or phrase; it is used effectively in many cases, such as posing a question: "Are you going to the store?"; often, it is used ineffectively in poetry, making it sound artificial and stilted: "To the hounds she rode, with her flags behind her streaming"

irony: a situation or statement in which the actual outcome or meaning is opposite to what was expected

L

loose sentence: a sentence that is grammatically complete before its end, such as "Thalia played the violin with an intensity never before seen in a high school music class"; the sentence is grammatically complete after the word *violin*

M

metaphor: a **figure of speech** in which one thing is referred to as another; for example, "my love is a fragile flower"

metonymy: a **figure of speech** that uses the name of an object, person, or idea to represent something with which it is associated, such as using "the crown" to refer to a monarch

mode: the method or form of a literary work; the manner in which a work of literature is written

mood: similar to **tone**, mood is the primary emotional attitude of a work

motif: main theme or subject of a work that is elaborated on in the development of the piece; a repeated pattern or idea

myth: one story in a system of narratives set in a complete imaginary world that once served to explain the origin of life, religious beliefs, and the forces of nature as supernatural occurrences

N

narration: the telling of a story in fiction, nonfiction, poetry, or drama; one of the four **modes of discourse**

naturalism: a literary movement that grew out of realism in France, the United States, and England in the late-nineteenth and early-twentieth centuries; it portrays humans as having no free will, being driven by the natural forces of heredity, environment, and animalistic urges over which they have no control

O

objectivity: an impersonal presentation of events and characters

onomatopoeia: the use of words that sound like what they mean, such as *hiss* and *boom*

oxymoron: a **figure of speech** composed of contradictory words or phrases, such as "wise fool"

P

parable: a short tale that teaches a moral; similar to but shorter than an **allegory**

paradox: a statement that seems to contradict itself but that turns out to have a rational meaning, as in this quotation from Henry David Thoreau: "I never found the companion that was so companionable as solitude."

parallelism: the technique of arranging words, phrases, clauses, or larger structures by placing them side by side and making them similar in form

parody: a work that ridicules the style of another work by imitating and exaggerating its elements

periodic sentence: a sentence that is not grammatically complete until its last phrase, such as, "Despite Glenn's hatred of his sister's laziness and noisy eating habits, he still cared for her."

persona: a fictional voice that a writer adopts to tell a story, determined by subject matter and audience, e.g., Mark Twain

personification: the attribution of human qualities to a nonhuman or an inanimate object

persuasion: a form of argumentation, one of the four **modes of discourse;** language intended to convince through appeals to reason or emotion

point of view: the perspective from which a story is presented; common points of view include the following:

- **first-person narrator:** a narrator, referred to as "I," who is a character in the story and relates the actions through his or her own perspective, also revealing his or her own thoughts

- **stream of consciousness narrator:** like a first-person narrator, but instead placing the reader inside the character's head, making the reader privy to the continuous, chaotic flow of disconnected, half-formed thoughts and impressions in the character's mind

- **omniscient narrator:** a third-person narrator, referred to as "he," "she," or "they," who is able to see into each character's mind and understands all the action

- **limited omniscient narrator:** a third-person narrator who reports the thoughts of only one character and generally only what that one character sees

- **objective narrator:** a third-person narrator who only reports what would be visible to a camera; thoughts and feelings are only revealed if a character speaks of them

protagonist: the main character of a literary work

R

realism: a nineteenth-century literary movement in Europe and the United States that stressed accuracy in the portrayal of life, focusing on characters with whom middle-class readers could easily identify; it is in direct contrast with **romanticism**

regionalism: an element in literature that conveys a realistic portrayal of a specific geographical locale, using the locale and its influences as a major part of the plot

rhetoric: the art of using language effectively; involves (1) writer's purpose, (2) his or her consideration of the audience, (3) the exploration of the subject, (4) arrangement and organization of the ideas, (5) style and tone of expression, and (6) form.

rhetorical modes: *exposition, description, narration, argumentation*

romanticism: a literary, artistic, and philosophical movement that began in the eighteenth century as a reaction to neoclassicism; the focal points of the movement are imagination, emotion, and freedom, stressing subjectivity, individuality, the love and worship of nature, and a fascination with the past

S

sarcasm: harsh, caustic personal remarks to or about someone; less subtle than **irony**

simile: a **figure of speech** that uses *like*, *as*, or *as if* to make a direct comparison between two essentially different objects, actions, or qualities; for example, "the sky looked like an artist's canvas"

speaker: the voice of a work; an author may speak as himself or herself or as a fictitious persona

stereotype: a character who represents a trait that is usually attributed to a particular social or racial group and who lacks individuality

style: an author's characteristic manner of expression

subjectivity: a personal presentation of events and characters, influenced by the author's feelings and opinions

suspension of disbelief: the demand made that the reader accept the incidents recounted in the literary work

symbolism: the use of symbols or anything that is meant to be taken both literally and as representative of a higher and more complex significance

synecdoche: a **figure of speech** in which a part of something is used to represent a whole, such as using "boards" to mean a stage or "wheels" to mean a car

syntax: word choice or **diction**

T

theme: the central idea or "message" of a literary work

tone: the characteristic emotion or attitude of an author toward the characters, subject, and audience

U

unity: quality of a piece of writing; see also **coherence**

V

voice: the way a written work conveys an author's attitude

Peterson's
Book Satisfaction Survey

Give Us Your Feedback

Thank you for choosing Peterson's as your source for personalized solutions for your education and career achievement. Please take a few minutes to answer the following questions. Your answers will go a long way in helping us to produce the most user-friendly and comprehensive resources to meet your individual needs.

When completed, please tear out this page and mail it to us at:

> Publishing Department
> Peterson's, a Nelnet company
> 2000 Lenox Drive
> Lawrenceville, NJ 08648

You can also complete this survey online at **www.petersons.com/booksurvey.**

1. **What is the ISBN of the book you have purchased? (The ISBN can be found on the book's back cover in the lower right-hand corner.)** _____

2. **Where did you purchase this book?**
   - ❑ Retailer, such as Barnes & Noble
   - ❑ Online reseller, such as Amazon.com
   - ❑ Petersons.com
   - ❑ Other (please specify) _____

3. **If you purchased this book on Petersons.com, please rate the following aspects of your online purchasing experience on a scale of 4 to 1 (4 = Excellent and 1 = Poor).**

	4	3	2	1
Comprehensiveness of Peterson's Online Bookstore page	❑	❑	❑	❑
Overall online customer experience	❑	❑	❑	❑

4. **Which category best describes you?**
   - ❑ High school student
   - ❑ Parent of high school student
   - ❑ College student
   - ❑ Graduate/professional student
   - ❑ Returning adult student
   - ❑ Teacher
   - ❑ Counselor
   - ❑ Working professional/military
   - ❑ Other (please specify) _____

5. **Rate your overall satisfaction with this book.**

Extremely Satisfied	Satisfied	Not Satisfied
❑	❑	❑

6. **Rate each of the following aspects of this book on a scale of 4 to 1 (4 = Excellent and 1 = Poor).**

	4	3	2	1
Comprehensiveness of the information	❑	❑	❑	❑
Accuracy of the information	❑	❑	❑	❑
Usability	❑	❑	❑	❑
Cover design	❑	❑	❑	❑
Book layout	❑	❑	❑	❑
Special features (e.g., CD, flashcards, charts, etc.)	❑	❑	❑	❑
Value for the money	❑	❑	❑	❑

7. **This book was recommended by:**
   - ❑ Guidance counselor
   - ❑ Parent/guardian
   - ❑ Family member/relative
   - ❑ Friend
   - ❑ Teacher
   - ❑ Not recommended by anyone—I found the book on my own
   - ❑ Other (please specify) _____

8. **Would you recommend this book to others?**

Yes	Not Sure	No
❑	❑	❑

9. **Please provide any additional comments.**

_____

_____

_____

_____

Remember, you can tear out this page and mail it to us at:

Publishing Department
Peterson's, a Nelnet company
2000 Lenox Drive
Lawrenceville, NJ 08648

or you can complete the survey online at **www.petersons.com/booksurvey.**

Your feedback is important to us at Peterson's, and we thank you for your time!

If you would like us to keep in touch with you about new products and services, please include your e-mail here: _____